The MAILBOX®

SUPERBOOK®
Preschool

Everything You Need for a Successful Year!

P9-CAM-518

- **Literacy**
- **Math**
- **Science**
- **Social and Emotional Development**
- **Seasonal and Holiday**

- **Centers**
- **Circle Time**
- **Music and Movement**
- **Classroom Displays**
- **Classroom Management**

And Much More!

Revised and Updated!

Managing Editor: Sharon Murphy

Editorial Team: Becky S. Andrews, Kimberley Bruck, Diane Badden, Thad H. McLaurin, Lynn Drolet, Kimberly Brugger-Murphy, Gerri Primak, Kelly Robertson, Karen A. Brudnak, Juli Docimo Blair, Hope Rodgers, Dorothy C. McKinney

Production Team: Lori Z. Henry, Pam Crane, Rebecca Saunders, Jennifer Tipton Cappoen, Chris Curry, Sarah Foreman, Theresa Lewis Goode, Greg D. Rieves, Eliseo De Jesus Santos II, Barry Slate, Donna K. Teal, Zane Williard, Tazmen Carlisle, Kathy Coop, Marsha Heim, Lynette Dickerson, Mark Rainey, Karen Brewer Grossman, Amy Kirtley-Hill, Ben Wooster

www.themailbox.com

©2007 The Mailbox®
All rights reserved.
ISBN10 #1-56234-732-2 • ISBN13 #978-156234-734-1

TABLE OF CONTENTS

Developmental Profiles of Preschoolers

Three-Year-Old 4

Four-Year-Old 6

What Do We Do in Preschool? 8

Welcome to School 9

Literacy

Listening & Speaking 16

Phonological Awareness 20

Print Awareness & Book
Knowledge 32

Letters 39

Literature 51

Math

Colors 63

Shapes 68

Sorting and Patterns 76

Numbers 80

Science

Animals 91

Plants 99

Weather 105

Social and Emotional Development

All About Me 113

Friendship & Kindness 121

Seasonal and Holiday

Fall 128

Fall Centers 133

Winter 140

Winter Centers 145

Spring 152

Spring Centers 157

Summer 164

Summer Centers 168

Greeting Cards 175

Open Reproducibles 179

Centers

Get Set for Centers 189

Anytime Centers 194

Transportation Centers 199

Ocean Centers 203

Pet Centers 207

Bug Centers 211

Making the Most of Every Center 215

TABLE OF CONTENTS

Circle Time 218

Developing Motor Skills

Fine Motor 228

Gross Motor 237

Dramatic Play and Role-Play 242

Music & Movement 248

Arts and Crafts

Art Explorations 254

Recipes for Arts and Crafts 262

Classroom Helpers

Classroom Displays 265

Assessment Tips 281

English Language Learners 285

Parents as Partners 289

Parent Conferences 298

Classroom Management 302

Index 317

DEVELOPMENTAL PROFILE OF A THREE-YEAR-OLD

Here's a ready reference on the range of abilities of a typical three-year-old child.

SOCIAL-EMOTIONAL

- Has short attention span; easily distracted
- Joins and plays with other children
- Takes turns/shares with encouragement
- Helps with simple chores
- Shows sympathy/concern for others
- Calls attention to own performance
- Shows enthusiasm for work/play
- Uses toys appropriately
- Prefers more challenging tasks
- Finds humor in absurd events/sights/sounds
- Identifies with parents

COMMUNICATION/LANGUAGE

- Knows first/last name, age, and gender
- Recites nursery rhymes; sings songs
- Uses 3- to 5-word sentences
- Tells a simple story
- Recalls elements from story just read
- Names pictures of familiar objects/items
- Follows 2- to 3-step sequenced directions
- Relates personal experiences
- Asks questions for information
- Answers simple logic/reasoning questions
- Describes attributes of objects/observations
- Takes turns in conversation

COGNITIVE

- Orders graduated containers/blocks/rings by size
- Understands simple opposites: big/little, long/short, fast/slow
- Sorts by one attribute (color or size)
- Counts up to five objects
- Matches pictures of like objects
- Recognizes/matches up to six colors
- Understands object function
- Matches simple shapes
- Understands simple time concepts (day/night)
- Groups objects by common attributes
- Understands same/different
- Understands positional concepts (on, in, under)
- Identifies real-life/pictured absurdities
- Repeats 3-digit and 3-word sequences

SPEECH MILESTONES

- Has vocabulary of almost 1,000 words
- Has 85% speech intelligibility
- Uses the following grammar forms:
  - pronouns (I, she, they)
  - auxiliary verbs (am, is, are)
  - noun and verb plurals
  - *-ing* endings (walk*ing*)
  - prepositions (in, on)
  - possessives (mommy*'s* shoe)
  - articles (a, the)
- Produces all vowel sounds
- Consistently produces sounds for *m, p, b, h, w*
- May produce sounds in front of mouth that typically are made in back (*t*up for cup)
- May produce simplified consonant blends (pane for *p*lane)
- May substitute more easily produced sound for another (wing for *r*ing)

FINE MOTOR

- Builds a 9- to 12-block tower
- Demonstrates hand preference
- Stabilizes paper with one hand; writes with other
- Draws vertical line, circle, and cross
- Draws recognizable picture
- Cuts continuously along a line
- Screws on lids
- Completes 5-piece puzzle
- Builds 3-block bridge
- Drives pegs into semisoft surface
- Rolls/shapes play-dough forms

SELF-HELP

- Puts on shoes (may be incorrect feet)
- Undresses, manipulating simple fasteners
- Unzips front zipper
- Fastens snaps
- Buttons/unbuttons large buttons
- Toilets self (with some help to clean/dress)
- Washes and dries hands
- Brushes teeth (with help)
- Eats independently
- Pours liquid from small pitcher into cup
- Spreads soft foods with a blunt knife
- Uses napkin to wipe mouth
- Serves self from container (some spilling)

GROSS MOTOR

- Walks up/down stairs, alternating feet (holds rail)
- Walks several steps on tiptoe
- Walks line on floor
- Balances on one foot for several seconds
- Throws ball overhead
- Catches bounced ball
- Kicks ball
- Runs around obstacles
- Climbs easy playground ladders/equipment
- Performs consecutive and forward jumps without falling
- Rides tricycle

PLAY

- Begins cooperative play
- Organizes/engages in pretend play
- Sequences play to tell a story
- Assigns roles to props (dolls/puppets)
- Creates imaginary characters
- Uses different voices for different play characters

DEVELOPMENTAL PROFILE OF A FOUR-YEAR-OLD

Here's a ready reference on the range of abilities of a typical four-year-old child.

SOCIAL-EMOTIONAL

- Has extended attention span; easily distracted
- Prefers playing with peers rather than alone
- Spontaneously takes turns/shares
- Chooses/identifies special friends
- Accepts responsibility
- Shows awareness of/concern for another's feelings
- Talks about own feelings, emotions, attitudes
- Uses appropriate social responses (says thank you, raises hand)
- Controls/expresses emotions in acceptable ways
- Responds appropriately to small-group instruction
- Shows interest in own body/exploring gender differences

COMMUNICATION/LANGUAGE

- Plays with words and sounds (rhymes, repetitions, nonsense words)
- Asks/gives meanings of new words
- Sings songs/rhymes of 30 or more words
- Uses up to 8-word sentences
- Retells stories with essential elements in logical sequence
- Answers content questions about story (facts may be confused)
- Follows three unrelated commands in order
- Asks variety of questions
- Responds appropriately to many question forms (answers may be incorrect)
- Describes past events
- Describes objects by shape, size, color
- Describes own activities
- Uses quantity terms (all, some, most)

COGNITIVE

- Knows own street and city
- Groups by two characteristics (shape, color)
- Classifies objects into categories (food, toys)
- Knows and names up to six colors
- Understands one-to-one correspondence
- Counts/creates sets up to ten
- Imitates simple patterns
- Completes up to 10-piece puzzles
- Matches/identifies simple shapes
- Sequences three pictures to tell story
- Has expanded knowledge of time concepts (today, tomorrow, yesterday)
- Understands directional concepts (top/bottom)
- Repeats 4-digit and 4-word sequences
- Completes sentences about simple analogies (Fire is hot, but ice is cold.)
- Understands comparatives (big/bigger)
- Predicts outcome of story/event

SPEECH MILESTONES

- Has vocabulary of over 1,500 words
- Has 100% speech intelligibility (not error free)
- Uses the following grammar forms:
    possessive pronouns (his, her, their)
    regular past tense with -ed (walked)
    irregular past (came instead of comed)
    no and not appropriately
    contractions (it's, there's)
    prepositions (beside, around, between)
    future-tense verb forms (will)
    connector words (and, but, because)
- Consistently produces sounds for n, ng, f, k, g, t, d, y (as in you)
- Produces consonant blends with 90% correctness

FINE MOTOR

- Uses mature grasp on pencil
- Copies simple shapes (square, triangle, diamond)
- Draws stick figure
- Draws person with up to six recognizable parts
- Uses irregular/uneven strokes to copy letters/ numbers
- Creases paper
- Puts paper clip on paper
- Cuts out circle and other simple shapes
- Performs simple sewing on lacing card
- Uses key to open padlock
- Puts pegs in pegboard

SELF-HELP

- Dresses/undresses with little help
- Knows front and back of clothes
- Buttons small buttons
- Engages separating zipper
- Laces shoes (may not tie laces)
- Hangs up coat
- Blows/wipes nose without help
- Washes face
- Toilets self independently
- Uses fork/spoon skillfully
- Uses blunt knife to cut easy foods
- Gets drink from water fountain
- Puts away personal belongings; cleans up

GROSS MOTOR

- Walks up/down stairs, alternating feet (without holding rail)
- Walks on tiptoe for up to ten feet
- Walks balance beam without falling
- Hops on one foot
- Jumps forward up to ten times without falling
- Skips, alternating feet
- Gallops
- Catches a thrown ball
- Kicks rolling ball toward target
- Pumps legs while swinging

PLAY

- Plays cooperatively with peers for extended periods
- Involves others in pretend play
- Represents more realistic situations in pretend play
- Enjoys playing dress-up
- Builds large block structures around which play is centered
- Begins playing group games with simple rules

WHAT DO WE DO IN PRESCHOOL?

- **Circle time** is a group gathering during which we share our ideas, plans, and observations. Circle activities are designed to stimulate youngsters' thinking, enrich their social skills, and expand their attention spans.

- **Gross-motor activities** give children the opportunity to use their muscles—as well as their imaginations—as they engage in fun, healthy exercises such as running, jumping, and climbing.

- **Fine-motor activities** help improve small-muscle development and eye-hand coordination. Some common items found in the fine-motor/manipulative area include puzzles, pegboards, crayons, and scissors.

- **Art activities** help youngsters creatively express their thoughts and feelings. They help reinforce fine-motor skills and concept development in areas such as colors, shapes, and size relationships.

- **Dramatic-play activities** help children express themselves, practice life skills, improve social skills, increase self-esteem, build vocabulary, and solve problems. And, well, dramatic play is just plain fun!

- **Music activities** promote youngsters' listening skills, creative expression, and social skills. In music, children can explore sound, volume, tempo, and rhythm.

- **Science activities** offer children many hands-on opportunities for observation, exploration, investigation, making predictions, and experimentation.

- **Sand and water activities** allow youngsters to experiment with textures and the properties of different substances. These activities also promote the development of other skills, such as math, science, and language.

- **Block play** gives children experience with many different concepts such as shape and size discrimination, spatial relationships, number skills, balance, organization, cause and effect, and classification. Cooperative play skills, problem solving, and creativity are also promoted in block play.

- **Storytime** is designed to help youngsters develop an appreciation and enjoyment of literature. Reading activities enhance children's vocabulary and comprehension skills, and also expand their knowledge base.

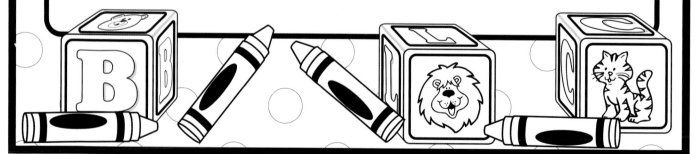

Welcome to School

Circle of Names

Ease the challenge for youngsters who are learning the names of classmates with this whole-group game. Sit with your students in a circle and roll a ball to a student. Instruct her to pick it up and stand. Then have her step back, hop three times, and announce her name. Encourage youngsters to reply, "Hi [child's name]!" Next, have her sit down and roll the ball to a different classmate. Continue in this manner until each child has had a turn. To play again at a later date, roll the ball to find out students' favorite colors and foods.

Bumper to Bumper

Preschoolers zoom into a brand-new year with these personalized headbands! Cut a class supply of two-inch-wide strips out of construction paper or bulletin board paper to make headbands. Also cut out several colorful copies of the car cards on page 12. Program the cars with individual letters to spell each child's name.

To begin, give each child a paper strip and his letter cars. Help him unscramble the letter cars to spell his name and glue the cars, in order, on the strip. When the glue dries, size the headband to fit and tape the ends. Encourage youngsters to wear the headbands as they travel around the room meeting new friends.

Who's Here Today?

This inviting idea will have your little ones practicing name-recognition skills as you take attendance. Prepare an attendance chart by gluing a picture of each student onto a separate library-card pocket. Attach the pockets to a large sheet of tagboard; then laminate it for durability. Use an X-acto blade to slit the laminating film across the opening of each pocket. Next, cut a supply of index cards in half; then personalize a half for each child in your class. Tape each child's name onto a separate wide craft stick. Place the chart and the sticks near the entrance of your classroom.

At the beginning of the year, assist each child in locating his personalized stick and then placing it in his corresponding pocket. Later in the year, request that each child locate his stick and place it in his pocket by himself. With this method you'll be able to see at a glance who is present and who is not.

Preschool Pals

The new school year will be loaded with compliments with this friendship-building idea! Select an object, such as a stuffed animal, to be your classroom's positive pal. When you observe a student being kind or complimentary to another child, call attention to the behavior and introduce the pal. Give the pal to the youngster and discuss other behaviors that build friendships. When class resumes, encourage the child with the pal to be on the lookout for acts of kindness. When he sees a classmate demonstrating a good deed, have him quietly pass the pal. Since youngsters may be hesitant to give up the pal, be sure to recognize both students for their praiseworthy behavior. Friendships and kindness are sure to spread throughout the year with this contagious positive praise!

Puzzle Power

Welcome little ones while fostering self-esteem with these personable preschool puzzles. Mount enlarged photocopies of children's individual snapshots on pieces of tagboard. Laminate them if desired. Then cut each picture into several pieces according to your children's abilities and store each puzzle in a separate, resealable plastic bag. This activity provides *two* scoops of self-esteem—one for the child who succeeds at completing a puzzle, and one for the person whose picture is recognized. It's so nice to meet you!

A Handy Parent Resource

Here's an informational resource your parents will love! Type up all those things parents will need or want to know, such as a list of themes for the year, planned field trips, students' names, birthday party guidelines, school vacations, discipline plans, and a class schedule. Then, at the beginning of the school year, give each family a folder containing copies of the information. Parents will appreciate having this valuable information organized in one place for them.

Melodies With Motion

The beginning of the year is the perfect time to establish routines! So use these upbeat songs to keep youngsters tuned in at the beginning and end of each day. Lead the happy hello morning melody to capture students' attention as you greet them with a warm welcome. Then bid a nice farewell with the friendly good-bye song!

Hello, Hello, Hello

(sung to the tune of "If You're Happy and You Know It")

Hello, hello, hello,
Hi to you!
Hello, hello, hello,
Hi to you!
I'm so glad you came today;
We will learn and work and play!
Oh, hello, hello, hello,
Hi to you!

If desired, personalize this song by substituting a different child's name for the word *you* in the second, fourth, and last lines. Repeat the song as many times as necessary to mention each child in your class.

Good-Bye Song

(sung to the tune of "She'll Be Comin' Round the Mountain")

Oh, it's time to say good-bye to all my friends.
(Wave good-bye.)
Oh, it's time to say good-bye to all my friends.
(Wave good-bye.)
Oh, it's time to say good-bye.
Give a smile and wink your eye.
(Smile and wink.)
Oh, it's time to say good-bye to all my friends.
Good-bye, friends!
(Wave good-bye.)

Check out the skill-building reproducibles on pages 13–15.

Car Cards

Use with "Bumper to Bumper" on page 9.

Student Information Card

Student no.

First name

Last name

Address

Student's birthdate

City

State

Zip

Mother's name

Mother's phone

Mother's email

Father's name

Father's phone

Father's email

Comments: _____

_____

Medical concerns: _____

_____

Emergency contact

_____

Emergency phone

Transportation to and from school: _____ walks _____ rides bus (#_____) _____ other

©The Mailbox® • *Superbook*® • TEC61046

Note to the teacher: Make one copy of the "Preschool Is Cool!" certificate and program it with your name; then make a class supply and write each child's name on a certificate to welcome him to your class. Make a class supply of the student information card and send one home with each student for his guardian to complete and return to school.

13

Nametags

TEC61046

TEC61046

TEC61046

TEC61046

Note to the teacher: Make a class supply of one of these nametags to coordinate with a thematic unit. Or use several of the designs together to divide your class into small groups. Color, label, cut out, and then laminate the nametags for durability.

TEC61046

TEC61046

TEC61046

TEC61046

©The Mailbox® • *Superbook*® • TEC61046

Note to the teacher: Make a class supply of one of these nametags to coordinate with a thematic unit. Or use several of the designs together to divide your class into small groups. Color, label, cut out, and then laminate the nametags for durability.

15

Listening & Speaking

The Follow-Along Song

Spotlight following directions with this catchy song! Lead students in singing the song, encouraging them to move as described. Continue in a similar way with other verses, substituting the action with a different action suggested below. **Listening**

(sung to the tune of "The Hokey-Pokey")
Let's [raise our hands up high].
It's not so hard to do.
Let's [raise our hands up high]
Because it's fun for me and you.
Let's listen to directions so we know just what to do.
Listening is fun—it's true!

Suggested actions: stretch our arms out wide, stand on tippie-toes, turn round and round

Careful Listening

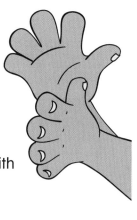

Get little ones listening and moving with this nifty circle-time rhyme! Have students chant the first two lines of the rhyme below. Then encourage youngsters to listen carefully as you chant the final three lines of the rhyme. Prompt students to complete the movement or movements described. Continue in the same way, substituting the underlined portion of the chant with other one-step directions provided. When youngsters are comfortable following one-step directions, repeat the process with the two-step directions shown. **Listening**

Children: Teacher, teacher, tell us true.
           Tell us one thing we should do.
Teacher: Listen in a careful way.
           [Clap your hands].
           That's what I say.

One-step directions: stomp your feet, pat your head, turn around, sit right down
Two-step directions: hop then sit, twirl then jump, clap then nod

Listen and Do

Youngsters need to listen carefully to complete this stellar activity! Give each child a copy of page 18 and provide access to crayons, black water-color paint, and a cup of water. Then have students listen carefully as you guide them through the steps below to complete the page. **Listening**

Steps:
1. Color the rocket ship blue.
2. Draw orange flames coming out of the bottom of the ship.
3. Draw a line from the astronaut to his ship.
4. Color the stars yellow.
5. Color the moon white.
6. Color the mouse brown.
7. Paint over the picture with black water-color paint to make a black background.

The Same Game

Youngsters speak up to share information with this visual discrimination game! To begin, choose two volunteers and have them stand. Encourage youngsters to study the volunteers, looking closely at their clothing, shoes, hair, and eyes. Invite a child to use his best speaking voice to share something that's similar between the two youngsters, prompting him to use appropriate eye contact as he shares the information. Continue in the same way with other volunteers. After several rounds of this game, give youngsters a pat on the back for sharing information with the class. **Speaking**

Tell All About It!

To prepare for this idea, cut out a copy of the prompts on page 19. Then place them in a decorated box or bag. To begin, invite a child to remove a prompt from the bag. Read the prompt aloud and then invite the youngster to answer the prompt. Continue in the same way with other youngsters. When all of the prompts in the bag have been used, place them back in the bag for a repeat of this fun activity! **Speaking**

They're both wearing tennis shoes!

Talk about a food ...like.

Talk about your favorite animal.

Tell about your favorite book.

...out a time ...ved with a

Note to the teacher: Use with "Listen and Do" on page 17.

Use with "Tell All About It!" on page 17.

Talk about the food you had for breakfast.

TEC61046

Talk about your trip to school.

TEC61046

Tell about a time you played with a friend.

TEC61046

Talk about your favorite food.

TEC61046

Talk about a food you do not like.

TEC61046

Tell about your favorite book.

TEC61046

Talk about your favorite animal.

TEC61046

Tell us about the people in your family.

TEC61046

Tell us about a toy you like to play with.

TEC61046

Phonological Awareness

Green Light

Preschoolers give rhyming word pairs the green light! Give each child a green paper circle to represent a green light. Next, explain that you are going to say a pair of words. Further, explain that if the words rhyme, each child should give the pair a green light by holding up his circle. Then recite the verse shown and slowly say a pair of words. Scan students' responses for accuracy. Continue in this manner for several rounds. **Rhyming**

Do these words rhyme?
Tell me true!
Give a green light if they do.

nap
cap

Rhyme Puzzles

This self-checking center activity is just right for independent rhyming practice! To prepare, color and cut apart a construction paper copy of the puzzles on pages 25 and 26. Scramble the pieces and store them in a bag. Place the bag at a center. A child assembles each puzzle by matching the pairs of pictures whose names rhyme. **Rhyming**

Fill in the Blank

Youngsters supply rhyming words in this small-group activity. Color and cut apart a construction paper copy of the cards on pages 27 and 28. Show a card to the students in a small group and give a partial description as shown. Next, help a volunteer supply the rhyming word that completes the description. When the description is complete, review the two rhyming words. Continue in this manner with the remaining cards. **Rhyming**

This is a cat wearing a…

Hat!

Pass It, Rhyme It

Grab a beanbag and sit with students in a circle for this rhyming game. Recite the chant shown and then name a word that has several rhyming words, such as *mat*. Pass the beanbag to the child beside you. The student supplies a word that rhymes with yours. After you confirm her choice, she passes the bag to the next child, who also names a rhyming word. Play continues in this manner until no more rhyming words can be supplied. If desired, recite the chant again and name a different word. **Rhyming**

We love rhymes, have you heard? Give a rhyme for this word!

Listen, Look, and Rhyme

In advance, obtain small objects or toys that are rhyming pairs. Place three pairs of items on a tray. Invite youngsters to name the items and help them locate the rhyming pairs. Then secretly remove one item. Present the tray again and name the missing object's rhyming partner as a clue. For example, if the tray contains a shell and a bell and you remove the shell, you would say, "The missing object rhymes with bell." Invite a child to guess the missing object. After confirming her answer, encourage youngsters to announce the rhyming pair. Then return the object to the tray and secretly remove a different item to play again. **Rhyming**

Special Sentences

Give each youngster a handful of Unifix cubes. Announce a sentence that includes a student's name. Have each child place one cube in front of him for each word he hears in the sentence. After one cube has been placed for each word, have each student link his cubes together. Next, instruct students to touch each cube as you repeat the sentence. Continue the activity using different sentences. **Word awareness**

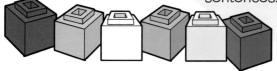

Deshaun plays nicely with his friends.

How Many Jumps?

This activity has little ones putting their whole bodies into syllabication! Use masking tape to outline three boxes on the floor, making sure to keep them small enough for a child to jump easily from one to the next. Have a student stand at one end of the row of boxes. Say a word; then help him jump into one box for each word part as you slowly repeat the word. For example, the word *pencil* would require the child to jump into the first and second boxes. Continue with different words until each child has had a turn to jump his way through a word. **Syllables**

Pen-cil!

Soaring With Syllables

Youngsters learn how many syllables are in their names with this high-flying activity! Use the patterns on page 29 to make a class supply of construction paper kite and bow cutouts. Personalize a kite for each child and then ask her to color it. Have her say her name and help her determine the number of syllables. Direct her to count out a matching number of bow cutouts and color them as desired. Help her tape a length of yarn to the back of the kite and then bows equal to the number of syllables in her name. **Syllables**

Sarajane

Sounds Like Me!

This class book featuring student photos is sure to be a favorite! Help each child select a classroom item that begins with the same sound as her name. Snap a photo of the child with her item. Glue each photo to a sheet of colorful construction paper and add text similar to that shown, emphasizing the matching beginning sounds. Bind the pages into a booklet and then read it aloud with student help. **Beginning sounds**

Rayna has a rabbit.

Do They Match?

Here's an easy game that's just right for transitions! Say a pair of words. Invite a volunteer to tell you whether the words share the same beginning sound. If she is correct, send her to the next activity. If she is incorrect, repeat the words while emphasizing the initial sounds and invite her to try again. Continue in this manner until each child has had a turn. **Beginning sounds**

Table, tap.

They match!

In the Box

Obtain several objects that begin with the same sound. Place the items in a box. During group time, invite a child to remove an item from the box and name it. Then lead little ones in singing the song shown, inserting the child's name, the name of the object, and the object's beginning sound. Continue until all of the items have been taken out of the box, each by a different child. **Beginning sounds**

(sung to the tune of "Sally the Camel")

[Ethan], our friend, has a [football].
[Ethan], our friend, has a [football].
[Ethan], our friend, has a [football].
So, [/f/ football /f/]
[/f/, /f/, /f/, /f/].

Rob and Randy

The Same Game

Focus your students' listening skills with this phonological awareness activity. Announce a pair of names. If the names begin with the same sound, have the youngsters give thumbs-ups. If the beginning sounds are different, have the students give thumbs-downs. Continue in this manner until each child's name has been used. **Beginning sounds**

Sound Stew

Review beginning sounds with this circle-time activity. With great fanfare, show students a plastic pot and spoon. Tell them that you're making Sound Stew. Next, pretend to put an object into the pot, give it a stir, and say, "I'm putting in a [hat]." Pass the pot and spoon to the child beside you and help her pretend to add to the stew an item with the same beginning sound as yours. Then she passes the stew to the next child, who adds another item to the stew. When a child cannot think of another item whose name begins with the same sound, supply a new beginning sound and continue play. **Beginning sounds**

Moon!

Towering Sounds

Youngsters use blocks to build beginning-sound awareness! Gather a small group in your block center. Place a block on the floor and say a word that begins with a consonant, such as *mouse*. Have a volunteer stack a block on top of yours while saying a word with the same beginning sound. Invite each child to take a turn adding a block to the tower until the group cannot think of another word or the tower falls. Repeat with different beginning consonant sounds. **Beginning sounds**

Check out the skill-building reproducibles on pages 30 and 31.

TEC61046   TEC61046   TEC61046   TEC61046

TEC61046   TEC61046   TEC61046   TEC61046

Rhyme Puzzles

Use with "Rhyme Puzzles" on page 20.

TEC61046

TEC61046

TEC61046

TEC61046

TEC61046

TEC61046

TEC61046

TEC61046

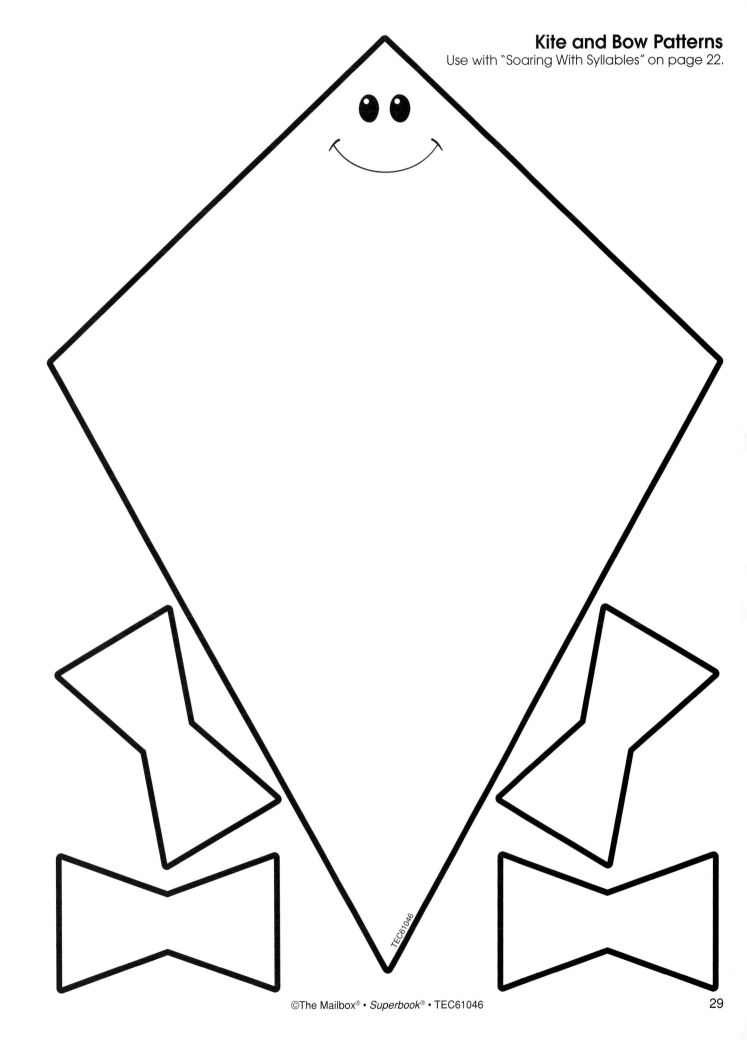

TEC61046

Mr. Cat

🖍 Color the pictures that rhyme with .

Mouse at Play

Color the pictures that begin like .

Peekaboo Bugs

When these ladybugs take flight, students' names are revealed! For each student, cut out a red construction paper copy of the ladybug pattern on page 37 (wings), a black construction paper circle of equal size (body), and a smaller black circle (head). Program each body with a student name. Then use two brads to fasten a head and wings to each body as shown.

To play peekaboo with these bugs, lead youngsters in singing the song below. At the end of the verse, open up a ladybug's wings to reveal a student name. When the little one recognizes her own name, have her jump up and say, "Buzz! Buzz!" Continue in this manner throughout the week until each child has had a turn. **Name recognition**

(sung to the tune of "Shoo Fly")

A name is hidden here.
A name is hidden here.
A name is hidden here.
When it flies it will appear!

Swimming With Names

To prepare, program a construction paper fish cutout (pattern on page 209) with each student's name. Cut a wavy slit in the center of a large sheet of blue bulletin board paper (water). Gather youngsters around the water and slide the front end of a fish through the slit until the first letter is revealed. Encourage each youngster to identify the letter and determine if it is the first letter in her name. Continue in this manner until each of the letters is in full view. When a little one recognizes her own name, invite her to "swim" to the water. Then have her select a new fish cutout for another round. **Name recognition**

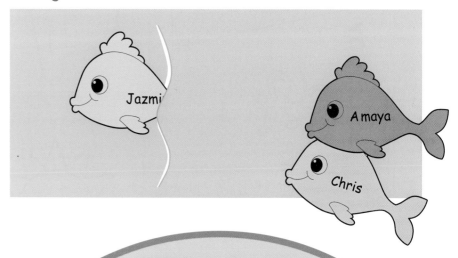

Names Adrift

Students make name clouds with this hands-on craft. For each child, use a white crayon to program a large sheet of blue paper with his name. Help each youngster trace the first letter in his name with glue. Then have him gently pull a cotton ball apart and place the cotton on the glue. Have him complete the rest of the letters in the same manner. Display the completed cloud crafts side by side to resemble the sky. Finally, encourage each youngster to find his name in the clouds! **Name recognition**

Cereal Box Lotto

Cereal boxes make perfect gameboards for this small-group game. In advance, obtain the front panel of a different cereal box for each group member. Then make a letter card for each letter in each cereal's name. To play, give each student the front panel of a cereal box and five small paper squares to use as game markers. Display a letter card. If a child finds a matching letter, she covers it with a marker. Continue displaying letters until one player has used all of her markers. If desired, have youngsters exchange boards and play again. **Concepts of print**

Letters Galore

Little ones sort different styles and shapes of print at this center. Select two letters you would like to feature. Then gather stickers, magnetic and foam letters, die-cuts, and magazine cutouts of the featured letters. Store the letters in a bag and place the bag at a center. When a youngster visits the center, he sorts the letters into two piles. For more advanced students, feature three or four letters at the center. **Concepts of print**

Colorful Words

Student descriptions link words to print with this crafty idea. Prepare a page with clip art and a sentence starter similar to the one shown. Copy it to make a class supply. Help each youngster read the sentence starter. Then write the color word of her choice to complete the sentence. Have her trace the color word with a corresponding crayon and color her picture to match. If desired, bind the completed pages into a book and read your little ones' work at storytime! **Concepts of print**

"Bee" on Track

This busy bee helps preschoolers follow print from left to right. To prepare, glue a construction paper bee cutout (pattern on page 38) to a craft stick to make a pointer. Write the poem shown on chart paper. Use the pointer to track each word in the poem as you read it aloud. As soon as you read the last word, quickly move the bee behind your back. Then select a volunteer to "fly" to the chart and track print in the same manner during a rereading of the poem. For added fun, have remaining youngsters buzz like bees while the volunteer travels to the chart! Concepts of print

> Follow this funny little bee
> From word to word and you will see.
> He moves along from left to right,
> And when he's done, he's out of sight!

The duck is yellow.
The pig is pink.
The cat is orange.
The frog is green.

Between the Words

This giraffe is sure to help youngsters recognize the spaces in a sentence. To prepare, glue a yellow construction paper cutout of the giraffe pattern on page 38 to a craft stick. Write several sentences on chart paper. Then invite a volunteer to move the giraffe from the beginning of the sentence to the space behind the first word. Read the word. Then have him move the giraffe to the next space and read that word aloud. Continue in this manner to read the entire sentence. For more practice, select a new volunteer to lead the giraffe to each space that separates the words.
Concepts of print

Special Endings

Share the front cover of a selected big book. Show students how a telling sentence ends with a period. Invite youngsters to squeeze into little balls to show what a period looks like. Then, tracking the words while you read aloud, encourage little ones to transform into human punctuation marks at the end of each sentence. **Concepts of print**

All About Books

Invite students to participate during this book-handling tune. To begin, demonstrate for students the motions of handling a book as they correspond with the song. After singing several rounds with students, give each youngster a book and encourage her to act out the motions while singing the tune. **Book awareness**

(sung to the tune of "Do Your Ears Hang Low?")

Is it upside down?
Should you turn your book around?
Can you open it up now?
Oh, can you show me how?
Point to where we will start;
Now go to the ending part.
Let's look at this book.

Undercover Cover

The front cover of this book is sure to keep students guessing! Mask the front cover of a book. Read aloud the disguised book, stopping from time to time to discuss important events. At the book's end, have youngsters design a front cover that offers information about the story. When each paper is complete, reveal the cover and invite youngsters to compare their drawings to the book's cover. Book knowledge

The Happy Duck

Stick It!

Sticky notes are the perfect tool to alert young readers to parts of a book. In advance, place a sticky note on the edges of different parts of a book you would like to feature, such as the front cover, the back cover, the title page, where the story starts, and where the story ends. During a group reading of the story, call attention to the sticky notes. Explain that each note represents a special book feature. Encourage youngsters to identify the special part of the book featured. **Book knowledge**

Authors and Illustrators

Introduce young readers to the very important people who write the words and draw the pictures in books. **Book knowledge**

(sung to the tune of "Three Blind Mice")

Books! Books! Books!
Books! Books! Books!
With lots of words,
And pictures too!

The author writes all the words we read.
The illustrators add the art we need.
Reading a book is a wonderful deed.
So we love books!

I am going to get a meatball at the Meatball Station.

John

Environmental Print Books

Students are the main characters visiting well-known sites in this class book! Keep a photograph of each child in your work area. Gather a class supply of pictures of familiar environmental print; then place the pictures in a bag. Working with one student at a time, give him his photo and ask him to remove a picture from the bag. Then have him pretend that he is going on a trip to the pictured site; ask him to say it in a complete sentence. Write his response on a sheet of paper. Next, help him glue the corresponding pictures to his page. Finally, bind the completed pages into a class book for a real adventure in reading! **Print awareness**

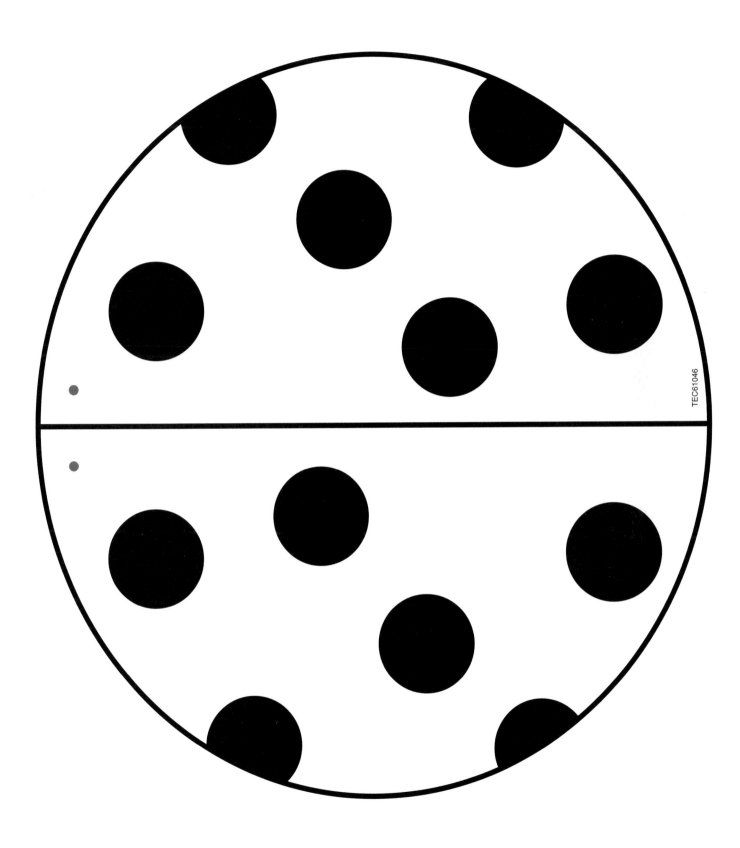

TEC61046

Bee and Giraffe Patterns

Use the bee with "'Bee' on Track" on page 34. Use the giraffe with "Between the Words" on page 34.

TEC61046

TEC61046

Letters

a b c d e f g h i j k l m n o p q r s t u v w x y z

Hop to It!

To prepare for this small-group activity, use the patterns on page 45 to make a green construction paper frog and several lily pad cutouts. Tape the frog cutout to one end of a ruler to make a pointer. Label each lily pad with a different letter and spread them out in your small-group area. Have youngsters help you recite the rhyme below. At the end of the rhyme, name one of the letters on a lily pad. Ask a child to "hop" the frog pointer to that letter. Continue in this manner until each child has had a turn. **Letter recognition**

Little frog, little frog, hop, hop, hop!
On this letter, will you please stop?

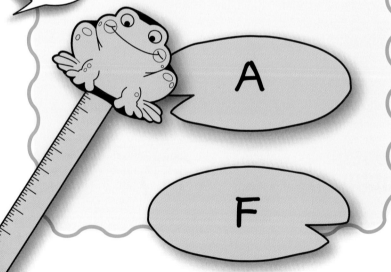

Fill the Candy Jar

Use the patterns on page 46 to make a supply of colorful construction paper candy cutouts. Program each candy with a different letter; then place the candies faceup on a table with a large tagboard-jar cutout. Ask a child to find a candy labeled with a specific letter. Have him put it on the jar. Repeat the activity with different students until all of the candy is on the jar. **Letter recognition**

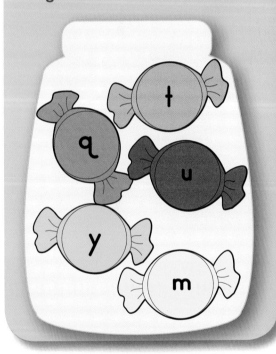

Letter Placemats

Serve youngsters a helping of literacy at snacktime! Randomly program a sheet of paper with six or eight different alphabet letters. Copy to make a class supply. Give each child a copy of the resulting placemat and a serving of bite-size snack foods, such as cereal, apple chunks, or fish-shaped crackers. To begin, announce a direction that links a snack and one of the letters. For example, you might say, "Put two cereal pieces on the letter *B*" or "Put an apple chunk on the letter *T*." After youngsters find the letters, invite them to enjoy their snacks. **Letter recognition**

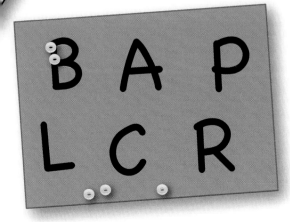

Feels Like a *B* to Me!

Youngsters focus on the shapes of letters with this center activity. Program a paper strip with a few different letters and then place a matching set of letter manipulatives in a bag. Place the bag and strip at a center. A student reaches into the bag, removes a letter, and traces it with his finger, noting the shape. Next, he uses his finger to trace over the letters on the strip to help him determine the match. Then he places the magnetic letter below the matching letter on the strip. He continues in this manner until all the letters are matched. **Letter matching**

The Letter Game

Youngsters practice important matching skills in this letter game. To prepare, cut 26 five-inch squares from each of two different poster board colors. Print a different letter on each square so that you have an alphabet-card set in each color. Prior to circle time, place the letter cards of one color set around the room in plain sight. Then, during circle time, give each child one card from the other color set. Sing the "Alphabet Song," replacing the ending with "We can sing the letter names. Now let's play the letter game!" At this time, invite each child to find the letter matching the one she is holding. After all the matches have been found, ask each child to show and name her letter pair. **Letter matching**

Spot-and-Dot Letters

To prepare, write a letter near the top of a sheet of paper and circle it. Then write the featured letter several more times and add other letters randomly. Copy the sheet to make a class supply. Give each child a copy and a bingo dauber. Point out and name the featured letter. Each time a child sees the letter on her sheet, she names the letter and then dots it with the bingo dauber. **Letter matching**

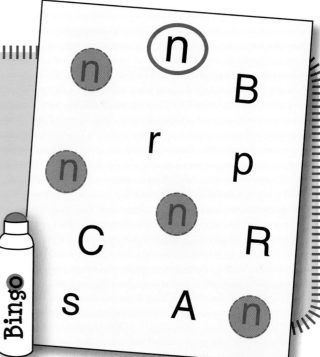

Letter Detectives

To prepare, cut out a tagboard copy of the magnifying-glass pattern on page 47. Place a selection of magnetic letters on the board and place the matching letter cards nearby. Invite a child to be the letter detective. Have the detective look through the magnifying glass to examine the magnetic letters and match one with the appropriate card. Then invite a different detective to the board. Continue in this manner until each letter has been matched. **Letter matching**

Bear Hunt!

Youngsters will eagerly hunt these bears at circle time! In advance, use the patterns on page 46 to make 26 bear cards. Label each card with a different alphabet letter and then hide them in your classroom. During circle time, display an alphabet strip on the floor. Then invite students to go on an imaginary bear hunt and tiptoe around the room in search of bears. When a child finds a bear, he places it below the matching letter on the strip. Continue in this manner until all the bears are found and the letters are matched. **Letter matching**

A B C D E F G H I J

Bees and Blossoms

Invite little ones to buzz on over to this letter-matching center! In advance, cut out several colorful copies of the flower and bee cards on page 48. Program each flower with a different uppercase letter. Write a matching lowercase letter on each bee. Then place both sets of cards in a center. A child chooses a bee and flies it to the corresponding flower. He continues in this manner until each bee and flower are matched. **Uppercase and lowercase letters**

Musical Letters

Arrange a class supply of uppercase-letter cards in a circle on the floor. Play some lively music as students march around the letters in the same direction. After a few moments, stop the music to signal each child to sit behind a letter. Write a lowercase letter on the board. The child sitting behind the matching uppercase letter jumps up. Then erase the letter and start the music for another round of play! **Uppercase and lowercase letters**

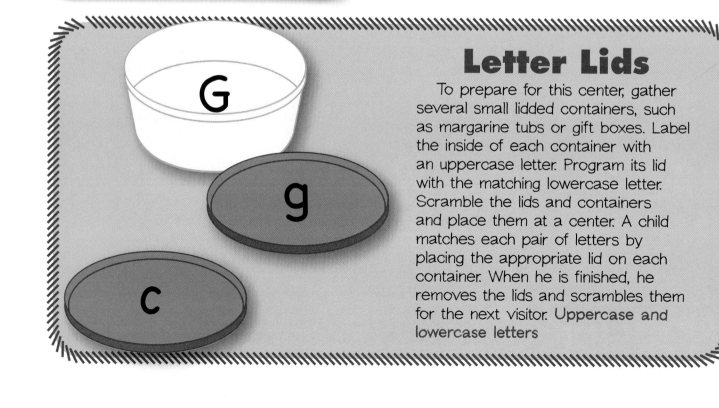

Letter Lids

To prepare for this center, gather several small lidded containers, such as margarine tubs or gift boxes. Label the inside of each container with an uppercase letter. Program its lid with the matching lowercase letter. Scramble the lids and containers and place them at a center. A child matches each pair of letters by placing the appropriate lid on each container. When he is finished, he removes the lids and scrambles them for the next visitor. Uppercase and lowercase letters

Tabletop Trails

This center is sure to help little ones build letter-formation skills! Use masking tape to form a desired letter on a tabletop. Have a child at this center line up small manipulatives, such as counters, blocks, or links, along the tape trail to form the letter. **Letter formation**

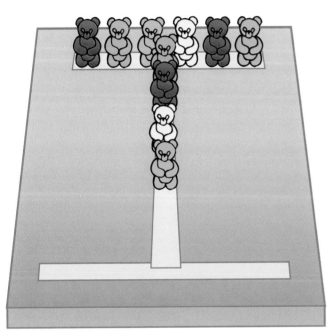

Lots o' Dots

Go dotty with this small-group activity! Program a sheet of copy paper with the letter of your choice by making small pen dots about an inch apart. Give each child a copy of the prepared letter sheet and a bingo dauber. Show him where to begin the letter and then encourage him to make a bingo dot atop each dot on his paper. **Letter formation**

Rainbow Letters

This letter-formation project doubles as beautiful artwork! Give each child a sheet of construction paper. Arrange crayons and containers of thinned tempera paints for easy student access. Have each child use different colors of crayons to form a chosen letter several times on her paper. Then invite her to paint over the entire page with thinned tempera paint. When the pages are dry, youngsters will have an assortment of colorful letters with an artistic flair! **Letter formation**

Disappearing Letters

This partner activity is exciting for preschoolers! Have one child use a paintbrush and water to paint a desired letter on a chalkboard. Direct the partner to use a crayon to write the same letter on a sheet of paper as many times as possible before the water letter disappears. Have partners switch roles and continue in this manner for several rounds.
Letter formation

Parachute Pick-up

In an open area, have students hold the edges of a parachute and pull it taut. Toss a class supply of letter cards onto the parachute. Invite youngsters to bounce the letters until they all fly off; then direct students to lay the parachute down. Next, have each child pick up a letter card. Help him identify his letter before replacing the card on the parachute. Continue in this manner for several rounds. **Letter identification**

Treasure Hunt

Preschoolers search for sparkly letters at circle time! In advance, use glitter glue to write each desired letter on a separate card. While students are away from the classroom, hide the cards around the room. Designate a shallow container, such as a box lid, as a treasure chest. During circle time, have students hunt for the cards. Help each child identify the letter on his card before adding it to the treasure chest. Continue in this manner until all the cards are found. Letter identification

Check out the skill-building reproducibles on pages 49-50.

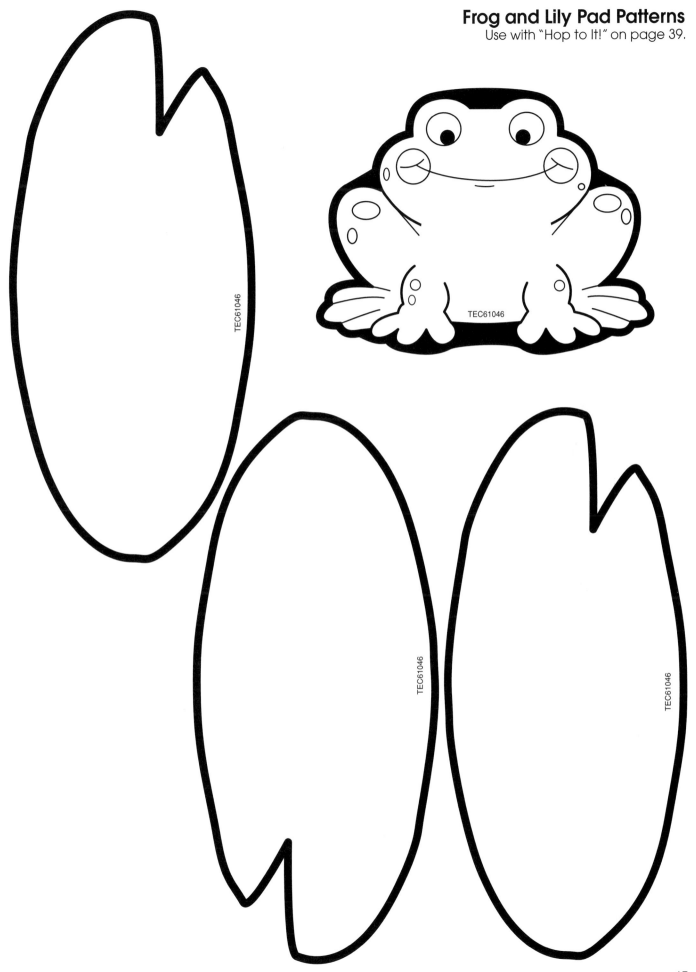

TEC61046

TEC61046

TEC61046

TEC61046

Candy Patterns
Use with "Fill the Candy Jar" on page 39.

Bear Cards
Use with "Bear Hunt!" on page 41.

Cut out.

TEC61046

Flower and Bee Cards

Use with "Bees and Blossoms" on page 42.

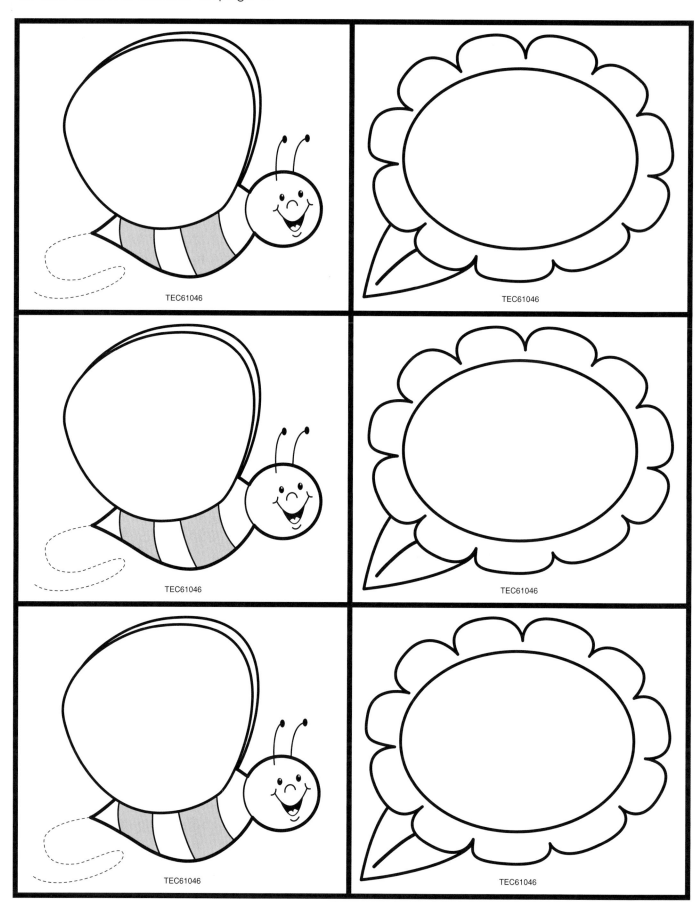

TEC61046

TEC61046

TEC61046

TEC61046

TEC61046

TEC61046

Name _____

Hanging Out

✂ Cut. 🔖 Glue to match.

F

T

M

M   F   T

Name _____

50

Alphabet Soup

🖍 Trace.

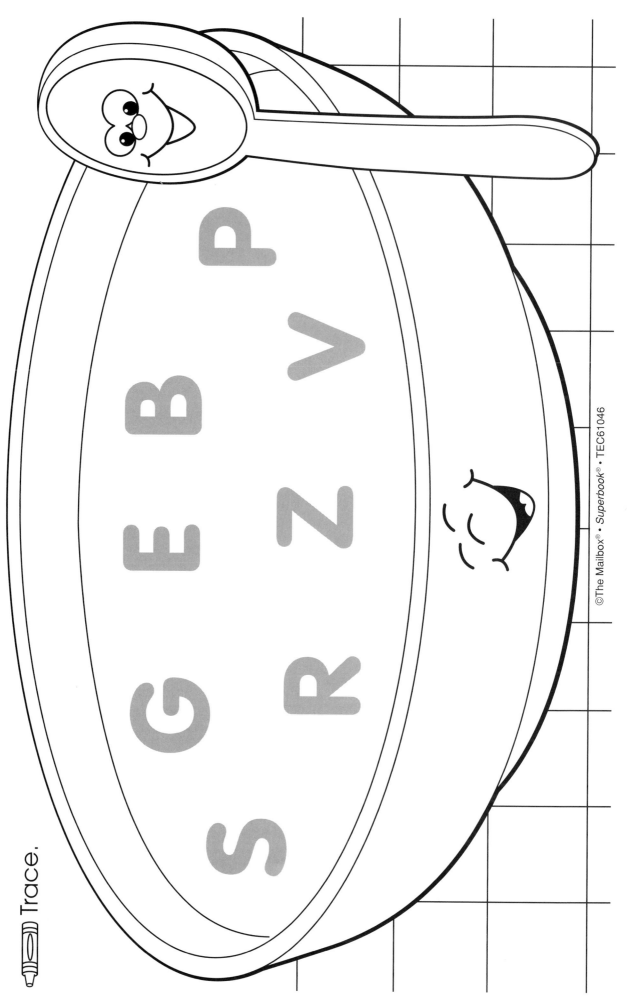

Literature

Brown Bear, Brown Bear, What Do You See?
Written by Bill Martin Jr.
Illustrated by Eric Carle

What does this brown bear see? It sees a wide variety of animals — from white dogs to yellow ducks to green frogs!

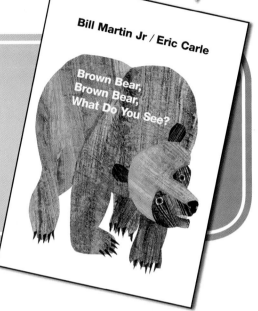

Bill Martin Jr / Eric Carle

Brown Bear, Brown Bear, What Do You See?

Noisy Animals!

Little ones hear the animals in the story with this sing-along story innovation! Open the book to the first page; then lead students in singing the first verse of the song to the right. Turn the page and lead little ones in singing the second verse. Continue singing the song, turning the pages in the book appropriately and making up each new verse to reflect the animals and the noises they might make.

(sung to the tune of "The Farmer in the Dell")

Brown Bear hears a bird.
Brown Bear hears a bird.
Listen to it tweet, tweet, tweet.
Brown Bear hears a bird.

Red Bird hears a duck.
Red Bird hears a duck.
Listen to it quack, quack, quack.
Red Bird hears a duck.

Brown bear, brown bear, what do you see?

I see 10 birds looking at me!

Counting With Brown Bear

For each child, program a 12" x 18" sheet of construction paper as shown. Have each youngster color and cut out a copy of the bear pattern on page 57. Encourage her to glue the bear to the left side of the paper. Next, help her count aloud as she makes ten red fingerprints on the right side of the paper. When the prints are dry, add details to the prints to resemble birds.

Where the Wild Things Are
Written and illustrated by Maurice Sendak

When Max gets into trouble for his wild behavior, he is sent to his room without his supper. That night, his room transforms into a jungle, and he sails to the land where the wild things are. Although he is named king of the wild things, he finds that he is lonely. So he returns to the place where he is loved best of all!

Crafty Wild Things

Youngsters make their own wild things reminiscent of those in the story! Stock a table with play dough, craft feathers, and craft sticks. Youngsters visit the center and use the items to make their own wild things. Have each student explain his wild thing to his classmates, describing its different characteristics.

Music and Movement

After a read-aloud of this book, revisit the pages that show the wild rumpus. Ask youngsters what type of music the monsters might be dancing to. Is it fast or slow? Is it loud or soft? When youngsters share their opinions, play a recording of music similar to the music the students described and invite them to dance around for their own wild rumpus. Next, play a different music selection and have youngsters alter their movements to reflect the music's qualities.

Sailing Through a Year

It took Max over an entire year to sail to the land of the wild things. With this idea, youngsters sail Max's boat while being introduced to the months in a year! Color and cut out a copy of the sailboat on page 58; then transform the cutout into a stick puppet. Write the months on a length of adding machine tape and post the tape on a wall. Invite a child to move the boat along the tape as you lead students in singing the song shown. Continue in the same way, inviting other youngsters to move the boat during the sing-along.

(sung to the tune of "Are You Sleeping?")
January,
February,
March,
April,
May and June,
Then July and August,
September, October,
November,
December.

January, February, March,

Green Eggs and Ham

Written and illustrated by Dr. Seuss

Do you like green eggs and ham? When Sam poses this question, it triggers a series of outlandish events designed to tempt the main character to try this colorful cuisine. The message of this rhyming tale is one that children have undoubtedly heard before: You won't know if you like it until you try it!

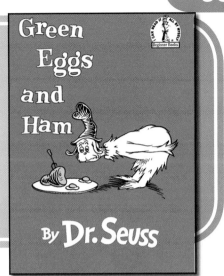

Eating Together

With whom would your little ones like to eat green eggs and ham? You'll find out with this writing activity! Cut out a copy of the egg and ham patterns on page 59 for each child. Invite each child to share her green eggs and ham with the person or animal of her choice. Use a black marker to write the child's words on the ham and eggs as shown, so that the phrases are similar to those in the story. Invite each child to color the ham and yolk green. Then display the eggs and ham on a large frying pan cutout.

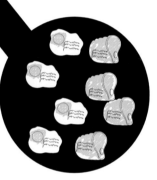

Would you like them with your mom?

I would like them with my mom! Kayla

Taste Test

In advance, make a simple graph similar to the one shown. Also, make a batch of scrambled eggs; then tint half of the batch green. Give each child a small amount of green eggs and a small amount of regular eggs. After each child tries the eggs, have him decide which color he prefers. Then have him place a sticky note with his name in the appropriate column. When each child has had a chance to add his sticky note, discuss the results of the graph.

Which color eggs do you prefer?	
green	white
juan	billy
nick	susy
jenny	joey
	mikey

"Egg-cellent" Dramatic Play

Make green eggs and ham from craft foam. Use a permanent marker to add details to the ham as desired. Place the eggs and ham at your dramatic-play center along with spatulas, frying pans, and plastic plates. Invite little ones to whip up batches of green eggs and ham and then offer them to their classmates as they pose the question: "Do you like green eggs and ham?"

The Very Hungry Caterpillar

Written and illustrated by Eric Carle

Strawberries! Oranges! Chocolate cake! Throughout the week this little caterpillar consumes a great quantity of unusual foods. Suddenly this caterpillar is no longer little, and he's ready for the next stage in his life.

Munch!

The very hungry caterpillar has been munching on all of these leaves! Place leaf cutouts at a center along with several hole punchers. Near the center, post a supersize tree cutout minus foliage. Invite a youngster to visit the center and punch several holes in a leaf cutout. Then invite him to attach his cutout to the tree. After each child has had several opportunities to add leaves to the tree, attach a caterpillar cutout to the display.

Crawl and Fly

Have youngsters revisit the changes that take place in the book with this movement activity. Invite students to crawl on the floor like caterpillars as you play an instrument, such as rhythm sticks, very slowly. Next, stop playing the instrument and tell students to lie very still in their cocoons. Finally, play a different instrument, such as a jingle-bell bracelet, and have them "emerge" from the cocoons and fly around the room like butterflies.

Extending the Menu

What else might the hungry little caterpillar like to eat? Youngsters will let you know with this writing activity. Make a copy of page 60 for each child. Have each youngster draw a food item on the caterpillar's tummy that she feels he might enjoy eating. Write the name of her food item in the space provided. Then invite her to color the rest of the picture. If desired, bind the pages together with a cover titled "Tasty Suggestions."

I think the caterpillar should try

spaghetti and meatballs . Yum!

Jamberry
Written and illustrated by Bruce Degen

A little boy and a bear frolic through a whimsical land where they look for tasty berries for jam! The rhyming story follows the characters as they romp through a jam-filled land with strawberry sheep, raspberry rabbits, and many other playful critters!

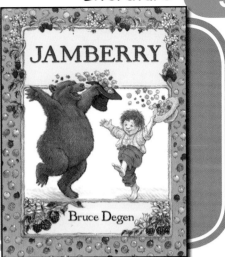

A "Berry" Tasty Treat

Before reading the story, introduce youngsters to different berries with this simple snack. In advance, mix together blueberries, raspberries, and chopped strawberries. Gather a supply of vanilla yogurt and granola. To begin, help youngsters identify the different berries. Then invite each child to put a spoonful of berries, yogurt, and granola in a cup. Invite each student to eat the snack. Then have students settle in for a read-aloud of this fun book.

Blueberries!

The bear in the story fills his top hat with berries. Have youngsters add blueberries to this top hat to practice position words! Give each youngster a copy of page 61 and four blue sticky dots. Have each student color his hat. Then instruct him to place a blueberry in a particular location on the page. For example, you might say, "Place the blueberry on the hat" or "Place the blueberry below the hat." Continue in the same way for each remaining blueberry.

Jamberry by Bruce Degen
Look at our sweet-smelling strawberry lambs
Prancing around in some strawberry jam!

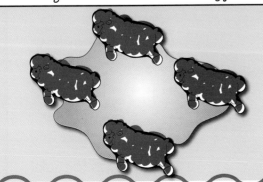

Strawberry Lambs and Jam

The wonderful smell of strawberries will fill the room with this "scent-sational" display idea! To make strawberry paint, mix two packets of unsweetened drink mix with ⅓ cup of water. Make several tagboard copies of the lamb patterns on page 62. Help each child cut out a lamb. Then invite him to paint it with the strawberry paint to resemble the lambs in the book. Display the lambs on a large pink puddle shape attached to a wall. Then add the text shown to the display.

Caps for Sale
A Tale of a Peddler, Some Monkeys and Their Monkey Business
Written and illustrated by Esphyr Slobodkina

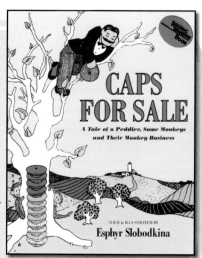

One day, a cap peddler takes a long walk carrying his merchandise stacked atop his head. Eventually, he rests under a tree and falls asleep. When he wakes, he's shocked to find out that a mischievous troupe of monkeys has taken his caps. His humorous efforts to retrieve his precious caps and the surprising conclusion make this tale a favorite.

Create a Cap

The peddler in the story has a variety of colorful caps for sale. Encourage each youngster to make a beautiful new cap to add to his merchandise! Enlarge a copy of the cap on page 62; then make a copy for each child. Help each student cut out her cap and glue it to a sheet of construction paper. Invite her to decorate the cap as desired. Then have the youngster describe her cap as you write the information on the paper as shown. Display the finished projects with the title "Class Caps for Sale!"

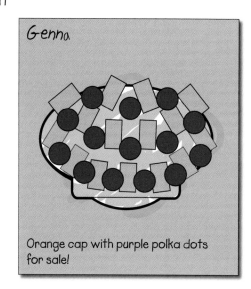

Genna

Orange cap with purple polka dots for sale!

Monkey See, Monkey Do

The monkeys in the story copy the peddler's actions. Give little ones a chance to act like the monkeys with this copycat game. Help each youngster make a cap headband similar to the one shown (pattern on page 62). Have each youngster don his cap. Then perform an action, such as stomping your feet, and encourage youngsters to copy you. Continue in the same way with several other actions.

Counting Caps

In advance, make a six-page booklet for each youngster. Title the first page "Counting Caps." Then program each remaining page with a circle and the text shown. Give each child his booklet. Have him decorate the circle on the first page to represent himself. Then have him press his thumb on a colored ink pad and make one print above his head to resemble a cap. Encourage him to use a crayon to add a brim to the cap. Continue in the same way with each remaining page, adding caps to reflect each number in the text.

1 cap for sale!

TEC61046

Sailboat Pattern

Use with "Sailing Through a Year" on page 52.

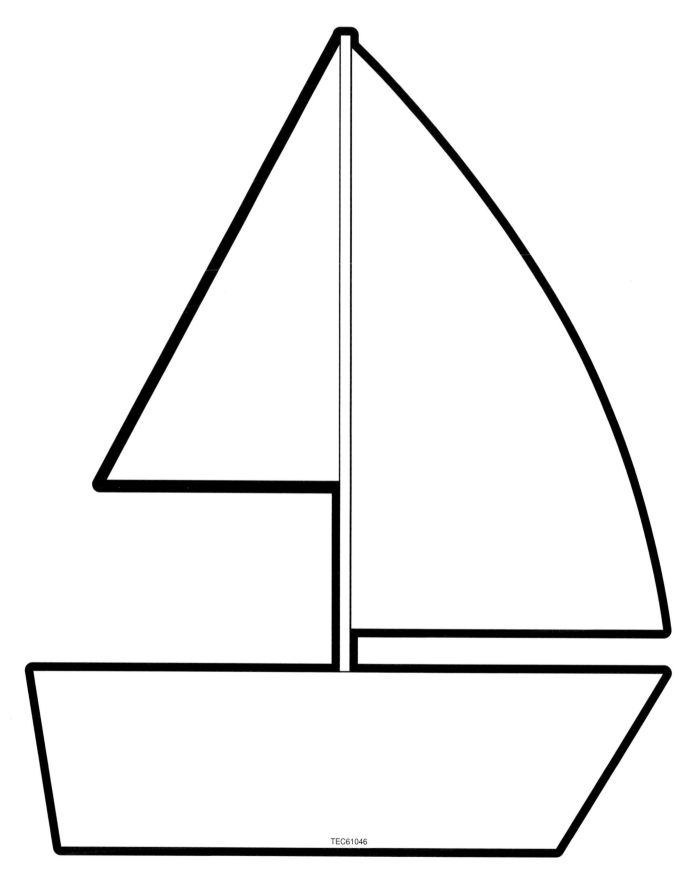

TEC61046

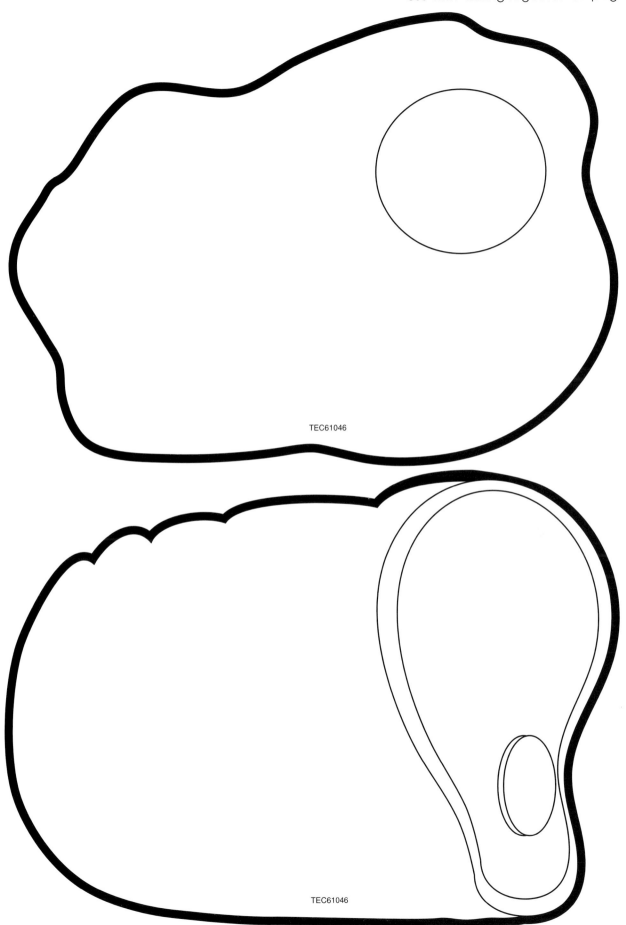

TEC61046

TEC61046

I think the caterpillar should try

_____. Yum!

60

Note to the teacher: Use with "Extending the Menu" on page 54.

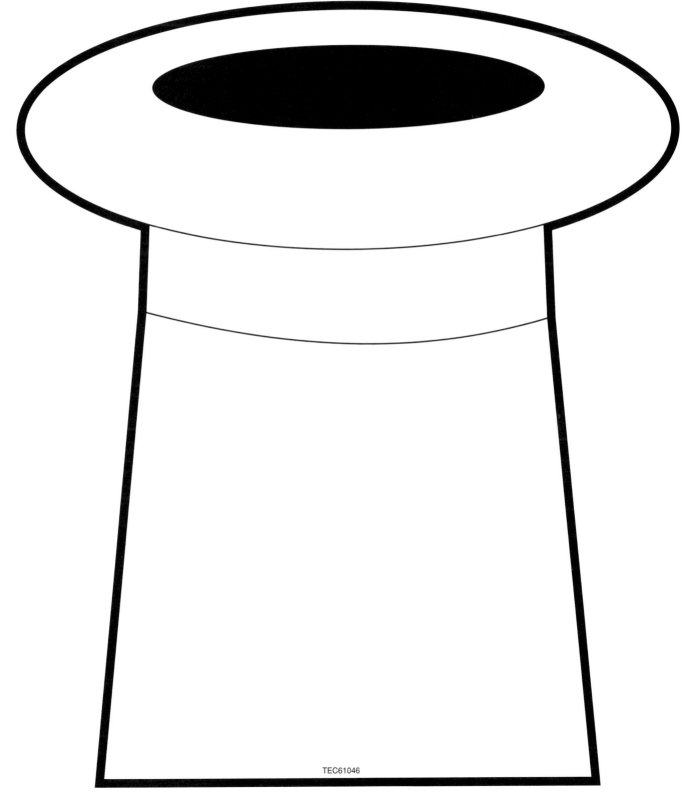

TEC61046

©The Mailbox® • *Superbook*® • TEC61046

Note to the teacher: Use with "Blueberries!" on page 55.

61

Lamb Pattern
Use with "Strawberry Lambs and Jam" on page 55.

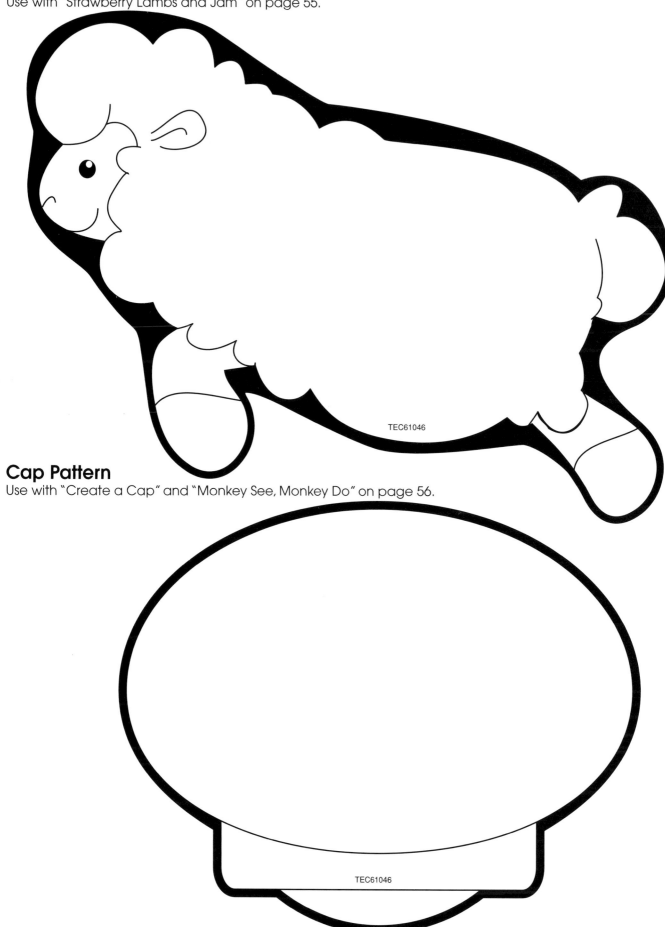

TEC61046

Cap Pattern
Use with "Create a Cap" and "Monkey See, Monkey Do" on page 56.

TEC61046

Colors

Color Spy

Lead your little ones outside for a game of I Spy with a colorful twist. In advance, help youngsters make special spyglasses. Provide each child with a length of cardboard tube, a paintbrush, and tempera paint in the color currently being studied. Have each child paint the outside of his tube; then set all the tubes aside to dry thoroughly.

When the tubes have dried, have each child pick up a special color-seeking spyglass and follow you outdoors for a walk around the school. Instruct your students to be on the lookout for items in that special color. If desired, carry a clipboard with paper and pencil and make a list of all the items your students identify. When you return to the classroom, review the list and praise your preschool color spies!

blue   Meg

blue

baby blanket

plates

ball

ribbon

Crayon Clues

A box of crayons will help you get started with this color-search idea. Ask each child in a small group to select a crayon. Have her identify the crayon's color; then write the color word and the child's name at the top of a sheet of plain paper. Tape the crayon to the paper. Ask each child to find items in your classroom that match her crayon's color. As a student discovers an item, write that item's name on her page. After each child in the group has found several items, collect the papers and review the colors with the group.

Colorful Photos

In a flash, your preschoolers will be practicing color identification and matching skills with this activity! Ask each child to name her favorite color; then ask her to find as many classroom items as she can in that color. Have her gather all the items on a tabletop. Then snap her picture with the objects. Select a half sheet of construction paper in the same color and mount the developed photo in the center. Group all the photos showing the same color together and add a sized-to-match top sheet (again in the same color) labeled with the color word. Stack each color grouping together and bind the book with a cover that bears the title "Our Classroom Color Book." Share the book with your students, helping them identify each color and the items shown in each photo.

A Looking Glass

The world will look mysterious and magical when youngsters peer at it through rose-colored—or blue- or green- or yellow-colored—glasses! To make these special looking glasses, make a class supply of the frame pattern on page 66 on heavy tagboard. Have your assistant or a parent volunteer help you cut out each frame, including the center section. Then ready your art table with the cutout frames, several colors of plastic wrap or cellophane, glue, and crayons.

Working with one small group at a time, ask each child to begin coloring a frame. Have him choose and identify a color of plastic wrap or cellophane. Assist the child in cutting a piece of the see-through material to fit over the opening of a frame; then help the child tape the wrap or cellophane in place. Invite youngsters to peer through their special looking glasses and describe what they see. Encourage each child to trade glasses with a friend for another colorful view of your classroom.

Colorful Sort

For a fun circle-time activity, fill a sock and a small basket with colored bear counters. Have a student take one bear from the sock; then have him find a matching-colored bear in the basket. Have several other children point out objects in your classroom that are the same color. Continue in this manner until each color has been matched.

Color in the Classroom

Each time you introduce a new color, use this activity to encourage your little ones to search for it in your classroom. Using construction paper in the current color of study, cut out a class supply of letters corresponding to the color word's beginning letter. For example, if you are focusing on red, cut a class supply of Rs from red construction paper. Place tape and the cutout letters in a basket in your circle-time area. Then ask a child to take a letter cutout and a small piece of tape. Have her find something red in your classroom and tape the letter cutout to the object or picture. Continue until every child has had a turn, giving assistance as necessary.

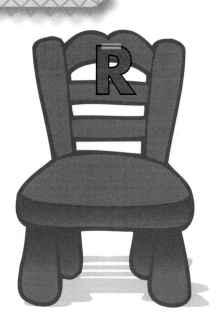

Floating Foam Shapes

Purchase several sheets of colorful craft foam from your local craft store. Cut various shapes from the foam and float these shapes in your water table. Also, provide containers in various shapes such as square baskets or round plastic containers. Ask youngsters to sort the foam shapes into the corresponding shaped containers.

Get Movin'

Incorporate some movement into your shape study. Use masking tape to outline one or more basic shapes on the floor of your classroom (or draw the shapes with chalk on a sidewalk or blacktop area). Invite youngsters to perform various movements on each shape outline, such as "Jump around the square" or "Tiptoe around the triangle."

Hokey-Pokey Shape-Up

It's time to shape up youngsters' recognition of shapes with a few rounds of "The Hokey-Pokey"! In advance, cut a variety of shapes from tagboard. To begin, give each child a shape cutout. When each student hears her shape named in the song, she performs the named actions. Each time you repeat the song, use a different shape name for the underlined word until each child has had the opportunity to participate. That's what it's all about!

(sung to the tune of "The Hokey-Pokey")

You put your [square] in. You take your [square] out.
You put your [square] in. And you shake your [square] about.
You do the hokey-pokey, and you turn yourself around.
That's what it's all about!

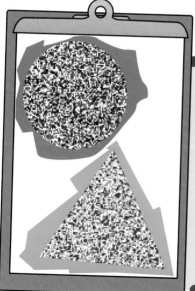

Shape Rubbings

To prepare for this activity, cut sheets of sandpaper into basic shapes, peel the paper off a supply of crayons, and gather a few clipboards. Working with two or three children at a time, have each child choose a sandpaper shape and identify it. Use a piece of rolled masking tape to secure each child's shape to a clipboard. Then clip a sheet of white copy paper over the shape. Demonstrate how to rub the length of a crayon across the paper to make the shape "magically" appear. Continue with different crayon colors and shapes on the same or different sheets of paper.

Sponge-Around Shapes

Invite little ones to make unique shape pictures with this painting method. To prepare, cut a variety of shapes from tagboard, set out several shallow trays of tempera paint, and attach a supply of one-inch square sponges to clothespins. Working with two or three children at a time, have each child choose two or three shapes and identify them. Next, have him arrange them on a 12" x 18" sheet of white construction paper. Use rolled pieces of masking tape to secure the shapes. Then have the child dip a sponge into the paint color of his choice and sponge all around the edges of one shape. Have him repeat the procedure with other paint colors on the other shapes. Then remove the tagboard shapes. Display the finished artwork on a bulletin board.

I see a square looking at me.

Square, square, what do you see?

I See Shapes!

Review all the shapes your little ones have studied with the reproducible booklet on pages 71–72. You may choose to use only some of the pages, and they can be placed in any order, with the exceptions of the cover, the first page, and the last page. To prepare, duplicate the desired booklet pages for each child; then cut them apart and staple the booklets together. For each child, cut out a construction paper copy of the shapes on page 72.

When you are ready for students to complete their booklets, set out glue, the shape cutouts, and crayons. Give each child a booklet. Read through the booklet together, asking each child to glue the correct shape to each page. Then have each child draw shapes on her booklet cover and her last page. Encourage youngsters to take these booklets home to share identifying shapes with their families.

Shapes Everywhere

Give little ones opportunities to hunt for a specific shape both at home and at school. Prepare a note to parents similar to the one shown, and make a copy for each child. When youngsters bring in their items, hold a shapely sharing session so they can tell about the objects they found.

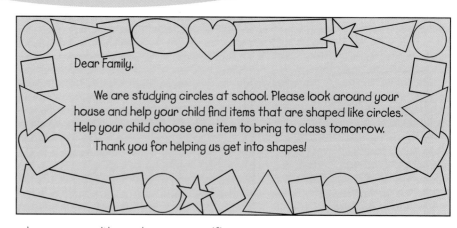

Dear Family,

We are studying circles at school. Please look around your house and help your child find items that are shaped like circles. Help your child choose one item to bring to class tomorrow.

Thank you for helping us get into shapes!

Then extend the shape hunt to your classroom with a shape-specific spy game. Provide a large plastic magnifying glass. Hand the glass to one child at a time and ask him to look around your classroom until he spies an item that matches a predetermined shape. Have him point to the shape or use his finger to outline the shape. If desired, write the shape name on a sticky note and invite the finder to attach it to the item he found.

Check out the skill-building reproducibles on pages 73–75.

I See Shapes!

by _____

Circle, circle,
what do you see?

I see a square looking at me.

I see a rectangle looking at me.

Square, square,
what do you see?

Rectangle, rectangle,
what do you see?

I see a triangle looking at me.

Triangle, triangle,
what do you see?

I see lots of shapes
looking at me!

Circles

Lollipop Land

Trace.

Draw a ◯.

Name _____

All Aboard!

Trace.

Draw a □.

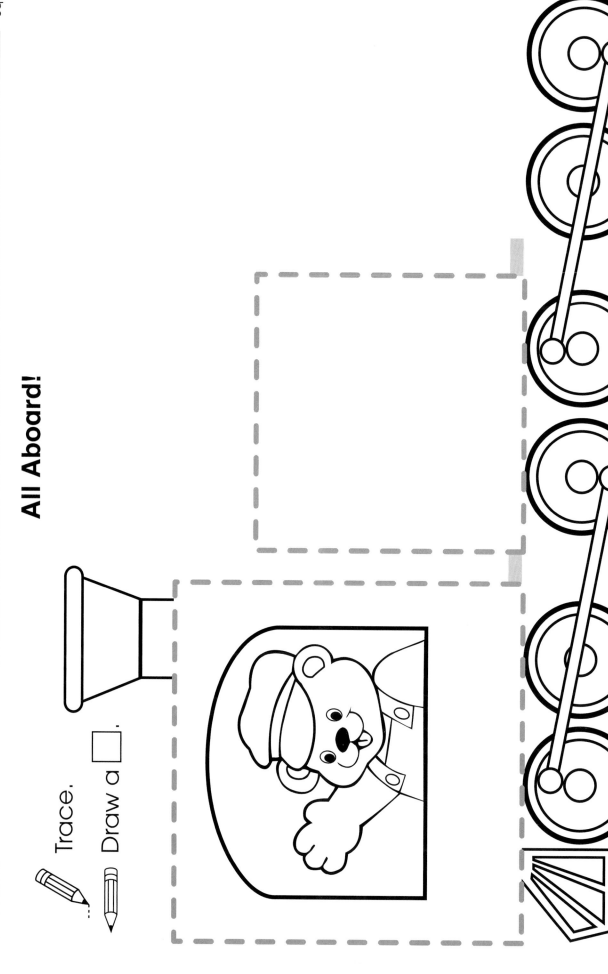

Name _____

It's a Party!

✏ Trace.

✏ Draw a △.

Sorting and Patterns

Sort It Out!

Youngsters sing and sort a variety of critter counters! Teach students the song below. Next, show your group several different types of animal counters. Name one type of animal and substitute it in the song where indicated. As you sing together, invite student volunteers to sort accordingly. Repeat the song, substituting a different animal until all the counters are sorted by type. **Sorting**

(sung to the tune of "Shortnin' Bread")
Find all the [bears] and put them together.
Put all the [bears] together right now.
Find all the [bears] and put them in a pile.
The [bears] are all together; see them smile!

What Shape? What Color?

Reinforce sorting by attribute with this shapely small-group activity! In advance, make one red paper copy and one green paper copy of the cards on pages 78 and 79. Cut apart the cards and arrange them faceup in your group area. Gather a small group of students and select a card. Next, name one attribute that describes the shape on the card, such as shape, color, or size. Encourage volunteers to sort the cards according to that attribute. Continue naming attributes and sorting together; then invite a student to select an attribute by which the rest of the group may sort the cards. *Sorting*

Picture This

Provide plenty of sorting fun with people pictures! Place a supply of student photos (or magazine pictures) in a center. A child in this center selects an attribute, such as gender, hair color, or clothing, and sorts the pictures accordingly. If desired, have each child describe his method of sorting before beginning the next round. **Sorting**

Red, Blue, Red, Blue

Looking for a fun way to identify and copy patterns with your preschoolers? This is it! On your flannelboard, display three red and three blue felt circles in an AB pattern (beginning with red). Teach youngsters the song shown as you point out the pattern. Next, ask a volunteer to extend the pattern with additional felt circles. If desired, substitute different-colored felt shapes and repeat the activity. **Patterns**

(sung to the tune of "Did You Ever See a Lassie?")

First a red one, then a blue one,
A red one, a blue one,
Then a red one and a blue one.
Now what did we make?

A pattern, a pattern,
A colorful pattern.
Oh, a pretty color pattern
Is just what we've made!

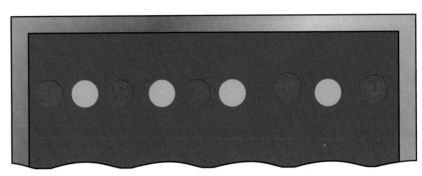

Paper-Chain Patterns

Add a new dimension to patterns with this simple, decorative activity! Stock a center with two colors of paper strips. Begin a paper chain in an AB pattern; then tape one end to a tabletop. A child in this center identifies the pattern, selects the next color strip, and adds a link to the chain. She continues extending the pattern in this manner as time allows. Then display the completed chain around your classroom to reflect youngsters' hard work. **Patterns**

On the Spot

Try this center activity to help youngsters easily extend patterns! Prepare a paper strip for each child by gluing shape cutouts to begin an AB pattern. Draw small, evenly spaced dots on each strip to guide the child as he extends the pattern. Place the prepared strips and a supply of similar cutouts at a center. A child selects a strip, identifies the pattern, and chooses the cutouts needed to extend it. He places a dab of glue on each dot and tops it with the appropriate cutout. **Patterns**

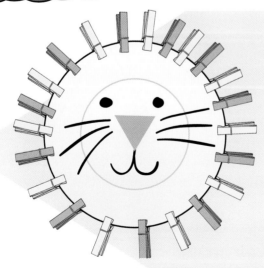

Roaring Into Patterns

Giving a lion a mane makes patterning fun for little ones! Draw a lion face on a yellow paper plate. Place the plate in a center with a supply of yellow and orange plastic clothespins. Clip clothespins to the lion face to start an AB pattern. A child in this center identifies the established pattern and extends it to complete the lion's mane. He reads his pattern to check his work and then removes most of the clothespins to prepare the center for the next visitor. **Patterns**

Shape Cards

Use with "What Shape? What Color?" on page 76.

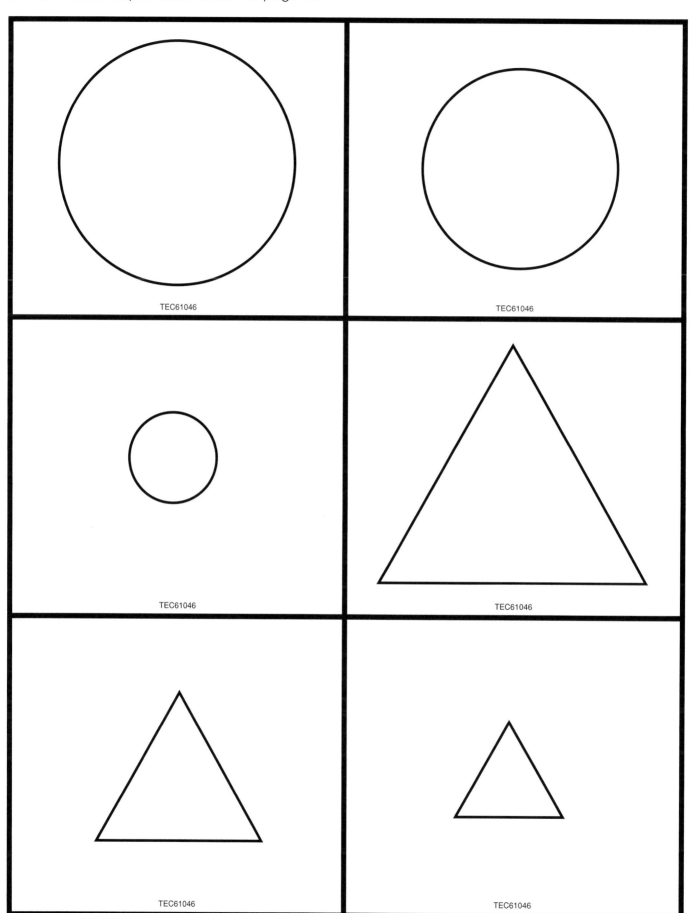

TEC61046

TEC61046

TEC61046

TEC61046

TEC61046

TEC61046

TEC61046

TEC61046

TEC61046

TEC61046

TEC61046

TEC61046

1² ³ 4 ⁵ # Numbers 6⁷ 8⁹ 10

Clothespin Cards

To prepare for this nifty center, cut sturdy cardboard into a variety of basic shapes. Label each shape with a different numeral from 1 to 10. Then attach a corresponding number of stickers around the edge of the shape. Place the shapes in a container with a supply of clothespins; then set the container in a center. For each shape, a child counts the stickers to help her identify the number. Then she attaches a clothespin to each sticker. Lead the youngster to notice that she has the same number of clothespins as stickers on each shape. For additional practice with one-to-one correspondence, have each child complete a copy of page 89. **One-to-one correspondence**

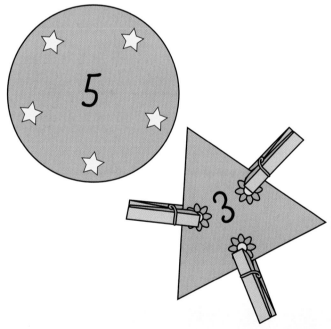

Mice Are Nice!

Here's an engaging game youngsters are sure to enjoy! Cut out three gray construction paper copies of the mouse cards on page 84 and gather two large foam dice. Cut a hole in a shoebox to resemble a mouse house. Then gather a small group of children around the prepared props. Have one child roll the dice as all the youngsters chant, "Roll the dice, count the mice!" After the child counts the number of dots on the dice, he counts the corresponding number of mouse cards as he places them in the mouse house. He removes the cards and the youngsters play another round. *Counting*

Count It Out

This idea provides valuable counting practice, as well as an opportunity to follow directions. During a small-group time, ask each child, in turn, to perform a specific action with a named body part. For example, you might instruct a child to stomp her foot, blink her eyes, or bump her elbows together. After several practice rounds, challenge each youngster to perform the named action for a specific number of times based on her counting ability. Ask the child to count each of her movements aloud. **Counting**

Time to Hibernate!

This math idea will provide lots of counting fun. In advance, collect five baskets. Turn the baskets upside down; then program each basket with a different numeral from 1 to 5. Place the baskets and a supply of bear cutouts (patterns on page 85) in a center. To use this center, encourage a child to place the correct number of bears in each corresponding "bear cave." If desired, also have each child numerically sequence the bear caves.
Making sets

Snacking Sets

Pair students and then provide each pair with a folded sheet of construction paper and two cups of crackers. Have one child in the pair unfold the paper and arrange a set of crackers on one half of the paper. Then have her partner create the same set on the other half of the paper. Have them repeat the process several times and then nibble on their snack. **Making sets**

Handy Numerals

Brighten your room with this handy numeral display. Draw the outline of a different numeral from 1 to 10 on each of ten large sheets of white construction paper. Place one of the sheets of paper on a table. Paint a student volunteer's hand with a vivid color of washable paint. Guide her in pressing her hand along the outline several times in order to form the numeral. Stop and repaint her hand if necessary. Repeat this process for the rest of the numerals, using a different child and a different color of paint each time. After the paint dries, cut around the numerals, mount them onto colored pieces of construction paper, and display them in sequential order at students' eye level or use them as large numeral cards. **Number awareness**

Guess the Numeral

Use a set of the number cards (pages 86–88) to play this counting game with your little ones. During circle time have a volunteer pick a card from your hand and instruct him not to show it to the rest of the children. Direct him to select a set of students to stand in front of the group to match the numeral on his card, and assist him if necessary. Ask a seated volunteer to guess the numeral on the child's card. If he is correct, give the guesser the next turn to pick a card. **Making sets**

Housekeeping Counts

Pair items found in your housekeeping corner with the number cards (pages 86–88) to provide lots of opportunities for little ones to count and make sets. **Making sets**

- Stock the shelves with empty food boxes. Label each of ten paper grocery bags with a different numeral card. Instruct a student to pick a bag and fill it with the correct number of boxes.

- Fill a box with five of each of the following: paper plates, napkins, plastic forks, plastic spoons, and paper cups. Have a child choose a number card from one to five, lay it in the center of the table, and then set the table for the correct number of guests.

- Hang a clothesline in your housekeeping center. Place baby or doll clothes, clothespins, and the number cards inside a basket. Invite a youngster to hang a number card along with the matching number of clothing items on the line to "dry."

Counting Under Construction

Blocks are for building and counting with these activities!

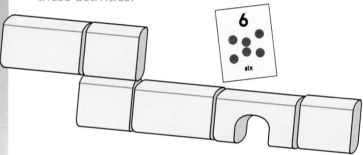

- Invite a student to choose a number card and then build a road with the corresponding number of blocks. Have him continue building until he has used the whole set of cards. **Making sets**

- Encourage a pair of youngsters to work together to build a block tower. When the tower falls, have the students count to find out how many blocks they used. Then challenge them to build a larger tower, using more blocks than before. **Counting**

- Designate a specific numeral from one to five (or ten with more advanced students). Instruct each member of a small group to build a structure that uses only the designated number of blocks. Share and compare the finished projects. **Making sets**

The Art of Counting

Try this palette of activities to keep little ones counting in your art center.
Making sets

- Spread out a set of the number cards (pages 86–88). Have a pair of children work together to place the correct number of crayons on each card.

- Encourage little ones to create pictures using a certain number of items such as four craft foam shapes, five feathers, seven star stickers, or ten toothpicks. If desired, use the story *Ten Black Dots* by Donald Crews as a springboard for this activity.

1, 2, 3...Dig!

Watch as youngsters get down to the nitty-gritty with these activities for the sand table.

- Label each of five small plastic flowerpots with a different numeral from one to five. Set them in the sand table with an assortment of 15 artificial blooms. Direct little ones to "plant" the correct number of flowers in each pot. **Making sets**

- Bury a set of ten plastic or wooden numerals in the sand. Have children in a small group find the numerals, sequence them (assist as necessary), and then count aloud as they point to each one. **Numbers**

Keep on Counting

Encourage parents to continue counting at home with their children. For each child, duplicate onto construction paper the parent note on page 86 along with a set of the number cards from pages 86–88. If possible include stickers or the stamp pad needed to complete the cards. Send the materials home in resealable plastic bags for durable storage. **Counting**

Check out the skill-building reproducibles on pages 89-90.

Mouse Cards

Use with "Mice Are Nice!" on page 80.

TEC61046

TEC61046

TEC61046

TEC61046

Dear Parent, 1...2...3...4...5

Here are some ideas to help your child learn to count at home:

- Count socks as you fold laundry.
- Count utensils as you set the table.
- Count flowers or trees outside.
- Count blocks as you build a tower.
- Clap and count as you listen to music.

To use the enclosed counting cards, draw dots or put stickers on the cards to represent each number. Cut out the cards. Help your child count the stickers and say the numbers.

TEC61046

Number Cards
Use with "Guess the Numeral," "Housekeeping Counts," and "Counting Under Construction" on page 82 and "The Art of Counting" and "Keep on Counting" on page 83.

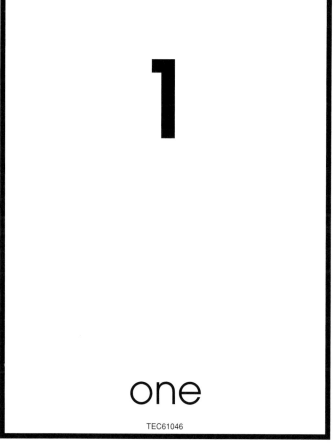

1

one

TEC61046

2

two

TEC61046

Number Cards

Use with "Guess the Numeral," "Housekeeping Counts," and "Counting Under Construction" on page 82
and "The Art of Counting" and "Keep on Counting" on page 83.

3

three

TEC61046

4

four

TEC61046

5

five

TEC61046

6

six

TEC61046

Number Cards

Use with "Guess the Numeral," "Housekeeping Counts," and "Counting Under Construction" on page 82 and "The Art of Counting" and "Keep on Counting" on page 83.

7 seven <small>TEC61046</small>	**8** eight <small>TEC61046</small>
9 nine <small>TEC61046</small>	**10** ten <small>TEC61046</small>

Name _____ One-to-one correspondence

Poultry in Paradise

 Cut.

Glue one  to each ☐.

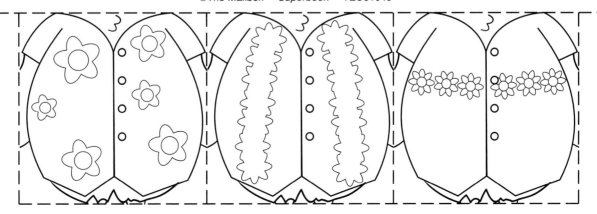

Easy as 1, 2, 3!

Trace.

Amazing Animals

Youngsters chant about many different types of animals with this rousing rhyme! What other animals can your students name?

Amazing animals, wild and tame.
How many animals can we name?

Zebras, dogs, and kangaroos,
Bats in caves, and cats who snooze.

Lions, tigers, growling bears,
Wiggly worms that have no hair.

Swans and cows and fuzzy sheep,
Whales that swim, and frogs that leap.

Horses, monkeys, butterflies,
Eagles that have such good eyes.

Two legs, four legs, six, or eight,
Even no legs—slithering snakes!

Amazing animals, large or small.
Can you guess? We like them all!

Home, Sweet Home

Little ones learn about animal homes with this booklet-making project. Give each child a copy of pages 95-97. Read the text on page one aloud; then help her find the appropriate animal, cut it out, and glue it to the page. Continue in this manner until the booklet pages are complete. When the glue is dry, stack the pages in order and staple them along the left side. To conclude the activity, discuss human and animal homes with youngsters; then lead them to conclude that homes can provide shelter and safety.

The Best Nest

Several types of animals, including birds and squirrels, make their homes in nests. If possible, take a walk with youngsters to look for nests in trees. Explain that these animals need a variety of materials to build their nests. Give the birds and squirrels in your area a helping hand by encouraging students to collect soft materials such as scraps of string, yarn, and clean fabric. You may also wish to cut facial tissues and used dryer sheets into strips. Have youngsters place the items in a shallow plastic tray, along with sturdy materials, such as small twigs, raffia, and straw. Then put the tray in a sheltered outdoor area near your classroom. Invite students to observe which items are chosen by the animals.

Fur, Feathers, and Scales

Little ones investigate different types of animal body coverings with this hands-on activity! To prepare, gather scraps of faux fur, craft feathers, and sequined fabric to represent scales. Also, color and cut apart a copy of the cards on page 98. Show youngsters the cards and help them identify each animal. Next, invite students to touch and feel the covering materials. Explain that the materials are similar to the coverings that these animals have on their bodies. Then invite youngsters to sort the animal cards according to the appropriate type of body covering.

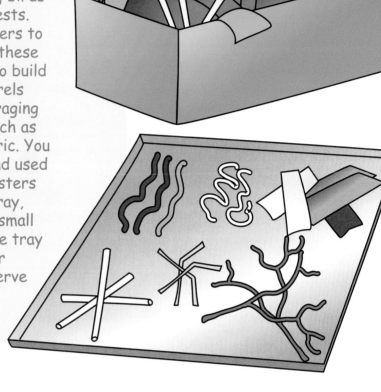

How Many Legs?

Lead little ones to understand that different kinds of animals have different numbers of legs. To prepare for this circle-time activity, place a variety of small animal toys, such as animal counters or stuffed animals, in a basket. Then pass the basket to a child, who removes an animal, identifies it, and counts the legs. Teach youngsters the song shown, substituting the animal name and appropriate number of legs where indicated. Repeat until each child has had a turn.

(sung to the tune of "The Farmer in the Dell")

A [cow] has [four] legs.
A [cow] has [four] legs.
Touch each leg and count them all.
A [cow] has [four] legs.

Quack, Meow, Roar!

Youngsters associate animals with their sounds in this wonderfully noisy game! To prepare, review a variety of animal sounds with students. Then seat little ones in a circle. Select a child to be the caller. He stands in the middle and makes an animal noise of his choosing. A volunteer names the animal that makes the sound. If she is correct, she becomes the caller for the next round. If she is incorrect, the caller repeats the sound and gives hints to help her guess correctly. Play continues in this manner until each child has had a turn to be the caller.

Animal Moves

Students explore how different animals get around in this movement activity! To begin, teach youngsters the poem shown. Then have students spread out in an open area and recite the poem together. Encourage youngsters to perform each movement as it is described.

I'll slither like a snake.
I'll pounce like a cat.
I'll wiggle like a worm.
I'll flap like a bat!

I'll jump like a rabbit.
I'll hop like a frog.
I'll scurry like a spider.
I'll run like a dog!

I'll swim like a fish.
I'll fly like a bee.
I'll waddle like a duck.
Then I'll move like me!

My owl has two legs and can see in the dark!

Play Dough Parade

This small-group activity will inspire plenty of thinking about animal characteristics! In advance, program a large die with numbers 0, 2, 4, 4, 6, and 8. Give each child a portion of play dough and eight craft sticks. A child rolls the die and announces the number that lands faceup. Each child uses his dough and sticks to form an animal with the matching number of legs. Then each student shares his animal, pointing out interesting characteristics and counting the legs aloud. Play continues in this manner until each child has had a turn to roll the die.

Home, Sweet Home

by

_____

A fish's home is in the water.

1

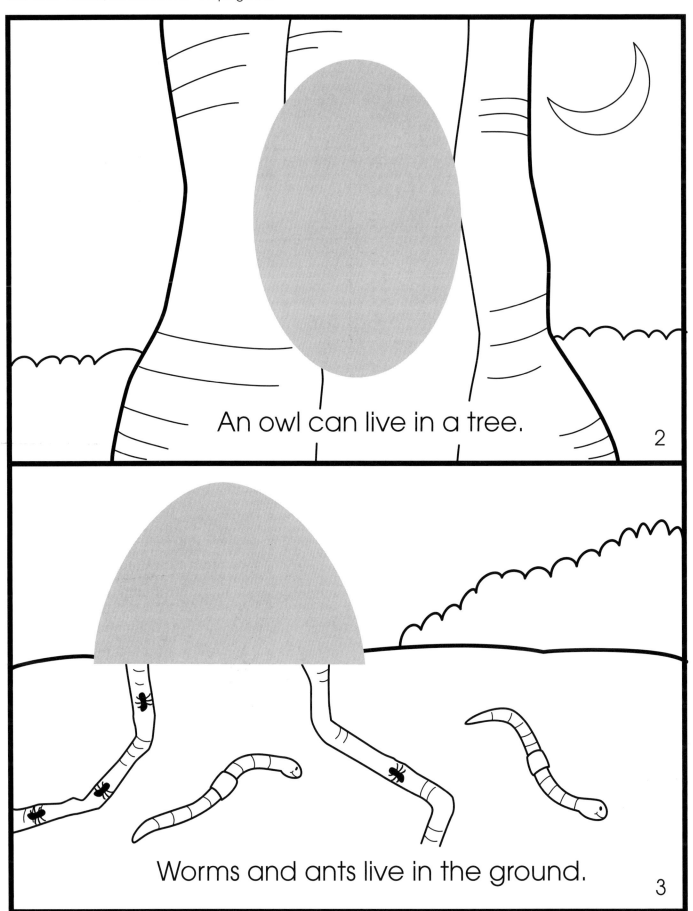

An owl can live in a tree.

2

Worms and ants live in the ground.

3

And this is a home for me!

4

Animal Cards

Use with "Fur, Feathers, and Scales" on page 92.

TEC61046

TEC61046

TEC61046

TEC61046

TEC61046

TEC61046

TEC61046

TEC61046

TEC61046

Plant Parts

Grow your students' plant knowledge and vocabulary with this flannelboard activity! In advance, color and cut out a copy of the plant parts on page 102; then prepare them for flannelboard use. Gather youngsters and present each piece as you name it. Next, teach youngsters the poem shown. As you say each line together, invite a different volunteer to identify the appropriate plant part and place it on the flannelboard. Repeat the activity so that each child has a turn.

Let's make a plant with all its parts.
These are the roots where growing starts.

This is the stem so tall and lean.
These are the leaves so small and green.

This is the flower that blooms so wide
And grows tiny little seeds inside.

Looking at Leaves

Youngsters compare leaves in this easy investigation. To prepare, cut apart two copies of the leaf cards on page 103. Color four cards light green, four cards medium green, and four cards dark green. Then gather youngsters and invite them to compare the leaves and describe ways in which they are the same and different. Help students sort the leaves by shape or color. Lead youngsters to conclude that leaves have similarities and differences. If desired, place the leaves in a center for further student investigation.

Posy Prints

Reinforce little ones' understanding of plant parts with this creative activity! To prepare, cut kitchen sponges into flower, stem, and leaf shapes. Place the sponges in your art area along with shallow pans of green, pink, and yellow paint. To make a posy print, a child dips the stem sponge into green paint and presses it onto a sheet of construction paper. Next, he prints green leaves growing from the stem. He then prints a colorful flower at the top of the stem and sets his project aside to dry. Later, have him identify each plant part as you label his project.

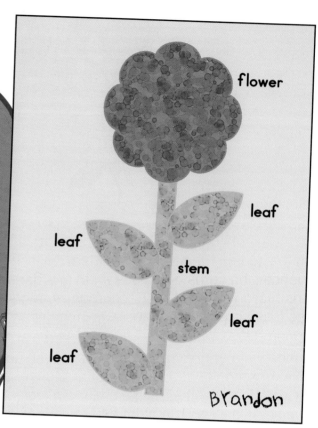

flower

leaf

leaf

stem

leaf

leaf

Brandon

Sun, Soil, and Water

Spotlight the importance of soil, sun, and water in this dramatic-play activity. Fill your sensory table with potting soil. Place plastic flowerpots, artificial plants and flowers, toy trowels, empty seed packets, craft foam seeds, a watering can, and children's gardening gloves nearby. Display a tagboard sun overhead. Gather youngsters around the table and explain that when a seed is planted in soil, watered carefully, and given the right amount of sunlight, it can grow into a plant. Then invite pairs of students to take turns pretending to work in the garden. Encourage them to discuss the process of planting a seed in the soil, watering it, and helping it grow into a plant.

How Does a Flower Grow?

Here's a song to help youngsters sequence the growth of a flower. In advance, color and cut out a copy of the cards on page 104. Teach youngsters the song shown; then display the cards in random order. Help students identify the picture on each card. Next, sing the song again, pausing at the end of each line to invite a volunteer to place the appropriate card in sequence. Follow up the activity by giving each child a copy of page 104. Have her color and cut apart the cards. Then help as needed while she sequences the cards and glues them in order to a construction paper strip. Encourage students to use their sequenced projects as props while they sing the song again.

Oh, How Does a Flower Grow?
(sung to the tune of "London Bridge")

Oh, how does a flower grow, flower grow, flower grow?
Oh, how does a flower grow in the garden?

First, there is a tiny seed, tiny seed, tiny seed.
First, there is a tiny seed in the garden.

Next, there is a little sprout, little sprout, little sprout.
Next, there is a little sprout in the garden.

Then, a bud grows on the stem, on the stem, on the stem.
Then, a bud grows on the stem in the garden.

Last, there is a pretty flower, pretty flower, pretty flower.
Last, there is a pretty flower in the garden.

Seeds and Plants

Youngsters take turns pretending to be gardeners and plants in this circle-time activity. Designate a group of youngsters to be gardeners and discuss how plants require good soil, water, and care. Designate the remaining students as seeds planted in the soil, and have them crouch down. Direct the gardeners to carefully walk among the seeds while pretending to water them. Invite the seeds to begin growing by slowly standing and stretching out their arms and hands to resemble stems and leaves. When the plants have grown tall under such good care, have youngsters switch roles and repeat the activity.

Plant Parts Patterns
Use with "Plant Parts" on page 99.

roots

stem

leaves

flower

TEC61046

TEC61046

TEC61046

TEC61046

TEC61046

TEC61046

TEC61046

Sequencing Cards

Use with "How Does a Flower Grow?" on page 101.

TEC61046

TEC61046

TEC61046

TEC61046

WEATHER

Weather Song

Whatever the weather, this little ditty is just perfect for your preschoolers!

(sung to the tune of "Twinkle, Twinkle, Little Star")

Stormy days and winds that blow,
White and fluffy falling snow.
Rain falls gently to the ground
And scatters colored leaves around.
Sunny days with bright blue skies,
Weather is a big surprise!

Daily Forecast

Little ones note the day's weather with this simple observation activity. Color, cut out, and laminate a copy of the weather cards on page 109. Program a sentence strip as shown. Display the strip in your group area and place the cards nearby. Each day, invite a student to look out the window and decide the type of weather. Next, help him use Sticky-Tac adhesive to mount the matching weather card to the strip. Then enlist student help to read the sentence aloud.

The weather is ☀ today.

What to Wear?

Youngsters make decisions about weather-appropriate clothing and accessories in this circle-time activity. In advance, gather a variety of items such as jackets, raincoats, umbrellas, coats, boots, mittens, scarves, hats, earmuffs, swimsuits, and flip-flops. Discuss temperature and conditions with youngsters, leading them to conclude that people dress for the weather. Then give a pretend weather forecast, such as "The weather will be warm and sunny with a temperature of 80 degrees." Hold up two items, such as a swimsuit and a raincoat, and ask students which item would be the better choice for the weather. Invite a volunteer to name the better option and explain why. Repeat with another forecast and choice of items. For additional practice with weather-appropriate choices, have each child complete a copy of page 112.

Spin the Wheel

Your little weather watchers are sure to enjoy this individual reporting activity! For each child, cut out the window on a construction paper copy of the window wheel on page 110. Have each student color a construction paper copy of page 111 and then help her cut out both wheels. Next, use a brad to join her wheels together where indicated. Then encourage her to observe the day's weather and turn the wheel to match it. Store the wheels near your classroom windows and encourage youngsters to check and report the weather daily.

Ask me about today's weather!

Weather Clues

Preschoolers identify various types of weather with this small-group activity. Provide each child with a set of the weather cards on page 109. (Keep a set of cards for yourself.) Direct each student to spread out his cards on the floor and stand behind them. Next, secretly draw a card and describe the weather conditions indicated. Instruct youngsters to stand behind the matching card. Scan for accuracy. Then continue with the remaining cards.

We could make a snowman in this weather!

A Cloud in the Sky

Clouds are often visible, whether the weather is sunny or rainy. Take youngsters outside on a breezy day to watch the clouds drift by. Explain to students that clouds are made of water vapor, or water that has evaporated and risen into the air. They can take on many shapes and be many sizes. Encourage little ones to describe and compare the clouds in the sky. Then invite each child to glue cotton balls to a sheet of blue construction paper to resemble a cloud he saw in the sky.

Ben

The Fog Song

Teach youngsters this little ditty about fog. Then venture out on a foggy morning to take a closer look at this type of weather!

(sung to the tune of "If You're Happy and You Know It")

If you would like to see some fog,
Look outside!
If you would like to see some fog,
Look outside!
There are clouds near the ground.
Oh, it's hard to see around.
If you would like to see some fog,
Look outside!

Looks Like Rain!

Illustrate rain with this simple demonstration. Explain to students that when a cloud absorbs too much water vapor, we get rain. Have each child place a dry cotton ball "cloud" in a shallow pan of water and observe as it becomes saturated. Then have her hold the cotton ball over the pan. Discuss the changes in the cotton ball cloud; it is wet and heavy, and cannot hold all of the water. The water drips away from the cotton ball as rain drips away from a cloud.

Windy Weather Windsock

These windsocks gently demonstrate the effects of wind. To prepare, cut a one-inch-wide ring from a two-liter plastic bottle for each child. Cut a class supply of 24-inch yarn lengths. Also, slit open the bottom of a quart-size resealable bag for each child and then fringe-cut the edges. Invite each child to decorate a prepared bag with stickers. Next, help her slide a ring inside her bag and staple it just below the seal. Punch two holes opposite each other and then thread a yarn length through the holes to make a handle as shown.

Take students outside and have each child hold her windsock by the handle. Explain to youngsters that wind is air moving around; it can't be seen, but we can see it moving objects such as the windsocks. Then invite students to observe the effects of wind. If it's a calm day, encourage little ones to run like the wind to make their windsocks fly!

Storm Tracking

Tracking an imaginary storm puts little minds at ease! Explain to students that the time between the lightning and thunder tells the storm's distance. As a storm approaches, the lightning and thunder arrive closer together. After the storm passes, the lightning and thunder are farther apart. Then tell youngsters that there's a make-believe storm coming and you need their help to decide how far away it is. Darken your classroom and then pulse a flashlight beam on the ceiling to simulate lightning. Slowly count aloud with students to five; then clap your hands to represent thunder. Continue in this manner, shortening the count between lightning and thunder until the storm arrives with great fanfare. Then reverse the activity, lengthening the time between the lightning and thunder until the storm passes.

Let It Snow!

Add a chill to the air when you create this winter weather wonder-land. Sprinkle foam packing pieces on the floor to create snow. Make a basic snowman shape by stuffing one large and one small white, plastic trash bag with more foam pieces or with newspaper. To make the snowman, insert half of a dowel's length inside the large bag before tying it shut. Then invert the small trash bag over the remaining part of the dowel and tie that bag shut. Provide winter clothing and accessories for children to use to dress the snowman as well as themselves. Use white athletic socks rolled into balls for soft snowballs.

Freezing Fun

Winter and cold weather go together in many areas. After a discussion of winter weather, lead students to conclude that it must be very cold outside for snow and ice to form. Then try this easy experiment to help little ones understand what freezes in cold weather. Fill each section of an ice cube tray with a different substance that will freeze, such as water, milk, and mud. You may also wish to test other objects that are less likely to freeze, such as counting bears, doll clothes, and dry soil. Chart youngsters' predictions about what will freeze and then place the tray in a freezer, or outside if it's cold enough. Check often to observe the changes. Then have students check their predictions. Did everything freeze?

Check out the skill-building reproducible on page 112.

Use with "Daily Forecast" on page 105 and "Weather Clues" on page 106.

TEC61046

TEC61046

TEC61046

TEC61046

TEC61046

TEC61046

Window Wheel Pattern
Use with "Spin the Wheel" on page 106.

Cut out.

Ask me about today's weather!

TEC61046

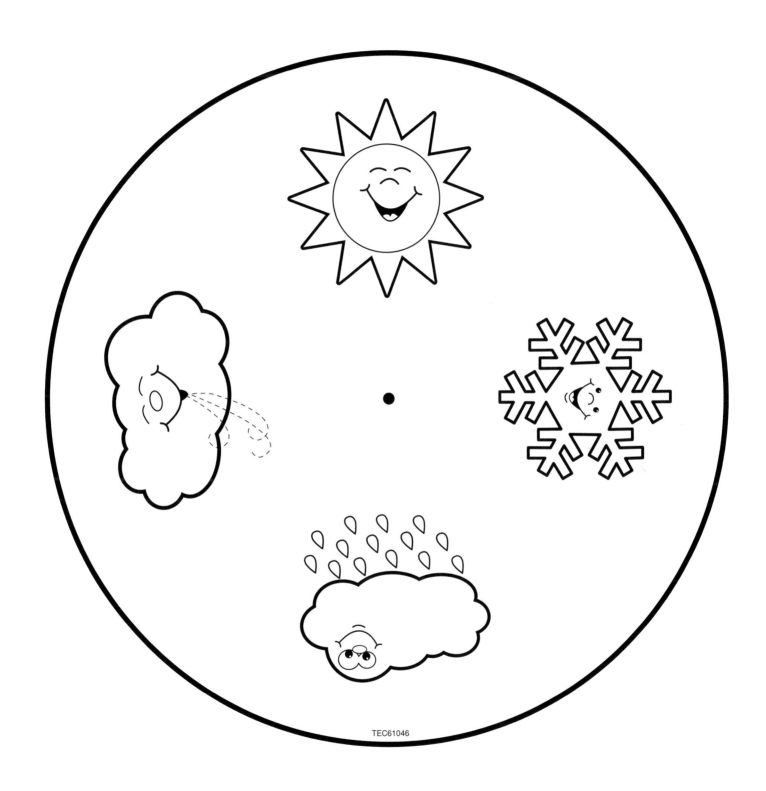

TEC61046

Name _____

Dressed for the Weather

✂ Cut. Match.

🔲 Glue.

All About Me

My Body Can

Use this rhyme about body parts and their movements to help youngsters become aware of their bodies. It's also great for transitions.

My little toes can tap, tap, tap.
My little hands can clap, clap, clap.
My little knees can knock, knock, knock.
My little feet can walk, walk, walk.

My head can nod.
My eyes can blink.
My lips can kiss—
And whistle, I think.

My arms can flap.
My fingers snap.
Now I can sit
And make a lap.

Where Does It Go?

Challenge students to think about their body parts with this game of associations. In advance, collect a variety of clothing accessories and wearable sports equipment, such as bracelets, necklaces, large rings, gloves, socks, caps, sunglasses, shoulder pads, knee pads, and elbow pads. Display all the items during group time; then ask a student to find an item that is worn on his hand, his knee, his head, or any other body part to which an item corresponds. After the child locates an appropriate item, invite him to model it for the class; then return the item to the collection. Continue in the same manner, giving each child an opportunity to select and model an item. Head, shoulder, knees, elbows—show us where each item goes!

Puzzled Parts

Make this life-size floor puzzle to help youngsters recognize the parts of the body. To begin, place a length of white bulletin board paper on the floor. Have a student volunteer lie down on the paper with his arms resting away from his body and his legs slightly spread. Trace around the child with a permanent marker. Invite small groups of students, in turn, to color the resulting outline. Glue the outline onto poster board; then cut the poster board to maintain the outlined shape. Puzzle-cut the outline into an appropriate number of body-part pieces for your students' abilities. To use, have a child or children in a small group put the body puzzle together, naming the different parts as they work.

Guess Who?

Raise self-esteem by describing each child's unique attributes and special abilities. Turn these descriptions into riddles for the rest of the group to solve. For example, you might say, "This child has short, brown hair. He likes to build with blocks. He can cross the monkey bars. He always uses good manners. His sister's name is Katrina. Who is he?" Be ready for lots of smiles and giggles as children hear about themselves in such a positive manner.

My Family and Me

Want to make your classroom burst at the seams with self-esteem? Then invite each of your youngsters to bring in a family photo to share with the group. Tape each photo to a large sheet of bulletin board paper. After each child shares information about his family, write down a few family-fact highlights beside his photo. Title your display "I Love My Family and My Family Loves Me!" Each youngster is sure to be pumped with pride!

y Family

d

Loves Me!

Erica has one brother named Alex and a new baby brother named Ian. Her mom is an artist and her dad is a dentist.

Joseph has one older brother named James. James and Joseph play baseball on the same team. Joseph's mother's name is Anita. She is a scientist.

Kate's parents own a toy store. She has one older brother named Todd.

Look at Me!

Provide an assortment of shatter-proof mirrors in your classroom to encourage exploration with facial expressions and body gestures, and to help children feel comfortable with and confident about themselves. Invite a pair of students to share a mirror and make comparisons about each other. Reinforce the unique and special qualities of each child. Try placing a full-length mirror in your dramatic-play area along with a couple of hand mirrors so that children can see how they look from behind. Include a mirror or two in the art area to encourage youngsters to create self-portraits. Look in the mirror; what do you see? A totally terrific, wonderful me!

Stargazing

For each child, cut a large star from yellow poster board. Label each point of the star with a different sentence starter listed below. Write on each child's star as she dictates her responses. Then ask her to draw a picture of herself in the center of the star. Put each child's star on the appropriate table or cubby. Or hang the stars from the ceiling to promote stargazing.

My favorite center is...
My favorite story is...
My favorite song is...
I like my school because...
My name is...

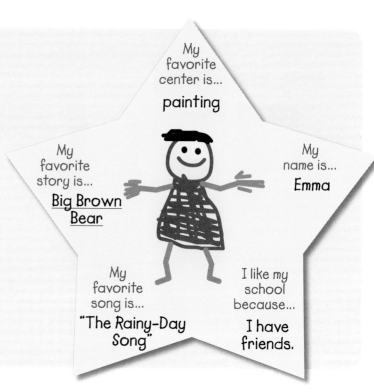

My favorite center is...
painting

My favorite story is...
Big Brown Bear

My name is...
Emma

My favorite song is...
"The Rainy-Day Song"

I like my school because...
I have friends.

Different Strokes for Different Folks

Have each child look through a magazine and cut out pictures of people who look different from her. Encourage her to tell you what's different about each person; then have her tell you something she likes about each person. Explain to the group that even though people look different, they are all special in their very own ways. Extend this idea by having youngsters glue their cutouts to a mural titled "All Different, All Special."

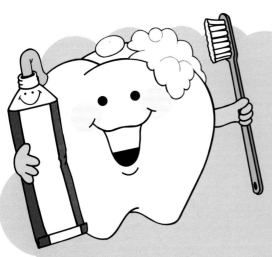

I Can Do Lots of Things!

Since your youngsters are growing up, there are lots more things they can do. Help little ones make a class list of things they are proud that they can do. Then sing the following song, inserting a different task each time you repeat the verse.

You Are Growing Up
(sung to the tune of "If You're Happy and You Know It")

You are growing up; now you can [brush your teeth].
You are growing up; now you can [brush your teeth].
You are growing up, it's true. We're so very proud of you!
You are growing up; now you can [brush your teeth].

I Know Where I Live

Help each of your little ones learn the name of her street with a project that gets parents and children working together. Cut a class supply of poster board strips in a color that matches the street signs in your community. Print each child's street name on a separate strip. Make a holder by cutting a slit into one end of a paper-towel tube. Insert a child's street sign into the holder. Place the holder on a table; then have the child sit on the floor below the street sign to give the appearance that the sign is taller than the child. Take a photo of each child sitting under her street sign. Glue the photo to a copy of the parent note on page 119. As each child is able to state this information at school, acknowledge her street-name savvy with a small treat such as a sticker or stamp.

Dear Family,
At school we are concentrating on learning personal information, including our street names. Please help your child memorize his or her street name. Take a walk to look at the street sign closest to your home. Discuss the importance of knowing the name of your street for safety reasons. Thanks for participating in your child's learning!

Elm Street

Kim Wells
March 12

I Know My Birthday

These birthday-present puppets are the perfect tool for helping your little ones learn their birthdates. Write each child's first name, last name, and birthday on a separate three-inch poster board square. Help each student count a number of stickers to indicate her age; then have her attach the stickers and a mini gift bow to the top of her square so it resembles a present. Glue a craft stick to the back of the completed square.

Have little ones bring their birthday puppets to your group area. Review each child's birthdate, emphasizing the different months (and perhaps sorting the children into groups by birth month). Next, explain that when you call a particular month, all the children born in that month may jump up and show their puppets. After you've called out all the months, invite everyone to sing your favorite birthday song.

Alex Bruce
June 11

A Personal Passport

This project is sure to get your little ones' seal of approval. Reproduce a class supply of the passport cover and information sheet on page 120. To make a passport for each child, fold a piece of blue construction paper in half; then glue the passport cover to the front. Invite each child to dictate his full name, parents' names, street name, and birthday. Write this information on a copy of the personal information sheet. Then glue it to the inside right of the passport. Glue the child's photo on the opposite side.

Use the passports for the activities described in "Show What You Know!" Then, after a few days, encourage each youngster to take his Personal Information Passport home and show off his knowledge to his family.

Show What You Know!

Give each youngster a chance to show off the personal information she knows. Keep the Personal Information Passports (made in "A Personal Passport") handy in your classroom for a few days. During transition times—such as on the way to the playground, on the way to circle time, or as children choose and go to centers—choose a child's passport and quiz her on a bit of personal information, such as her last name or her birthday. Use a rubber stamp to stamp the inside or back of her passport each time she correctly relates some personal information. When every child has several stamps in her passport, send the passports home to spark discussions with parents.

Dear Family,

At school we are concentrating on learning personal information, including our street names. Please help your child memorize his or her street name. Take a walk to look at the street sign closest to your home. Discuss the importance of knowing the name of your street for safety reasons. Thanks for participating in your child's learning!

©The Mailbox® • Superbook® • TEC61046

Note to the teacher: Use with "I Know Where I Live" on page 117.

119

Passport Cover and Information Sheet

Use with "A Personal Passport" on page 118.

PERSONAL INFORMATION PASSPORT

OFFICIAL

©The Mailbox® • *Superbook*® • TEC61046

PERSONAL INFORMATION PASSPORT

Name

Parents' or Guardians' Names

Street

Birthday

Friendship Song

Lead little ones in singing this song to remind them of some traits of a good friend.

(sung to the tune of "I'm a Little Teapot")
I'm your special friend and you're mine too.
You cheer me up when I'm feeling blue.
I'll make you laugh when you feel sad.
We're good friends and I'm so glad.

Super Snapshots

Capture images of students demonstrating qualities of friendship with this collection of photographs! Keep a camera on hand to take spontaneous photographs of children as they display qualities of friendship. (Try to snap at least one picture of each child.)

Once the pictures have been printed, punch a hole in the corner of each and slide the photos onto a metal ring. Each day, randomly choose a different photo to share with students. Then lead youngsters in a discussion of how the pictured child is being a good friend. After discussing all of the photos, put them on display for youngsters to review when they have some free time.

Wall of Kindness

Build kindness in the classroom, brick by brick. To prepare, place a supply of brick cutouts in a convenient location and title a display "Wall of Kindness." Each time you see a youngster exhibiting an act of kindness, write a sentence describing her deed on a brick. At the end of the day, share each programmed brick as you attach it to the display so it resembles a brick wall. Encourage youngsters to display kindness to build the wall as high as they can.

Rachel helped Max clean up.

Need a Friend?

Invite students to help bring a smile to a friend's face with these cheery cards. Copy a supply of the cards on page 125 onto colorful construction paper, cut them out, and place them in a designated spot in your classroom. To begin, lead a discussion about times when a friend may need to be cheered up, and ways to do that. Then share one of the cards and tell youngsters to be on the lookout for a friend who needs to be cheered up. When a child sees a friend in need, she gets a card from the stack and gives it to that student.

Smile!

Link by Link

Illustrate the importance of teamwork in the classroom by making this paper chain. Help each child write his name on a colorful paper strip; then have him decorate it as desired. Once each strip is complete, gather students in a circle. To begin a paper chain, help the first child use tape to form his strip into a link. As he does so, ask him to share a way that he can use teamwork in the classroom, such as by helping others. Then ask the remaining students to add a link to the chain in the same manner. Hang the finished project in the room to serve as a reminder of the importance of working together.

Handy Hearts

Youngsters put their hands together to make these special reminders of friendship. To prepare, program a piece of paper as shown and copy a class supply. Place the copies at a table along with paint brushes and paint. Invite two students to the area. Have each youngster choose a different color paint and use a paint brush to paint his friend's hand. Then help each youngster make an upside-down handprint on the paper to form a heart, as shown. After the students wash their hands, help each child write his friend's name in the blank on his paper.

Andy is my friend.

Close Classmates

Foster new friendships in your classroom with this idea. To prepare, puzzle-cut a colorful cutout for every two students, making each pair unique. (If you have an odd number of students, cut one into thirds.) To begin, ask each student to share something she enjoys doing with her classroom friends. List each response on chart paper. Then give each child half of a cutout and have her find the classmate with the other half. Encourage students in each pair to get to know each other better by participating together in some of the listed activities.

Share and Compare

This activity helps youngsters discover similarities and differences between themselves and their classmates. Working with one pair of students at a time, help each child write her name and her partner's name on a copy of page 126. Then have the partners use the appropriate crayons to color the corresponding spaces. Provide an ink pad to help each youngster add her thumbprint to the page. When the comparisons are complete, have each pair share its results with the group. Then lead a discussion to illustrate that even when two youngsters are different, they can still be friends.

Me	You
My name is Kelly	Your name is Melissa
My hair color	Your hair color
My eye color	Your eye color
My thumbprint	Your thumbprint

Beautiful Bracelets

Promote friendship and sharing by having youngsters make a gift for a friend. To prepare, cut a supply of colorful straws into smaller pieces. Pair students and give each child a length of yarn and several straw pieces. Have each child make a friendship bracelet for her partner by stringing straw pieces onto her length of yarn. When she is satisfied with her work, help her tie the ends of the yarn together and invite her to give her bracelet to her partner.

Good Choices

This activity gives little ones the opportunity to make good sharing choices. Discuss with your students reasons why some things are not appropriate for sharing with friends. As you name items, such as those shown, ask students to give you the thumbs-up sign if the item is appropriate for sharing or the thumbs-down sign if the item is not appropriate for sharing. Then ask children to suggest items for the rest of the group to evaluate.

- crayons
- your toothbrush
- books
- facial tissue
- toys
- medicine
- a drink from your cup
- a new game
- your apple

Sharing Song

Your little ones will be sharing smiles when they participate in this simple game. Gather your youngsters into a circle. Then ask one child to stand in the center of the circle and hold a classroom item such as a stuffed toy or a manipulative. Lead your little ones in singing the following song. As you end the song, invite the child in the center to hand the toy to another child and join the circle. The child given the item moves to the center of the circle. Continue playing until each child has had an opportunity to share the toy.

(sung to the tune of "Bingo")
There was a child, a special child, who liked to share with others.
S-H-A-R-E,
S-H-A-R-E,
S-H-A-R-E,
And [child's name] was [his/her] name-o!

Colorful Sharing

This activity helps youngsters discover the benefits of sharing with their friends. To prepare, give each child in a small group a copy of the coloring picture on page 127 and one crayon. (Make sure each student's crayon is a different color.) Invite your little ones to color their pictures. When a child requests additional crayons, tell her the only crayons available are the ones you've given out. Then lead youngsters to the idea of sharing or trading crayons with the other members of the group to create colorful pictures.

Smile!

TEC61046

Smile!

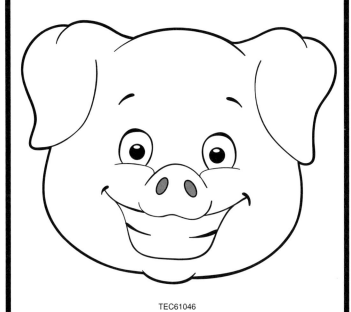

TEC61046

Smile!

TEC61046

Smile!

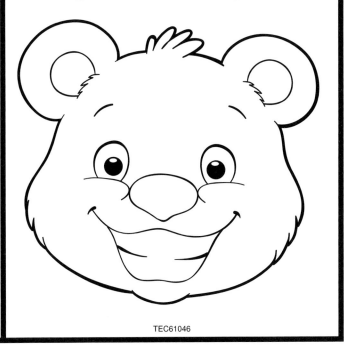

TEC61046

Me 	**You** 
My name is _____.	Your name is _____.
My hair color 	Your hair color 
My eye color 	Your eye color 
My thumbprint 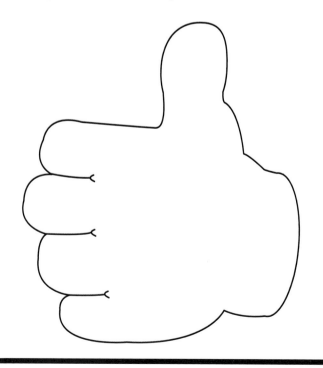	Your thumbprint 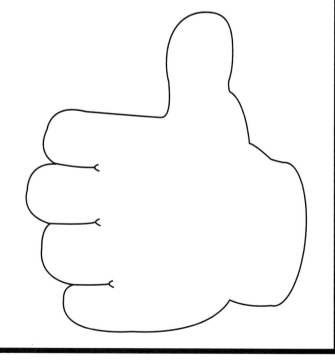

© The Mailbox® • Superbook® • TEC61046

Note to the teacher: Use with "Colorful Sharing" on page 124.

127

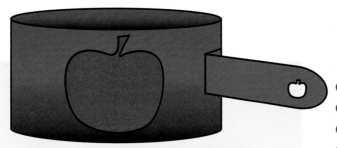

FALL

Johnny Appleseed Hats

Preschoolers pretend to plant seeds while wearing this fun hat! To make a hat, you will need:
- 9" x 3" construction paper rectangle
- black construction paper headband
- apple cutout

Have each child glue the apple cutout to the center of his headband. Help him round one end of the construction paper rectangle to resemble a pot handle. If desired, have him use an apple-shaped hole puncher to punch a hole in the rounded end of the handle. Fold down one inch of the opposite end of the handle to create a gluing tab. Help the child glue the handle to the headband. Encourage youngsters to wear their hats while they pretend to pack some seeds, clear the land, and plant orchards just like Johnny Appleseed!

Johnny Goes-a-Planting

This guessing game, similar to Who's Got the Button?, is sure to produce a bumper crop of smiles. Seat children in a circle. Invite a volunteer to be Johnny Appleseed and wear a pot on her head. Have this child stand away from the group with her back toward the circle. Give a child seated in the circle an apple seed (brown pom-pom) to hide in his hands. Have the remaining children pretend to hide seeds in their hands. Have Johnny return to the group and pretend to pour water on the hands of the child she thinks has the seed. If that child has the seed, he stands up and pretends to grow into a tree. He then becomes Johnny. If he doesn't have the seed, he opens his hands to reveal no seed. Johnny then has two more guesses to try and find the seed. If none of her guesses is correct, Johnny says, "Grow, apple tree, grow." The child holding the seed then stands up, pretends to grow into a tree, and takes his turn as Johnny Appleseed.

A Bushel of Preschoolers

Your youngsters are the center of attention in this 3-D apple craft. Give each student a cutout copy of the leaf pattern on page 134. Help him glue a photograph of himself in the center as shown. To make an apple, have each child stuff a paper lunch bag half full of crumpled newspaper. Help him gather the top of the bag together, twist to form a stem, and wind the stem with masking tape. Encourage him to paint the bag red, yellow, or green and paint the stem brown. After the bag dries, help him tape his leaf to the stem. Then arrange the apples to create an "a-peel-ing" display.

Maria   10-16-07

A Tree in Season

Use this year-round activity to document the seasonal changes of a tree while creating a special portfolio of each youngster's fine-motor skills. To begin, select a tree on or near your school campus—preferably one that exhibits lots of interesting changes throughout the year. At the beginning of the school year, introduce your class to the special tree. Ask students to carefully observe and then illustrate the tree. Write each child's dictated observations on her page. At least once a month, have students return to observe the tree; then repeat the process above. At the end of the year, sequence and bind each child's illustrations between two construction paper covers. Title the book "A Special Tree"; then share the book with the child's parents at the end-of-the-year conference, noting the child's progress in his fine-motor and observation skills. Like the tree's seasonal changes, the child's skill progression will be quite noticeable.

Leaf Sort

What sort of fun can be had in this detail-oriented sorting activity? "Leaf" it to youngsters to find out! To prepare, have students collect a large variety of fall leaves, either at school or at home. Place all the leaves in a basket; then attach a leaf representing each leaf type in the collection—such as oak, maple, or birch—to a separate box. Invite a small group to sort the leaves by type into the appropriate boxes. Then have them sort each leaf set by color onto corresponding sheets of construction paper. Finally, have the group sort each color set by size. After sorting the leaves, challenge each youngster in the group to select a leaf, then describe it using a combination of attributes. For instance, the child might describe her leaf as "a big yellow oak leaf."

oak

Apple Slices	Applesauce
My slice is white.	It looks kind of yellow.
Apples sound crunchy.	It's quiet.
The apple skin feels smooth.	

Apples to Apples

Children compare apple slices to applesauce with this tasty idea. In advance, ask parents to donate a bag of apples and a large jar of applesauce. Make a large chart as shown above. Give each child a peeled apple slice and encourage him to use his five senses to examine the slice. Record students' observations on the chart. Then give each child a taste of applesauce and record all comments as students again use their five senses. Then encourage youngsters to explain how the applesauce differs from the apple slices and how the fruit samples are the same.

Fall Follies

Fill your classroom with these swirling, twirling colorful leaves that will welcome fall with lots of smiles. Cut out a class supply of leaf shapes (patterns on page 135) from colored construction paper. Tape a craft stick to the back of each leaf. Then use the leaves with the activities listed below.

- Play lively classical music and invite each child to dance around in a designated area, performing some creative movements with his leaf.

- Play a game similar to Simon Says by giving directions to children who are holding specific-colored leaves. For example, "Red leaves, stand up," "Orange leaves, jump up and down," and "Yellow leaves, wiggle your noses."

- Direct each child in a small group to choose a leaf. Create a graph with the leaf choices. Compare to see which color is the group favorite.

Handfuls of Leaves

It won't be a mystery who makes these fall trees because they'll have youngsters' fingerprints all over them! To prepare, put a damp sponge in each of three separate trays; then squirt red, yellow, or orange paint over each sponge. To make a fall scene, have each youngster paint a tree onto a large piece of paper. Have her press her fingers into a paint-filled sponge, then onto the paper. She repeats this process to fill the tree and ground with leaves, wiping her fingers each time she changes paint colors.

Animals in Autumn

Use this poem as an introduction to a circle-time discussion about animals preparing for winter.

Six black crows get fat eating corn.
Five mice scurry on a frosty morn.
Four red squirrels hide nuts in a tree.
Three chipmunks stop and look at me.
Two brown beavers build their home all day.
And the little wild goose will soon fly away.

Pumpkin Song

(sung to the tune of "Twinkle, Twinkle, Little Star")

Pumpkin, pumpkin, big and round;
Pumpkin, pumpkin, on the ground.
Pumpkin, pumpkin, orange and fat;
Pumpkin, pumpkin, look at that!
Pumpkin, pumpkin, my oh my!
I can't wait for pumpkin pie!

Hold arms out wide.
Stoop down and touch floor.
Pat stomach with both hands.
Point ahead with eyes wide.
Smile.
Rub tummy.

Spider Mats

Every spiderweb is unique, and so is each of these student-painted ones! Invite each child to lay a sheet of black construction paper in the bottom of a rectangular pan or box lid. Using a large spoon, dip a golf ball in white paint and drop it on the paper. Direct the child to move the golf ball back and forth by repeatedly lifting and tilting the pan. When a desired result is achieved, remove the paper and set it aside. While the web is drying, help the child make a spider. To do this, have him twist four black pipe cleaners together in the center; then bend them to resemble spider legs. Help him squeeze a large puddle of glue onto the intersection of the legs; then place a large black pom-pom on top. To complete the spider, encourage him to put white hole-reinforcer stickers on the pom-pom. Then have him place the spider on the corner of his web.

Monster Stomp

Your little ones will stomp into basic concepts with this activity. Cut out a construction paper copy of the monster pattern and cards on page 136. Glue the monster to a small paper bag and store the cards inside. To play, pass the bag around at circle time. In turn, invite each child to remove a card from the bag. If the card has a shape on it, help him to identify it. If the card has a monster on it, the child yells, "Monster stomp!" and all students stand up and stomp around like big scary monsters. On your signal, the class sits down. Be sure to have each child return his card to the bag. To vary the game, replace the shape cards with color or number cards.

"Boo-tiful" Patterns

To prepare, duplicate onto orange construction paper a class supply plus several extra of the patterning card on page 137. Cut out each card, fold it along the dotted line, and tape the open side together. Give each child one of the two-sided cards. Then use the extra cards to create a pattern on the floor. Have students help you read the pattern aloud. Then invite each student, in turn, to place his card on its correct side to extend the pattern.

Finding Feathers

Can your students help the turkey find his lost feathers? Have several children stand in a row. Direct the seated children to close their eyes while you distribute a feather to each of two standing children. Have all the standing children cup their hands behind their backs, so that it appears that all are hiding feathers. Have the children in the seated group open their eyes; then invite volunteers to try to guess who is holding a feather. If a child guesses correctly, have her change places with the feather holder. When the feathers have been found, it's time for another round.

I am thankful for my mom.

Marissa

Gobbler Placemats

Circles and triangles make up these placemats that youngsters can use at a class feast. To make one, a child glues construction paper triangles to the back of a large brown circle to represent feathers. She then glues a yellow circle, two black circles, a red triangle, and an orange triangle onto the circle as shown to resemble the turkey's head. Write on the placemat as the child dictates a thankful thought; then personalize the placemat.

A Glimmering Ghost

In advance, collect a class supply of large cups with slick surfaces. Protect a work surface with waxed paper. To make a ghost, dip a 15-inch square of cheesecloth into a mixture of one part glue and one part water. Squeeze the cloth to remove as much of the liquid as possible. Drape the cheesecloth over an upsidedown cup. While the glue mixture is wet, sprinkle the ghost with clear glitter. Allow the ghost to dry overnight. The following day, detach the fabric from the cup. Draw eyes; then use fishing line to suspend the ghost. To have a ghost hunt, turn off the lights. Have youngsters use flashlights to search for glimmering ghouls.

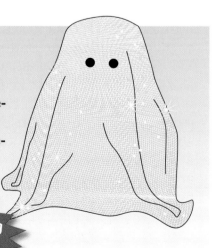

Check out the skill-building reproducibles on pages 138–139.

FALL CENTERS

Stuff your centers with these fall ideas and your little ones will be gobbling for more!

Building Area: Provide a set of interlocking building logs, craft sticks, clay, and broom straw for building the Pilgrims' homes. (Be sure to have books showing pictures of the Pilgrims' clapboard houses for children to use as references.)

Manipulative Area: Provide tubs of red, yellow, and orange play dough along with leaf- and fruit-shaped cookie cutters. Encourage youngsters to make colorful patterns with the resulting cutouts.

Writing Center: Cut an assortment of fall-colored paper leaves. Have students use scented markers to write letters, their names, and other familiar words on the leaves.

Housekeeping Area: Cover a table with a tablecloth that has a fall motif. Place a cornucopia full of plastic fruits and vegetables in the center of the table. Provide plates, cups, and napkins, and encourage children to set the table for a specific number of guests. Stock the kitchen shelves with real, unopened cans of food. Provide aprons for the cooks of this great feast.

Painting Center: Set out paint in fall colors. Add lemon extract to the yellow paint, cinnamon spice to the brown, and pumpkin spice to the orange. Encourage students to use vegetable and fruit halves to make prints or to paint with feathers instead of brushes.

Discovery Center: Peel, core, and cut two apples into ⅛-inch slices. String the slices from one apple and hang to dry. Soak the other apple slices in lemon juice before stringing. Let students observe the apples for several days to see which slices turn browner. Eat the dried apples at snacktime one day. Do they taste different from regular apple slices?

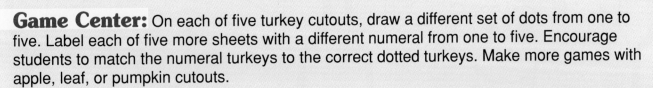

Game Center: On each of five turkey cutouts, draw a different set of dots from one to five. Label each of five more sheets with a different numeral from one to five. Encourage students to match the numeral turkeys to the correct dotted turkeys. Make more games with apple, leaf, or pumpkin cutouts.

Art Center: Gather a collection of real, colorful leaves. Have students glue the leaves on tagboard rings to create beautiful fall wreaths.

Sand/Water Table: Partially fill the table with a variety of fall leaves. Add several construction paper acorn cutouts (patterns on page 134). Encourage children to search through the leaf pile to find the nuts. If desired, include toy hand rakes for little ones to enjoy raking in the acorns!

Leaf Pattern

Use with "A Bushel of Preschoolers" on page 128.

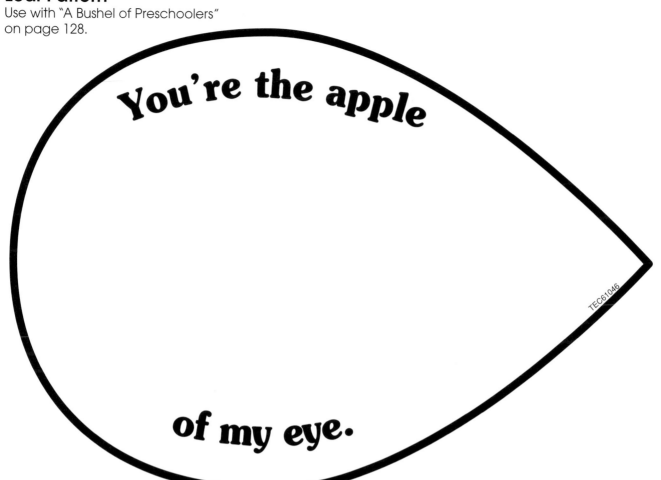

You're the apple

of my eye.

TEC61046

Acorn Patterns

Use with "Fall Centers: Sand/Water Table" on page 133.

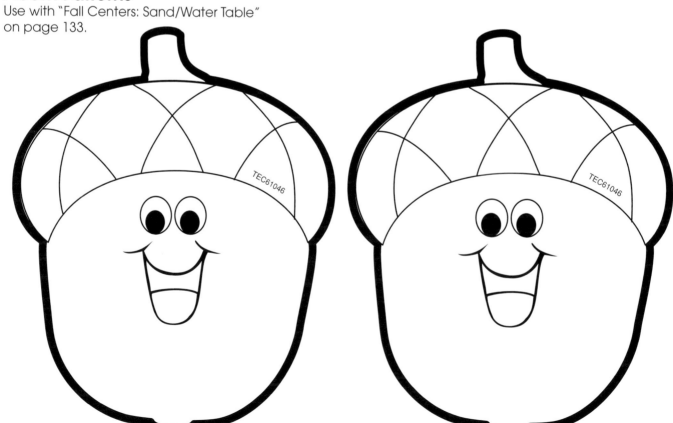

TEC61046

TEC61046

TEC61046

TEC61046

TEC61046

Monster Pattern and Cards

Use with "Monster Stomp" on page 131.

TEC61046

TEC61046

TEC61046

TEC61046

TEC61046

TEC61046

TEC61046

TEC61046

TEC61046

Spinning Spiderlings

Trace.

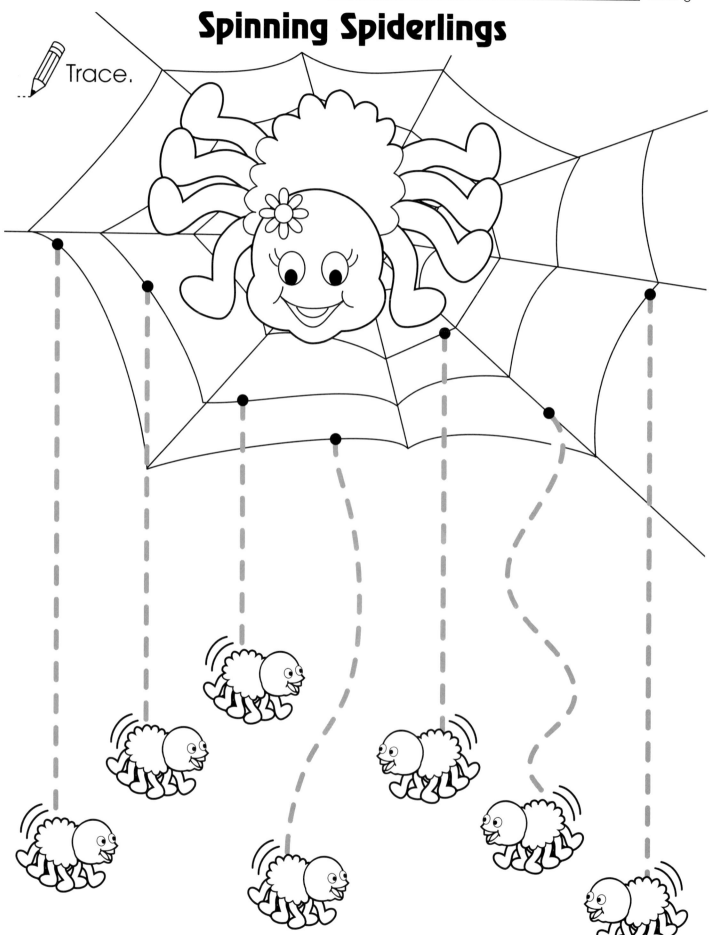

Looking for Acorns

Color the matching squirrels in each row.

WINTER

Snowfriends

Smiles and gleeful giggles will abound when your students dress a snowfriend using a real friend! Collect a variety of snowman-related items, such as a scarf, a hat, gloves, and a broom. Have students make a group circle. Invite a volunteer to be a snowfriend and to stand in the center of the circle. Lead students in singing the song below. Choose a student to find the named item(s) and place it on the snowfriend. Continue singing the song, each time choosing a different child to add each item of clothing, until the snowfriend is completely dressed and warm and toasty.

(sung to the tune of "Bingo")
There was a friend all made of snow,
And [Child's name] was his/her name-o!
Let's give her a [hat],
Let's give her a [hat],
Let's give her a [hat],
To keep her warm and toasty!

Let It Snow!

Practice counting, comparing, and predicting while discussing winter activities with your youngsters. To prepare, color and cut out the winter picture patterns on page 146. Glue each picture to the center of a separate small paper plate. Display the plates in front of your group; then have each child attach a clothespin to the plate that shows his favorite winter activity. Stop periodically as children are voting and discuss which activity has the most or fewest votes. About halfway through the voting, ask your students to predict which activity will come out on top. Count the votes together after everyone has had a turn. Were the predictions correct?

Fantastic Flakes

These snowflakes will have your room looking like a winter wonderland in a "flurry"! Provide each child with a paper doily and a variety of craft supplies (pom-poms, sequins, and ribbons) in cool colors, such as white, silver, and blue. Invite her to glue her choice of materials onto the doily to make a snowflake. When the glue is dry, spray a thin coat of adhesive on the doily; then sprinkle the entire surface with iridescent glitter. Tie a length of fishing line to each snowflake; then suspend all the shimmering flakes to create a wintry atmosphere.

Winter Weather Chant

After reciting this chant, have youngsters tell you different ways to get warm on a cold day.

It's cold outside!
The wind does blow.
The rain falls down.
The clouds drop snow.

It's warm inside!
The fire is bright.
The cocoa's hot.
Your hugs feel right!

It's cold outside—
Too cold to play.
It's warm inside;
Let's stay in all day!

Snowflake Ornament

To make a snowflake ornament, paint three snap-apart craft sticks white. When the paint is dry, stack and glue the sticks—one atop the other—to form a snowflake. Glue sequins onto the snowflake. Tie the center of a length of white yarn near the tip of one of the sticks; then tie the ends of the yarn together to complete the ornament.

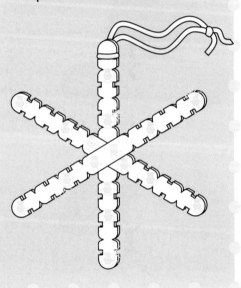

Super Scoopers!

The forecast for this activity is a flurry of excitement! Partially fill a plastic tub with cotton balls to represent snow. Place plastic shovels and pails near the tub. Encourage youngsters to slip on a pair of mittens and shovel the snow into the pails. Students are sure to enjoy scooping the snow while developing fine-motor skills at the same time!

Winter Wreaths

If you're looking for a craft that will make each child proud of his creative efforts, then these wreaths are winners. To make a Christmas wreath, cut out a paper plate's center. Have a child paint the rim of the plate green using a brush or sponge-painting technique. When the paint is dry, invite the child to spruce up his wreath by decorating it with gold, red, or green glitter glue; red dot stickers; or red pom-poms. Add a paper or fabric bow to the wreath. Punch a hole near the top of the wreath; then add a length of yarn for hanging.

To make a winter wreath, paint the plate rim blue. Splatter-paint the wreath white or decorate it with glitter, artificial snow, or cotton.

I'm a Little Candle

(sung to the tune of "I'm a Little Teapot")

I'm a little candle straight and tall,
Shining my light upon you all.

When the night is dark, then you will see
Just how bright my light can be!

Happy Holidays

Celebrate the season with this visual-discrimination activity. Gather a collection of winter holiday objects, such as an ornament, a menorah, a candle, a star, a dreidel, and a small wrapped gift. Arrange these objects on a tabletop for your group of students to see. Direct students to close their eyes while you remove an object. Invite youngsters to take turns guessing which item is missing. Have the correct guesser remove an object in the next round of play. For an added challenge, arrange the objects in a row. Give students a minute to study the lineup. Then cover the objects with a cloth and see who can remember which objects were first, second, third, and so on.

Gingerbread Ornament

Youngsters will run, run as fast as they can to make these cinnamon-scented ornaments. Place enough cinnamon and red glitter in a bottle of white glue so that the glue is tinted but still fluid. Squeeze the glue onto a gingerbread-cookie cutout (pattern on page 147) to decorate it. When the glue is dry, punch a hole near the top of the cutout; then add a ribbon loop for hanging.

Gifts of Love

I couldn't buy a gift for you
'Cause I am very small.

Put hands in pockets; shake head "no."
Point to self.

But I can give you some things—
The greatest gifts of all!

Shake head yes.
Hold hands out as if giving gift.

I can give you kisses.
I can hug you too.

Blow kisses.
Hug self.

I can give a friendly smile
And tell you, "I love you"!

Smile and wave.
Say "I love you" in sign language.

Treasured Triangle Tree

Transform a triangle into a keepsake with this activity. Cut a class supply of green construction paper triangles (trees) and small brown rectangles (trunks). Have each child use various shades of green paint to lightly sponge-paint a tree. When the paint is dry, have him glue a trunk to the bottom of the tree. To decorate the tree, help each youngster print colorful fingerprints on his tree to resemble ornaments. If desired, glue a star cutout to the top.

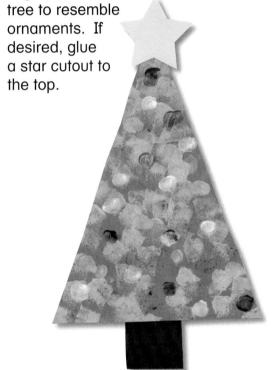

New Year's Party Hat

Ten, nine, eight...count down to New Year's fun with these festive party hats. To make one, use a variety of art supplies—such as markers, crayons, stickers, feathers, glitter, and confetti—to decorate a paper half circle that measures 12 inches on the straight side. To the bottom center of the undecorated side, tape icicle tinsel (used to decorate Christmas trees). Roll the half circle into a cone shape, making sure that the tinsel hangs out from the point of the cone. Staple the paper in place. To complete the hat, punch a hole in each side; then tie an 18-inch length of yarn to each side. Help each child tie on his party hat; then, as a group, count down to begin a New Year's class party!

Special Delivery

Set up a post office scenario for Valentine's Day. To create this scene, divide the area with a long table to separate the customers from the workers. On this counter, place various office supplies, such as pens, stamp pads, and rubber stamps. Include a scale for weighing packages as well as a cash register and play money. Provide different types of paper, envelopes, pencils, and crayons for customers to make their valentine mail. (Stamps from sweepstakes entries make great stamps for preschool mail.) Hang a class list nearby for children to use when addressing mail. Provide visors for the postal workers to wear. Other props could include an old handbag with a shoulder strap for carrying mail and a large divided box for sorting mail.

Valentine Song

(sung to the tune of "Merrily We Roll Along")

Won't you be my valentine,
Valentine, valentine?
Won't you be my valentine?
Here's a **card** for you.

Won't you be my valentine,
Valentine, valentine?
Won't you be my valentine?
Here's a **hug** for you.

Repeat the song as many
times as desired, substtuting
other gifts or gestures for
the boldfaced words.

Sweetheart Messages

To prepare for this game, cut out a class supply of construction paper heart messages using the patterns on page 148. To play, seat youngsters in a circle. Choose one child to be Cupid. Have Cupid stand a distance away from the group with her back toward the circle. Give a heart cutout to a child in the group and have him conceal it. Invite Cupid to return to the group by chanting, "Cupid, Cupid, what do you say? Do you know who has a message today?" Allow Cupid to guess who has the heart by asking children, "Do you have a heart today?" Once Cupid guesses correctly, the teacher then reads the message aloud and tapes the heart to Cupid's clothing. Cupid then rejoins the group and the guessed child becomes Cupid. Continue play until each child is wearing a heart.

Head Over Heels

Step right up for a valentine project that you'll fall head over heels in love with! In advance take a close-up of each child. Mix a small amount of dishwashing liquid with red tempera paint in a shallow pan. Place paper towels and a dishpan of warm, soapy water nearby. To make a valentine, ask a child to dip her bare feet into the paint. Have her press her feet one at a time onto a pink paper heart so that the heel prints overlap. Assist the child as she washes her feet. When the paint is dry, glue the heart onto a large piece of paper. Add the child's photo and the message shown. Who could resist such a sweet sentiment?

I'm Head Over Heels Crazy About You!

Check out the skill-building reproducibles on pages 150–151.

Winter Centers

Though the weather outside may be frightful, these winter centers are just delightful.

Building Area: Encourage children to plow into this winter scene. Supply the area with styrofoam packing pieces (snow) for toy construction vehicles to load, push, plow, and dump.

Manipulative Area: Knead iridescent glitter into white play dough for a glistening, snowy effect. Provide a snowman cookie cutter or a round cutter that children can use to create their own snowman forms. Set out a variety of decorative items, such as colored sequins and twigs, for embellishing the snow figures.

Writing Center: Encourage children to draw snowmen in different sizes. Provide a supply of dark paper, white crayons (or chalk), and assorted circle stencils for drawing snowy scenes. Then write as students dictate a sentence about their scenes.

Housekeeping Area: Add plenty of winter dress-up clothes and accessories. If your area is large enough, consider dividing it in half. On one side, create an outdoor scene by covering the floor with a white sheet. Add a sled; a small, artificial tree; and some sock snowballs. On the other side, arrange the furniture cozily around an imitation fireplace made by covering the back of a bookshelf with brick-patterned background paper. Stock the kitchen with warm foods and the cookware needed to prepare them, such as plastic mugs, spoons, a container of hot cocoa, a kettle, soup cans, bowls, pots, and a Thermos.

Painting Center: Use snowflake sponges for printing on dark-colored construction paper. Sprinkle sparkly glitter onto the wet paint for a shimmering finish.

Discovery Center: Bring in a snowball from outside or an ice cube from the freezer. Set it in a pie plate and invite students to observe and describe what happens.

Games Center: Cut out five copies of the snowman pattern on page 149. Label each snowman with a different numeral from one to five. Direct a student to place the correct number of cotton balls on each cutout.

Art Center: Add lots of white materials—such as doilies, cotton balls, coffee liners, felt, yarn, Styrofoam, and tissue paper—for interesting texture collages.

Sand/Water Table: Fill the table with crushed ice, white confetti, or mounds of shaving cream. Let little ones explore using shovels and buckets.

Winter Picture Patterns
Use with "Let It Snow!" on page 140.

TEC61046

TEC61046

Heart Message Patterns
Use with "Sweetheart Messages" on page 144.

BE MINE

HUG ME

SMILE

LOVE

I LIKE YOU

YOU ARE SWEET

TEC61046

©The Mailbox® • Superbook® • TEC61046

TEC61046

Home, Sweet Home

 Color.

Cut.

Glue.

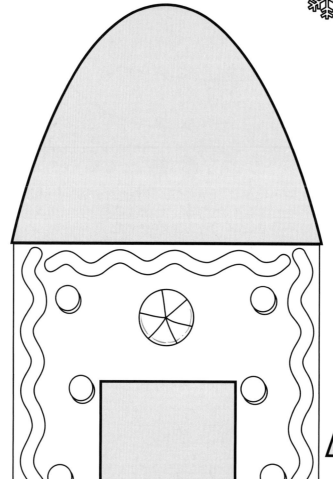

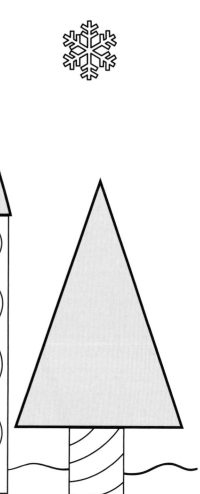

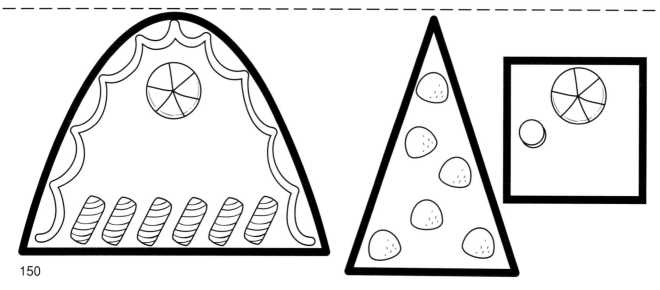

Penguin Pals

 Circle the matching letters in each row.

 S   P   S   G   S

 M   M   F   M   P

B   D   C   B   B

 R   X   R   J   R

 H   H   H   W   T

SPRING

Luck of the Leaves

This counting idea is worth its weight in gold! Cut out a green construction paper copy of the clover cards on page 158 and store them in a paper bag. Also, cut out five yellow construction paper circles to resemble gold coins. Place the coins, bag, and a pot cutout similar to the one shown in your circle-time area.

To play, have a volunteer take a card and help him count the leaves. If he counts three leaves, have him return the card to the bag and pass it to his neighbor. If he counts four leaves, encourage him to place a gold coin on the pot. Then have him return the card to the bag and pass the bag to his neighbor. Play continues until students strike it rich with all five coins on the pot.

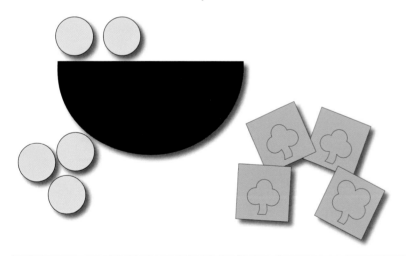

SPRINGTIME SONG

(sung to the tune of "Did You Ever See a Lassie?")

Hello, [spring]! It's good to see you,
To see you, to see you.
Hello, [spring]! It's good to see you!
It's springtime again!

Repeat the song, if desired, asking students to name other springtime objects to substitute for *spring,* such as *leaves* and *buds.*

Rainy-Day Watercolors

This simple project is inspired by April showers. Encourage students to look at pictures of spring flowers. Then instruct students to use watercolor markers to draw simple flowers on a piece of white construction paper. Next, have them paint water over the drawings, watching as the colors blend into a rainy-day garden.

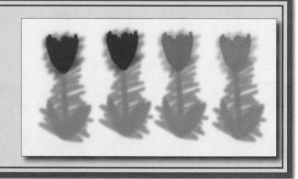

Rain, Rain, Rain

On a rainy spring day, introduce this musical raindrop activity. To prepare, cut out a blue construction paper copy of the raindrops on page 159 for each child. Have him arrange the drops in front of him. Call out a size and instruct the child to hold up his corresponding raindrop. Then sing the following song and have each child "rain" the appropriate raindrop.

*(sung to the tune of
"She'll Be Comin' Round the Mountain")*

I'm a teeny, tiny raindrop in a cloud.   *(Sing quietly.)*
I'm a teeny, tiny raindrop in a cloud.
I'm a teeny, tiny raindrop,
I'm a teeny, tiny raindrop,
I'm a teeny, tiny raindrop in a cloud.

I'm a medium-size raindrop in a cloud.   *(Sing in a normal tone of voice.)*
I'm a medium-size raindrop in a cloud.
I'm a medium-size raindrop,
I'm a medium-size raindrop,
I'm a medium-size raindrop in a cloud.

I'm a great big raindrop in a cloud.   *(Sing loudly.)*
I'm a great big raindrop in a cloud.
I'm a great big raindrop,
I'm a great big raindrop,
I'm a great big raindrop in a cloud.

Watch the Rain

(sung to the tune of "London Bridge")

Watch the rain come falling down,
Falling down, falling down.
Watch the rain come falling down.
Watch the rain fall.

Watch the rain fall on the [grass],
On the [grass], on the [grass].
Watch the rain fall on the [grass].
Watch the rain fall.

Repeat the verse as many times as desired, substituting other appropriate words—such as *trees, leaves,* and *birds*—for the underlined word.

Spraying Raindrops

Lots of oohs and ahs are sure to be heard with this rainy-day idea! In advance, fill a spray bottle with watered down blue paint to represent rain. Have each child glue an umbrella shape to a piece of paper. Encourage her to draw a picture of herself under the umbrella, holding the handle. When the drawing is complete, help her spray raindrops on her paper.

Quick Caterpillars

Youngsters will love making these creepy-crawly caterpillars. To make a caterpillar, glue one medium-size pom-pom to one end of a craft stick. When the glue dries, glue two small eyes on it. Then glue small pom-poms to the remainder of the craft stick.

A Terrific Transformation

Teach youngsters a simple, fun lesson on metamorphosis with this puppet. Hot-glue wiggle eyes and a pom-pom nose to the toe of a sock to represent a caterpillar; then turn the sock inside out. Hot-glue a decorated butterfly felt cutout onto the heel of the sock. To perform this chant with youngsters, slip the sock over your hand, caterpillar side out; then follow the suggestions provided to use the puppet with the rhyme.

Caterpillar crawled to the top of a tree.   *Crawl puppet up one arm.*
"I think I'll take a nap," said she.
So under a leaf she began to creep.
She spun a cocoon and fell fast asleep.   *Turn back cuff of sock to create cocoon.*

After six long months in her cocoon bed,
Spring came to say, "Wake up, sleepyhead!"
Caterpillar awoke with a happy sigh,
"Look at me now—I'm a butterfly!"   *Turn sock inside out to reveal butterfly.*

outside

inside

"Eggs-tra" Easy Bunnies

Is it an egg or is it a bunny? Your little ones will hop on over to change paper eggs into beautiful bunnies! Help each child brush a mixture of glue and water over a white construction paper egg cutout. Encourage him to cover the egg with a supply of light-colored tissue paper squares. Then help him brush over the finished egg with the glue mixture. When the egg is dry, trim the excess tissue paper edges. Then have each youngster glue bunny ears on his egg and use a black marker to add desired facial features.

Five Little Bunnies

Five little bunnies
(Hold up five fingers.)

Hopping in the sun.
(Hold up two fingers and make them hop.)

Eating all the farmer's carrots, one by one.
(Hold fingers up to mouth and pretend to nibble.)

Here comes Mr. Farmer;
(Make a scared face with a hand on each cheek.)

Ooooh, you'd better run!
(Shake one finger.)

5, 4, 3, 2, 1.
(Count down on fingers.)

A Pretty Basket

These baskets are so sweet—especially when they've been filled with Easter candies! Fold two same-size construction paper circles in half. Glue the circles together so that the sides overlap and two points meet to form a basket as shown. Glue a construction paper strip to the inside of the basket for a handle. Have students decorate the basket with markers or stickers. Fill the basket with Easter grass and goodies.

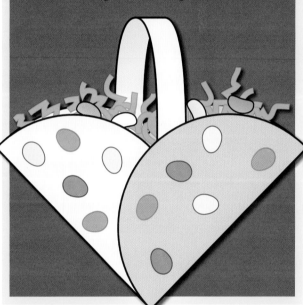

The rabbit is in front of the watering can.

Where's Peter?

Encourage students to use positional words with this rabbit search. After reading with your youngsters the classic story *The Tale of Peter Rabbit* by Beatrix Potter, draw students' attention to the part where Peter hides inside the watering can. Then show students a stuffed rabbit and a watering can and place them in a prominent classroom location. Each day, move the rabbit to a different place relative to the can. Invite volunteers to locate the rabbit and orally state its location. Students are sure to look forward to finding your little hopper each day!

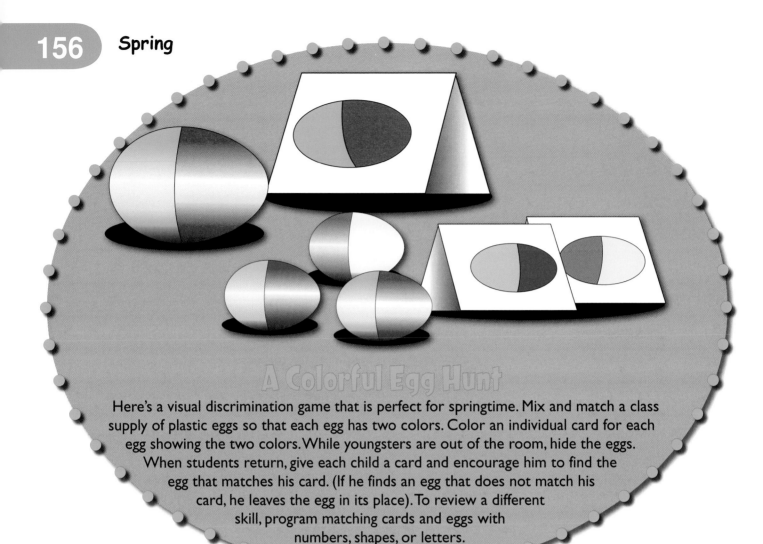

A Colorful Egg Hunt

Here's a visual discrimination game that is perfect for springtime. Mix and match a class supply of plastic eggs so that each egg has two colors. Color an individual card for each egg showing the two colors. While youngsters are out of the room, hide the eggs. When students return, give each child a card and encourage him to find the egg that matches his card. (If he finds an egg that does not match his card, he leaves the egg in its place). To review a different skill, program matching cards and eggs with numbers, shapes, or letters.

Mommy (or Daddy)

(sung to the tune of "Daisy, Daisy")

Mommy, Mommy,
You know that I love you.
You're my mommy—
Nobody else will do!
Oh, Mommy, when we're together,
We have the best time ever!
Oh, Mom, it's true:
I do love you!
Mommy, nobody else will do!

Use this song in celebration of Mother's Day. To use the song for Father's Day, simply substitute *Daddy* for *Mommy* throughout the song.

Check out the skill-building reproducibles on pages 162 and 163.

SPRING CENTERS

Gross-Motor Area: Have youngsters design a bunny trail using classroom blocks or cardboard bricks. Encourage little ones to hop high and low along the trail pretending to be a bunny who is happy to see the first signs of spring!

Math Center: Cut out five copies of the frog cards on page 160. Write a different number from 0 to 10 on separate lily pad cutouts. Have youngsters place the correct number of frogs on each lily pad.

Writing Center: Put a layer of mud in a tray for each center visitor. Encourage youngsters to practice writing their names, letters, and numbers in the mud using their fingers. (Provide craft sticks for little ones who prefer less mess!)

Dramatic Play: Little ones get rid of the dust bunnies with some spring cleaning! Supply the area with items such as a clean, empty bucket and a sponge; a mop; a broom; rags; and an empty spray bottle. If desired, provide some old clothing for children to use as scrub wear.

Paint Center: Pour equal parts of glue and white paint into a glue bottle. Prepare a second bottle with equal parts of glue and blue paint. Then, for each student, draw cloud shapes on colorful paper. Help a youngster squirt the white mixture to trace the cloud shapes. Then help him squirt the blue mixture on the paper to make raindrops.

Literacy Center: Write the name of each student on a separate card for children to copy. Then write each letter of each child's name on an orange triangle (carrot). Place the cards and carrots beside a stuffed bunny or bunny cutout. Encourage each youngster to spell his name using the carrots.

Game Center: Cut out two brown construction paper copies of the rabbit cards on page 161. Encourage partners to play a variation of the game Concentration using the bunny cards.

Art Center: Encourage each youngster to tear colorful paper scraps into small pieces. Have him glue the pieces onto a large sheet of paper in the shape of a flower. Then have him draw a stem to complete the flower.

Sand/Water Table: Gather several plastic containers. Poke holes in the bottom of each container, making sure to vary the size from container to container. Have youngsters pour water into the containers to explore how rain falls from different containers. Students are sure to discover that the water runs out of the containers with larger holes faster than it does in the ones with small holes!

Clover Cards
Use with "Luck of the Leaves" on page 152.

TEC61046

TEC61046

TEC61046

TEC61046

TEC61046

TEC61046

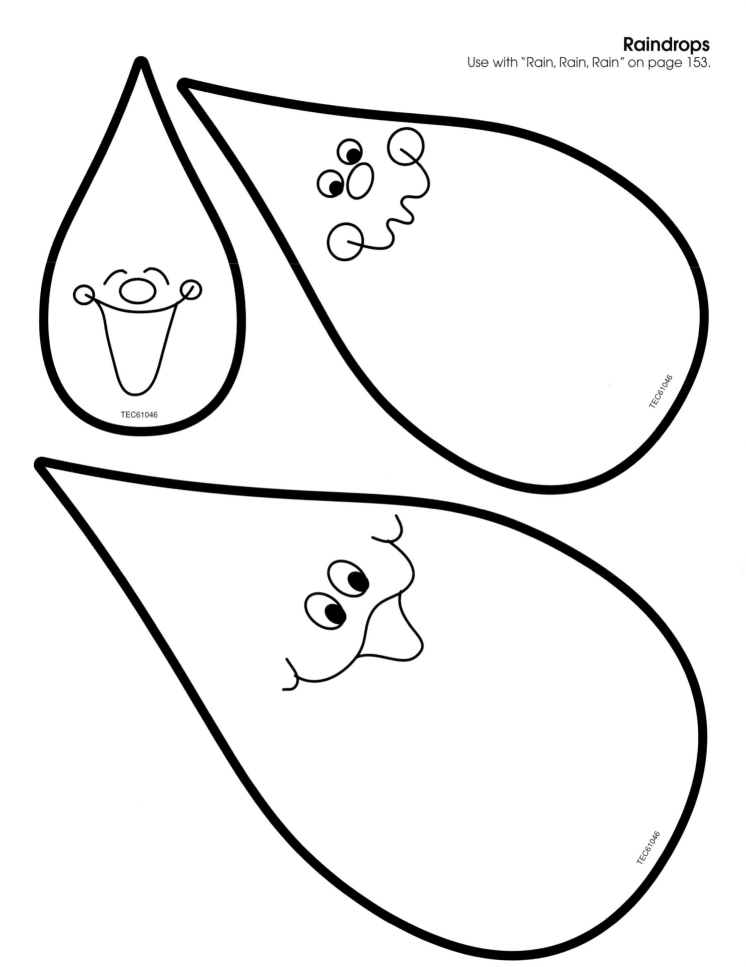

TEC61046

TEC61046

TEC61046

Frog Cards
Use with "Spring Centers: Math Center" on page 157.

TEC61046

TEC61046

TEC61046

TEC61046

TEC61046

TEC61046

TEC61046

TEC61046

TEC61046

TEC61046

TEC61046

TEC61046

TEC61046

TEC61046

TEC61046

TEC61046

TEC61046

TEC61046

Fancy Flowers

Trace.

The Toy Box

✂ Cut.

Glue to match the rhyming pictures.

Let's Go Outside

Let's go outside.	*Pretend to open door.*
It's summertime!	*Jump up and down and smile.*
We'll play at your house	*Point to an imaginary friend.*
And then play at mine.	*Point to self.*
Let's go outside.	*Pretend to open door.*
It's nice and hot.	*Fan face with hand.*
We'll get the hose	*Pretend to spray hose.*
And splash a lot!	*Make splashing motions with hands.*
Let's go outside.	*Pretend to open door.*
The sun is bright.	*Circle arms overhead to imitate sun.*
Let's play all day	*Skip or run in place.*
Till we say, "Good night!"	*Wave goodbye.*

Hoop It Up!

Summer is the perfect time to explore outdoor learning opportunities. Gather several plastic hoops, each in a different color; then cut out a large bulletin board paper circle corresponding to each hoop color. Position each hoop in a different outdoor space. For instance, one hoop might be placed in the grass, another in an area of soil, and another against a large tree trunk. Divide your class into the same number of groups as there are hoops; then have each group examine the area encompassed by its assigned hoop. Write students' observations on the corresponding circle cutout. Afterward, have students compare their observations of the outdoor areas.

IN THE GRASS:
—dirt under the grass
—ants crawling
—2 beetles
—little white flowers

Happy Father's Day

Each dad who receives this card will be surprised to find out that he had a hand in making it! For each child, fold a sheet of construction paper in half. Send the paper and a marker home with each child, along with a note requesting that the child's dad (or male caregiver) trace the outline of his hand on the front of the card. When the card is returned, write "Happy Father's Day" on the front of it and the poem shown on the inside. Encourage the child to write his name and draw a picture of his dad and himself in the card. Then assist him in pressing a paint handprint onto the front of the card inside the outline of his dad's hand.

Happy Father's Day

Hand in hand all through the day, You help me work and help me play!

Sam

Star-Spangled Banners

These bright banners remind students that red, white, and blue are the colors of the season. Using patriotic paint colors, a youngster paints a design on a white construction paper rectangle. When the paint is dry, he adds star stickers if desired. Then he tapes the banner to a paper-towel tube and waves his flag with pride!

Firecracker, Firecracker

Boom, boom, boom! An explosion of fun is in store when youngsters make these firecracker paintings. Arrange newspapers on the ground outside. To paint, a child puts a large sheet of black construction paper on the newspaper. She dips a paintbrush in red, white, or blue paint; then she splatter-paints the black paper. Using a different brush for each color of paint, she continues painting in this manner to create a shower of fireworks. While the paint is wet, she sprinkles on glitter. Oh, say, can you see these patriotic paintings on display!

Fourth of July Mobiles

Help students celebrate the season with this patriotic craft. To make a mobile, a student colors a prepared plate with red and blue markers. Next, she glues red, white, and blue streamers to the edges of her plate. Then she attaches a desired number of star stickers or cutouts to the streamers. For a decorative display, punch two holes in the center of the plate and suspend it by a length of yarn.

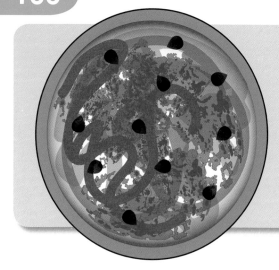

A Slice of Summer

After serving a watermelon treat, wash and dry the seeds for use on this sensory project. Just before painting, mix enough watermelon-flavored drink mix into red finger-paint so that it smells like the real thing. To make a project, a student fingerpaints on a fingerpainting-paper circle. Then he drops watermelon seeds onto the wet paint. When the paint is dry, he mounts the circle onto a slightly larger green construction paper circle.

A-tisket, A-tasket

What would your little ones pack if they were going on a picnic? Find out with this circle-time activity. Color a copy of the picnic cards on pages 169 and 170. Cut out the cards and store them in a small picnic basket. To begin, invite a youngster to remove a card from the basket and name the picture. If the card shows something that might be packed for a picnic, have him place the card in the middle of the circle. If the item should not be included, have him place the card behind him outside the circle. To continue play, encourage him to pass the basket as you lead youngsters in the song below.

(sung to the tune of "A-tisket, A-tasket")

A-tisket, a-tasket,
Let's pass the picnic basket.
I take a card and look and see,
Does it go on this trip with me?

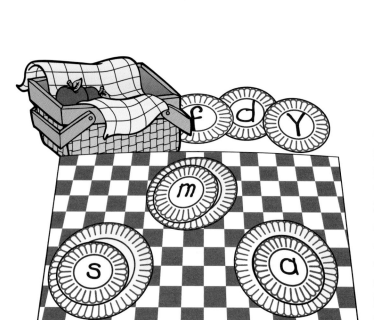

Picnic Plates

Little picnickers are sure to enjoy this alphabet-matching center activity. Program a set of large paper plates with uppercase letters and a set of smaller paper plates with the matching lowercase letters. Arrange the large plates on a blanket or a tablecloth at a center. Store the smaller plates in a picnic basket and place it on the blanket. When a youngster visits the center, she removes the plates from the basket and matches the corresponding letters to the larger plates. If desired, use stickers to program a set of spoons with pictures of beginning sounds that correspond with the letters on the plates for her to match.

Fishy Art

Students create a unique fish painting with this craft! For each student, copy the fish pattern on page 209 onto blue construction paper. Then cut out the fish and discard it. Set aside the resulting frame. To make a fish painting, a child folds a sheet of construction paper in half and unfolds the paper. He uses a paintbrush to drop several colors of paint onto one half of his paper. He refolds the paper, gently presses the sides together, and unfolds the paper. When the paint is dry, help him glue the prepared frame over his paper. Display the completed projects on a wall to create a lovely school of fish.

A Day at the Beach

Your youngsters will catch a wave of excitement when you have Beach Day in your classroom. Prepare by gathering a large beach ball, some pool floats, and a variety of other beach-related props.

Invite a child to choose a prop; then role-play a beach activity, such as surfing, swimming, or hunting for seashells. Next, play some beach music and invite youngsters to get in shape with some aqua aerobics by twisting and "swimming" to the music. Finally, end your fun in the sun with a groovy game of Beach Blanket Limbo, using a twisted beach towel as the limbo stick. Surf's up, dude!

In the Fish Tank!

Transform a table into a fish tank to create a unique reading area for little ones. Place goggles, fish-related books, and a large stuffed fish under a table. Then drape a clear, fish-printed shower curtain over the table to resemble a fish tank. Encourage each youngster, in turn, to take a trip to the tank, wear the goggles, and explore selected literature. Dive right in; the water is fine!

Check out the skill-building reproducibles on pages 173 and 174.

Summer Centers

Gross-Motor Area: Place carpet squares on the floor to represent islands and play some beach music. Encourage little ones to pretend to swim to the islands and pause at each to do a little summer dance.

Math Area: Label five large yellow circles (suns) with the numbers 1 to 5 and cut out 15 yellow strips (rays). Have youngsters place the corresponding number of rays around each sun.

Writing Center: Program a castle cutout (pattern on page 171) with each center visitor's name. Have youngsters trace their names in glue, sprinkle sand over the glue, and shake off the excess.

Dramatic Play: Paint a shower curtain to resemble a beach by the ocean. Color and cut out a copy of the animal patterns on page 172. Supply the center with shovels, pails, sunglasses, beach towels, and empty water bottles. Have youngsters place desired critters on the shower curtain and then pretend they are at the beach!

Literacy Center: Cut out several construction paper copies of the popsicle pattern on page 170. For each popsicle, program one half with an uppercase letter and the other half with the corresponding lowercase letter. Cut along the dotted line to make two halves. Have youngsters match the uppercase and lowercase letters to make cool treats!

Puzzle Center: Cut out a blue 4½-inch square, three each of red and white 11" x ½" strips, four 6½" x ½" red strips, three 6½" x ½" white strips, and 50 (or less, if desired) white stars. Have youngsters assemble the pieces to resemble the American flag.

Art Center: Cut eight one-inch slits in the end of a cardboard tube. Bend the cardboard outward, making eight tabs. A youngster brush-paints each tab and presses the tabs onto a sheet of paper to make a flower head. Then he adds details as desired. For a variety of colors, prepare one tube for each color.

Sand/Water Table: Place an assortment of beach erasers in your sand table along with shovels and pails. Label each pail with a number. Have students dig in the sand to shovel the correct number of erasers into the sand pails.

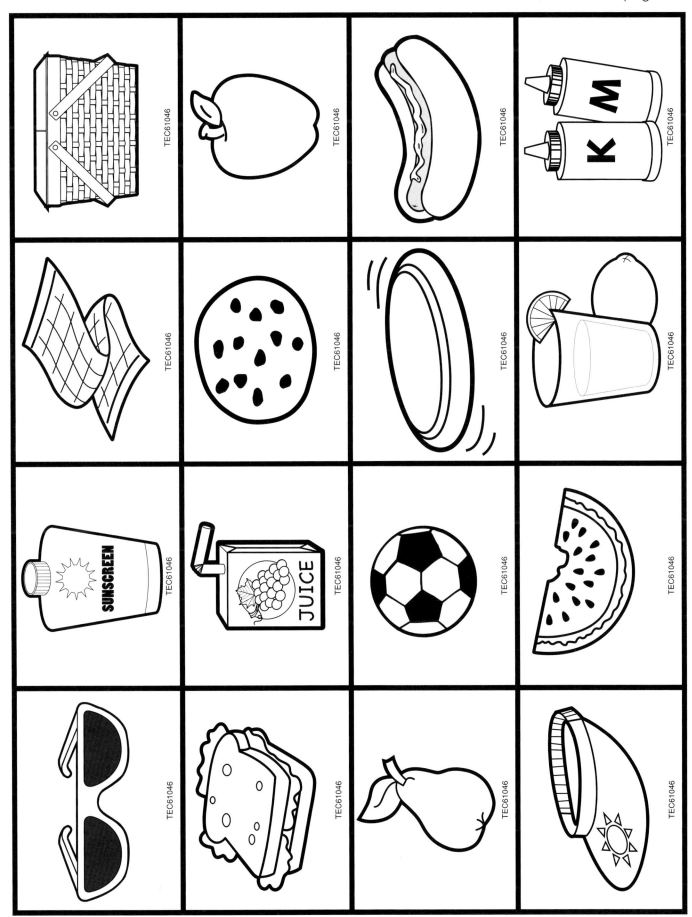

Picnic Cards
Use with "A-tisket, A-tasket" on page 166.

Popsicle Pattern
Use with "Summer Centers: Literacy Center" on page 168.

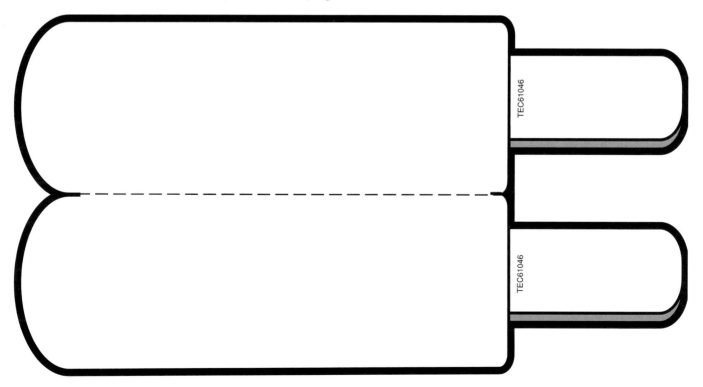

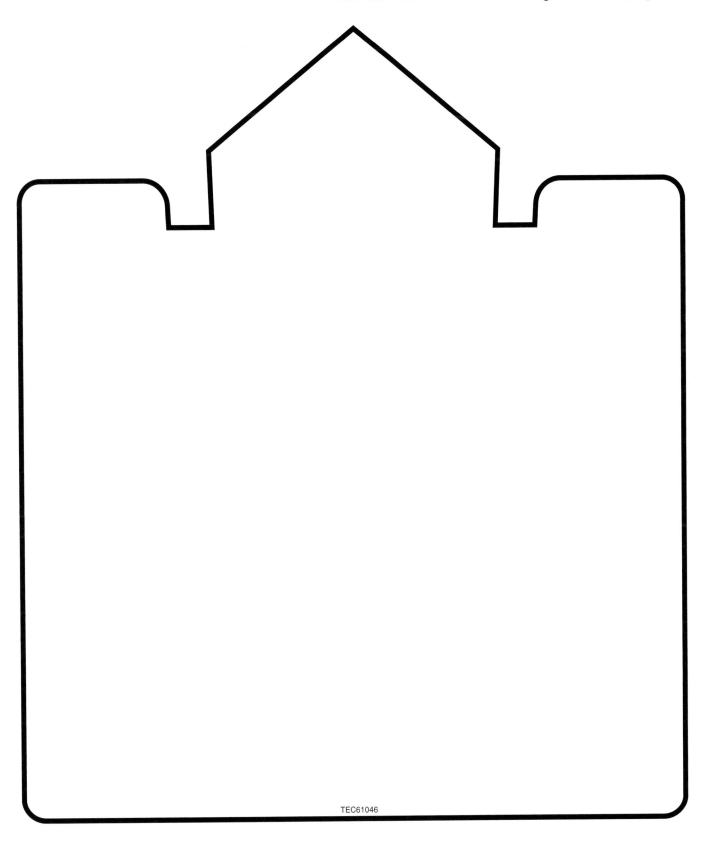

TEC61046

Animal Patterns
Use with "Summer Centers: Dramatic Play" on page 168.

Wonderful Waves

Trace.

Lion's Pride

SWEET SCOOPS

 Cut.

 Count to match.

 Glue.

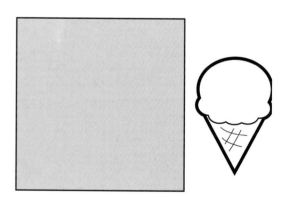

1   2   3   4

YOU'RE A TREAT!

TEC61046

Happy Halloween!

From Your Teacher

You add spice to our class. Happy Thanksgiving!

From Your Teacher

TEC61046

Note to the teacher: Make a construction paper copy of these cards for each child. Color the cards; then cut them out. If desired, spread glue in the middle of the pie on the Thanksgiving card; then sprinkle on some pumpkin-pie spice, cinnamon, or allspice.

BIRTHDAY WISHES
From Your Teacher
TEC61046

Happy Holidays!
From Your Teacher
TEC61046

Note to the teacher: Make a construction paper copy of these cards for each child. Color the cards; then cut them out. If desired, glue candy sprinkles to the cupcake.

U R
SPECIAL
2 ME!

From
Your Teacher

TEC61046

HAPPY
St. PATRICK'S
DAY

From
Your
Teacher

TEC61046

©The Mailbox® • Superbook® • TEC61046

Note to the teacher: Make a construction paper copy of these cards for each child. Color the cards; then cut them out. If desired, attach the valentine to a box of conversation hearts. Jazz up the St. Patrick's Day card by gluing green glitter to the shamrock.

177

"HOPPY" EASTER

From Your Teacher

TEC61046

GOOD LUCK IN "KINDER-GARDEN"!

From Your Teacher

TEC61046

Note to the teacher: Make a construction paper copy of these cards for each child. Color the cards; then cut them out. If desired, embellish the Easter egg with glitter.

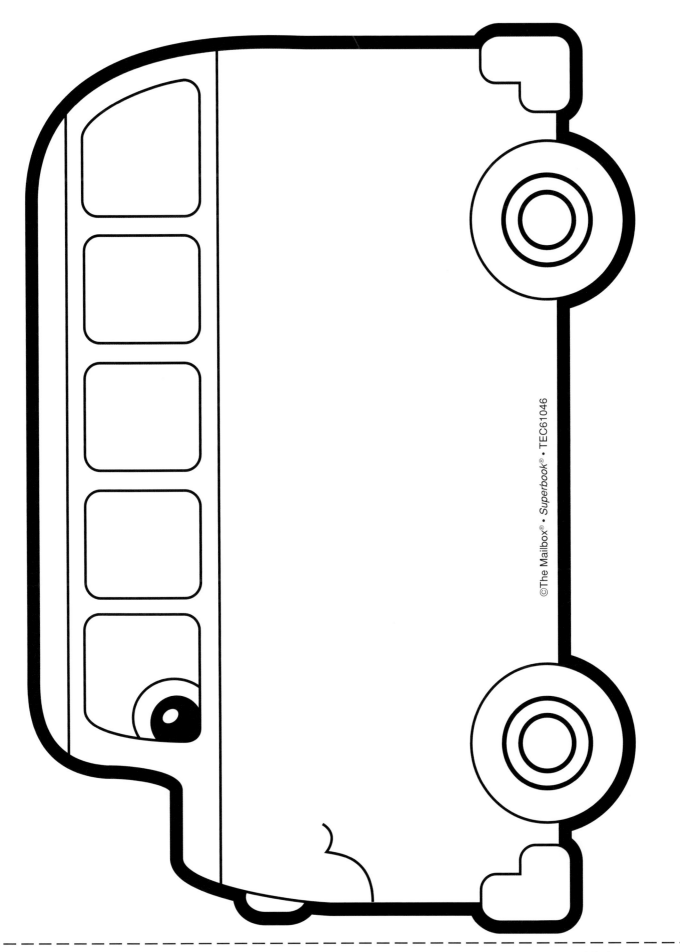

Programming Suggestions: Use a copy of this page for a newsletter, a parent note, a booklist, or a center game or label.

Programming Suggestions: Use a copy of this page for a newsletter, a parent note, a booklist, a center game, or a label.

TEC61046

Programming Suggestions: Use a copy of this page for a newsletter, a parent note, a booklist, a center game, or a label.

Programming Suggestions: Use a copy of this page for a newsletter, a parent note, a booklist, a center game, or a label.

©The Mailbox® • Superbook® • TEC61046

Programming Suggestions: Use a copy of this page for a newsletter, a parent note, a booklist, a center game, or a label.

©The Mailbox® • Superbook® • TEC61046

Programming Suggestions: Use a copy of this page for a newsletter, a parent note, a booklist, a center game, or a label.

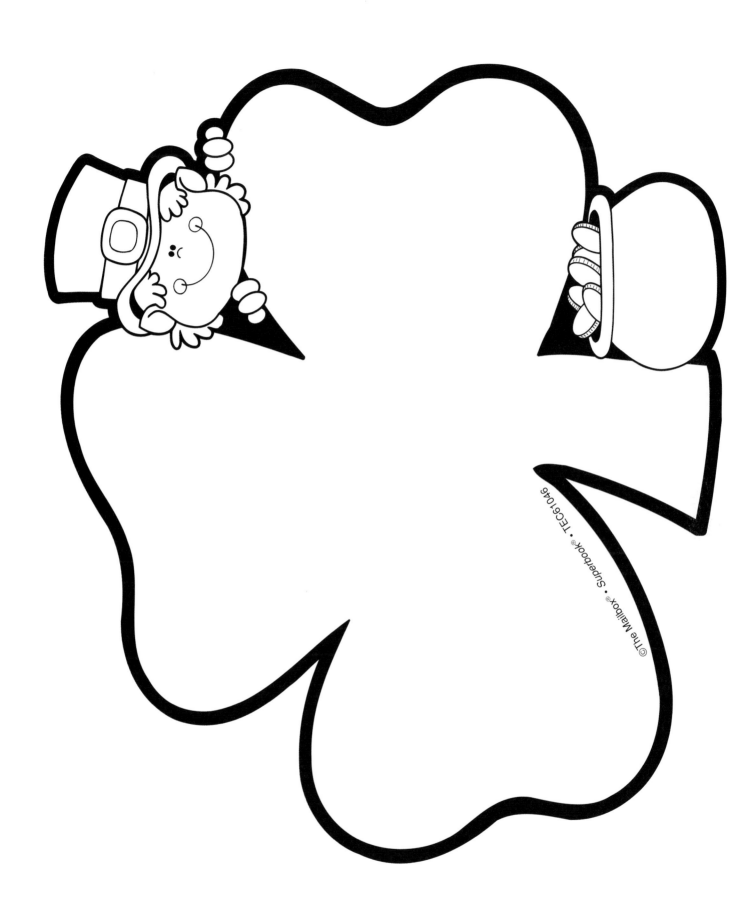

©The Mailbox® • Superbook® • TEC61046

Programming Suggestions: Use a copy of this page for a newsletter, a parent note, a booklist, a center game, or a label.

185

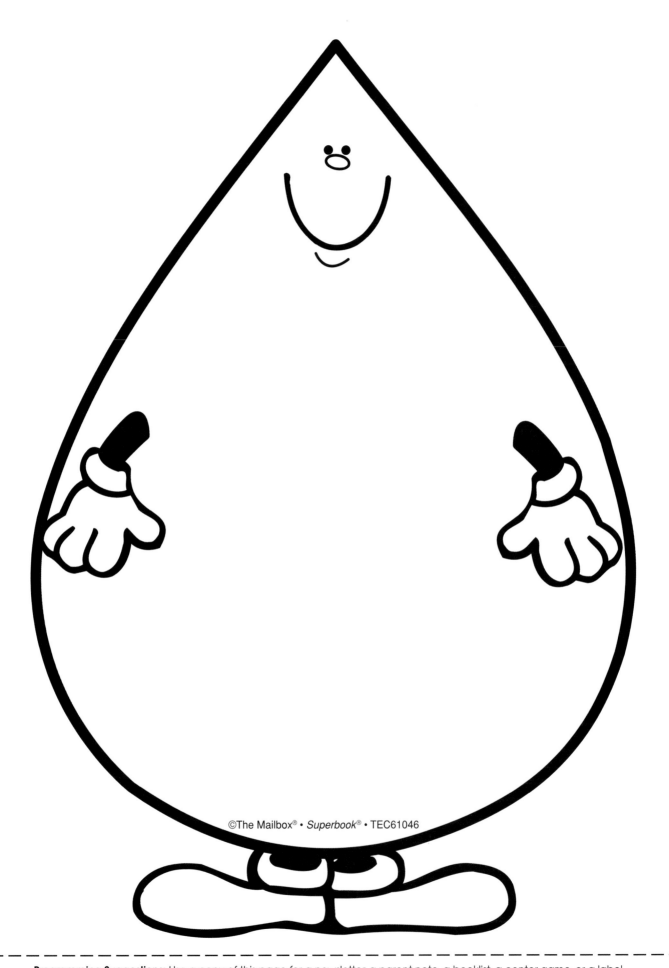

©The Mailbox® • *Superbook*® • TEC61046

Programming Suggestions: Use a copy of this page for a newsletter, a parent note, a booklist, a center game, or a label.

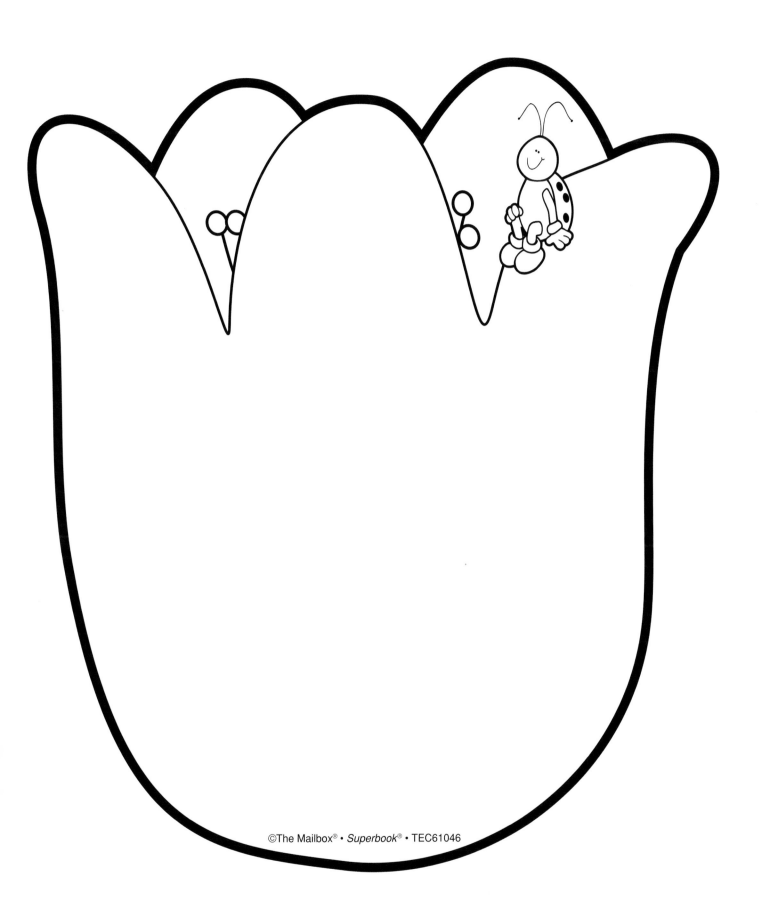

Programming Suggestions: Use a copy of this page for a newsletter, a parent note, a booklist, a center game, or a label.

Programming Suggestions: Use a copy of this page for a newsletter, a parent note, a booklist, a center game, or a label.

GET SET FOR CENTERS

Consider This...

Before you set up your classroom centers, ask yourself these questions:

How am I going to use centers in my teaching?

Will small groups complete guided lessons at various centers? Or will centers be strictly free play? Will the materials and activities you provide require supervision or can they easily be done independently?

How many centers do I have room for?

Consider the physical space and equipment you're working with. Where is the sink? Where are the electrical outlets? Do you have a portable sand table you could roll outside?

Are there some centers I may want to use only part of the time or seasonally?

If you live in a cold climate, do you want to use the water table only in warmer weather, when you can put it outside? Will the puppet center be open every day?

Will my choices for centers provide for a variety of learning styles?

Do you have both quiet and active centers? Do some centers provide for tactile learning? Are there centers where students can work independently and centers where students can interact with others?

What materials and equipment do I really need? How can I get them?

If you feel it's essential to have a class pet for your science area, can you get a local pet shop to donate one? Can you ask parents to provide materials or build a reading loft?

Once you've made some decisions about the *who, what, when,* and *how* of your classroom centers, turn the page for ideas on furniture arrangement, storage, and management. It's center time!

Use Your Imagination!

Once you've decided which centers to have, you're faced with the task of arranging your furniture to adequately define each area. Keep traffic flow and a clear view of all the centers in mind. The sides of a metal filing cabinet or the front of an air-conditioning unit can make wonderful magnetboards. Low bookshelves or milk crates can be pushed together to make room dividers. Cover the back of a bookcase with flannel to make a storytelling area or with Con-Tact covering to make a display area for bulletin board art. Use small area rugs to help define spaces. Place blocks on shelves near your circle-time area so that children can use the open, carpeted space for building during center time. With a little planning and creativity, you'll be set for centers in no time!

Lost-and-Found

Designate a box or basket as the lost-and-found. If a child finds a loose puzzle piece or any other manipulative and isn't sure where it belongs, have him place it in the lost-and-found. Periodically go through the lost-and-found and return items to their proper places.

Storage Solutions

Now you'll need to store all the wonderful materials you've collected for your centers. Take a photo or make a simple drawing of each material and glue one picture on each storage container to help little ones get things back into their proper places. Help preschoolers pick up on concepts of color, shape, pattern, and number by utilizing those concepts for storage with any of the following methods:

- Purchase plastic, tinted shoeboxes or storage boxes and designate a different shade for each center. For example, all math materials could go in blue boxes.

- Use sturdy boxes to store materials. Cover them with solid-colored Con-Tact paper; then label each container with a numeral or a shape on one side and a picture of the enclosed material on the other. Label a space on a shelf with the corresponding numeral or shape for each container.

- Cover storage containers with different patterns of Con-Tact paper. Then label a space on a shelf with each corresponding square of Con-Tact paper and have children match the patterns as they replace the containers.

- Label containers with pictures of the enclosed materials. Then label shelf space with corresponding pictures. Have children match the pictures as they replace the containers.

Round and Round We Go

If you plan on using your center areas for small-group lessons, you'll need an efficient way to rotate groups from center to center. Try designating a color for each group. Then cut out a balloon shape from each corresponding color of construction paper. Hang the balloon cutouts from clothespins attached to yarn lengths above each center. (Or, if you are not allowed to hang items from your classroom ceiling, simply place a balloon cutout in each center.) Then ask each child to go to the center with the balloon that corresponds to his group's color. When you are ready for each group to rotate, move the balloons and ask children to follow.

How Many?

During free-choice centers, you'll probably want to designate the number of children allowed in each center in order to avoid crowding and assure that there are enough materials for everyone. Prepare a simple poster to convey the limits to your preschoolers. To begin, prepare a small version of each of your center labels. Glue these to a sheet of poster board or a length of bulletin board paper as shown. Next to each center label, glue a library pocket. Label each pocket with a numeral to show how many children may visit that center at any one time. Then print each child's name on a separate craft stick.

To use this system, have each child insert the craft stick labeled with her name into one of the library pockets to indicate which center she plans to visit during free-choice time. Once the number of sticks in place equals the number on the pocket, that center is full.

It's a Theme Thing

If you extend your current theme to each of your classroom centers, you'll love this idea for helping keep track of which centers your little ones have visited. For each child, make a necklace using crepe paper streamers and a theme-related shape. For example, if your class is studying flowers, cut a flower shape for each child from heavy paper. Label each petal with a numeral or shape that corresponds to a label you've placed in a particular center. Over the course of your study, ask each child to wear his necklace as he visits each center. Then hole-punch the corresponding numeral or shape on his necklace. Each day at center time—as students wear their necklaces— you can tell at a glance whether a student needs to visit a particular center. When you move on to a new theme, send the necklaces home. The cutouts may spark discussions between parents and children about the thematic center activities little ones have completed at school.

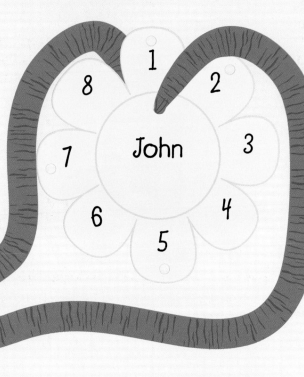

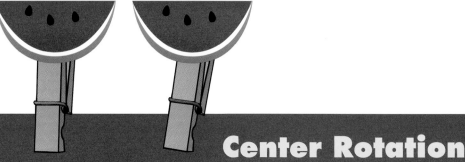
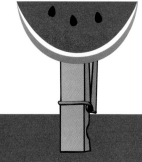

Center Rotation

Your little ones will feel independent as they select and change learning centers with this management system. From tagboard, cut a different-colored seasonal or geometric sign for each of your learning centers. Label each cutout with the center's name. For each center, make smaller matching shapes equal to the number of children who may visit the center at one time. Hot-glue each small shape onto a separate clothespin. Clip the clothespins to the appropriate signs. When visiting a center, a child removes a clothespin from the sign and clips it onto his clothing. When all the clothespins are removed from the sign, the center is full. When a child is ready to leave the center, he replaces the clothespin on the sign.

Who's Been Where?

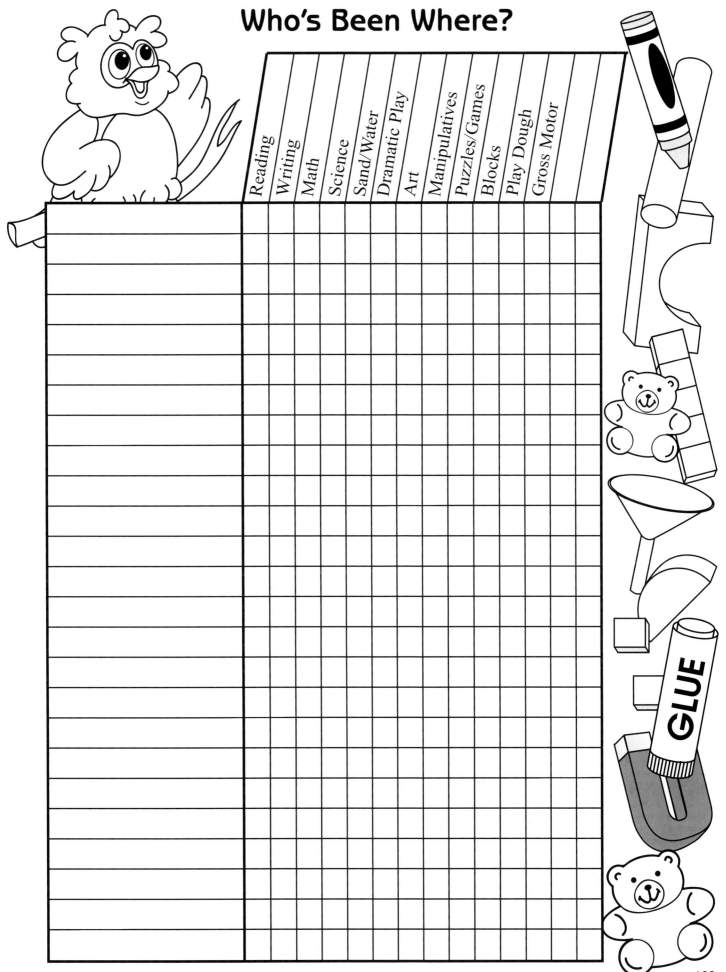

	Reading	Writing	Math	Science	Sand/Water	Dramatic Play	Art	Manipulatives	Puzzles/Games	Blocks	Play Dough	Gross Motor

ANYTIME Centers

Literacy Center

Copycat Letters

It's good to be a copycat at this partner center! Store a set of magnetic letters and a set of letter cards in a bag. Place the bag at a center. A child removes the letter cards, scrambles them, and places them facedown. Then she turns over a card and shows it to her partner. Her partner places the matching magnetic letter on the card. Next, the students switch roles and repeat the activity until the partners have matched a desired number of letters. If desired, have the preschoolers identify the letters as they make matches. **Visual discrimination**

Play Dough Center

Oat Dough

Surprise youngsters with this interesting dough. Mix regular uncooked oatmeal into your favorite play dough recipe. The rough texture of the oatmeal provides an unusual sensory experience. Invite students to shape, roll, and mold the dough while describing the texture. **Fine-motor skills**

Math Center

Serve It Up!

Youngsters flip at this pancake-themed center! To prepare, program each of several paper plates with a different shape. Program an equal number of tan craft-foam pancakes with matching shapes. Place the plates, the pancakes, and a small spatula at a center. A child spreads out the pancakes and plates; then she uses the spatula to transfer each pancake onto the appropriate plate. **Matching shapes**

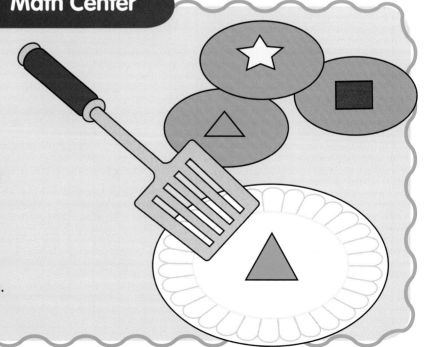

Math Center

Laundry Line

To prepare, make five colorful construction paper shirt cutouts. Number the shirts from 1 to 5; then store them in a laundry basket. Tie a length of yarn between two chairs to resemble a clothesline. Place the basket and a supply of clothespins nearby. A child hangs the shirts on the line in numerical order. After she counts each to verify the order, she removes the shirts and puts them back in the basket for the next center visitor. **Number order**

Art Center

Cooperative Mural

Use this versatile center with your current classroom theme. Make a blank mural by mounting a large sheet of bulletin board paper within easy student reach. Add a title to convey a desired theme. Place a container of crayons, chalk, and markers nearby. When a youngster visits the mural, he uses the supplies to draw and color a picture that corresponds with the theme. **Using art media**

Literacy Center

Alphabet Hopscotch

Transform a beach towel into a super space-saving center! Simply use fabric paint to outline a hopscotch path on a towel. Write a different letter in each box. When the paint is dry, spread the towel on a carpeted open area. A center visitor tosses a beanbag onto the path and hops to it, naming the letters as she goes. Then she retrieves the beanbag and tosses it again for another round. At the end of center time, just roll up the towel for easy storage. **Letter identification**

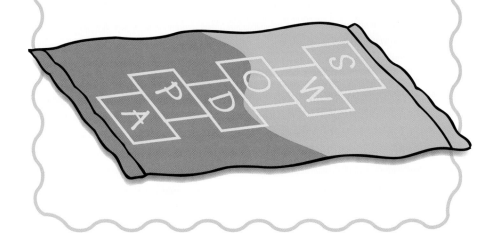

Math Center

Partner Patterns

Taking turns leads to some spiffy patterns! Place paper strips and a pair of different-colored bingo daubers at a center. A student uses a dauber to make one dot near the left edge of a strip. Next, his partner makes a dot of the other color. The twosome continues alternating turns, with each student stamping one dot per turn to create an *AB* pattern. If desired, encourage the partners to switch order and create another *AB* pattern in the same fashion. **Patterns**

Sensory Center

Flour Power

Scoop some all-purpose flour into your sensory table for a change of pace. The flour holds its shape much like wet sand and is soft to the touch. Add unbreakable measuring cups, spoons, and small baking pans. Then encourage a child to engage in some floury exploration. **Sensory experience**

Gross-Motor Area

Color Kingpin

Youngsters match colors in this bright twist on bowling. To prepare a set of pins, pour a few drops of liquid dish soap and a different color of tempera paint into each of six plastic bottles. Cap each bottle and swirl it to evenly coat the inside with the paint mixture. Pour out any excess paint and allow the bottles to dry overnight. Then recap the bottles and arrange them on a sheet of tagboard programmed with matching color dots. A child stands a desired distance from the pins and rolls a soft ball toward them. He resets the pins by matching the colors. For an added challenge, have preschoolers name each color as they reset the pins. **Matching colors**

Sand Table

Buried Treasure

Your pint-size pirates are sure to dig this matching center! To prepare, cut apart a yellow tagboard copy of the treasure cards on page 198. Bury the treasure in your sand table and place a plastic shovel nearby. A child uses the shovel to dig up the cards and match the pairs. When he has found all the treasure, he buries it for the next seeker. **Matching**

Gross-Motor Area

Sock Toss

Gather several pairs of socks and roll each pair into a ball. Place an empty laundry basket and several sock balls in an open area of the classroom. A child takes the sock balls and stands a desired distance from the basket. Then she tries to toss each sock ball into the basket. She tosses underhanded and over-handed for extra motor practice. When all of the sock balls have been tossed, the student counts the number of balls that landed in the basket. **Gross-motor skills**

Math Center

Set the Table

Preschoolers use their math skills to set the table! Program each of four paper plates with a different dot set. Program each of four plastic spoons with a different number to match a plate. Place the plates and spoons at a center. A child sets the table by placing the matching spoon next to each plate. **Matching numerals and sets**

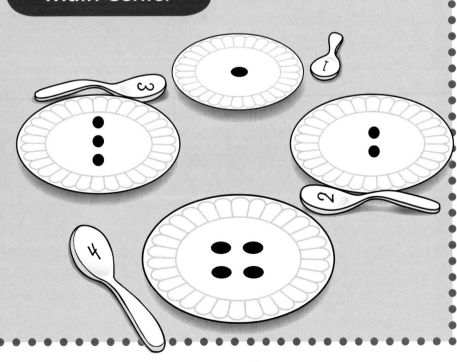

Treasure Cards

Use with "Buried Treasure" on page 197.

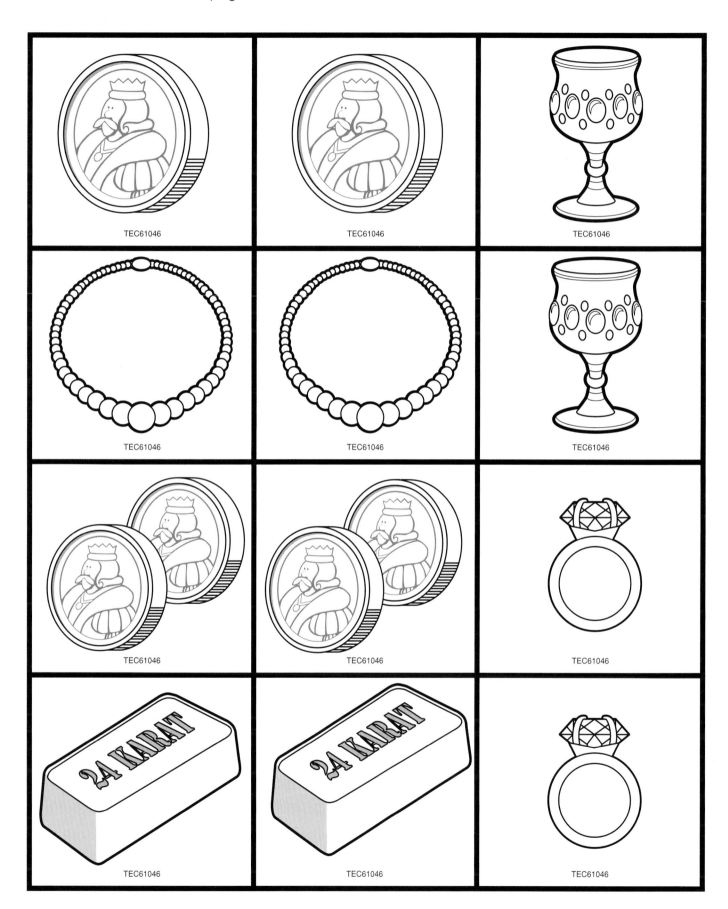

TEC61046

TEC61046

TEC61046

TEC61046

TEC61046

TEC61046

TEC61046

TEC61046

TEC61046

TEC61046

TEC61046

TEC61046

Transportation CENTERS

MATH CENTER

Special Delivery

Preschoolers drive delivery trucks to match shapes! To prepare, tape a different shape cutout to each of several small blocks. At a center, arrange the blocks to resemble a row of buildings. Program the front of an envelope to match each block. Place the envelopes and a small dump truck at the center. A child puts an envelope in the truck and drives the truck to the matching building. Then he delivers the envelope by placing it in front of the building. He continues with each envelope until all the deliveries have been made. **Matching shapes**

LITERACY CENTER

Flight Plans

To prepare for this partner center, tape a tagboard airplane cutout (pattern on page 201) and a tagboard cloud cutout each to a separate large craft-stick handle. Place the prepared cutouts at a center. Each child takes a cutout. The child holding the cloud directs the child holding the airplane (the pilot) to fly to different points around the cloud. For example, a child could say, "Fly over the cloud" or "Fly under the cloud." After several directions, the twosome switches roles and repeats the activity. **Following oral directions**

PUZZLE CENTER

Vehicle Matchup

Color and cut out a copy of the vehicle cards on page 202. Puzzle-cut each card to make a simple two-piece puzzle; then store the pieces in a bag. Place the bag at a center. A student puts each puzzle together to make a fleet of vehicles. Then she names each vehicle and states whether it travels in the air, on land, or in the water. **Matching**

WATER TABLE

Boats Afloat!

Preschoolers explore sinking and floating with boats and other vehicles. Place several toy boats near your water table along with several other vehicles that are less likely to float, such as small metal cars. A child chooses a vehicle, predicts whether it will float or sink, and then places it in the water. If it floats, he announces, "It floats like a boat!" Then he compares the result with his prediction. He repeats the activity with each remaining vehicle.
Making predictions

BLOCK CENTER

They're Off!

Stock your block area with several different-size toy cars and a set of blocks. When a pair of students visits the center, the children use the blocks to build a racetrack on a slick surface such as a tile floor or table. Each child chooses a car and races it with the others down the track. After a few races, the pair builds a new track and races again.
Exploration

DRAMATIC PLAY

Scrub-a-Dub

Give your youngsters a chance to wash toy vehicles in a pretend car wash. To make a car wash, remove the two end panels from an opened shoebox. To one end attach four-inch lengths of bright-colored ribbon. Place the car wash and several mini cars in a center and encourage students to drive their vehicles through the pretend water tunnel. **Imaginary play**

Green's
CAR WASH

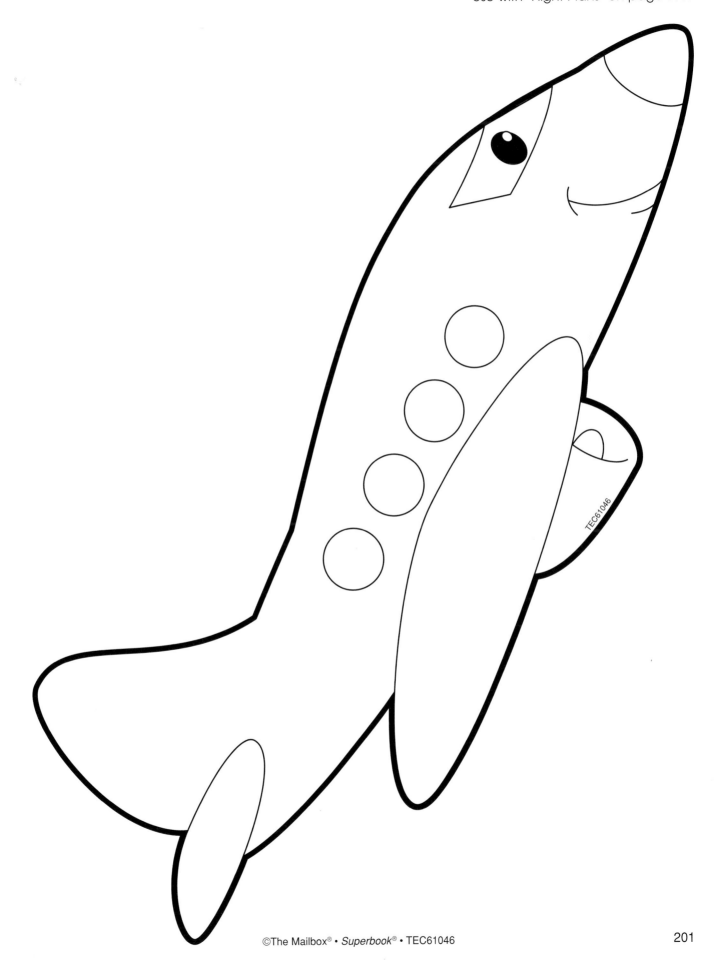

TEC61046

Vehicle Cards
Use with "Vehicle Matchup" on page 199.

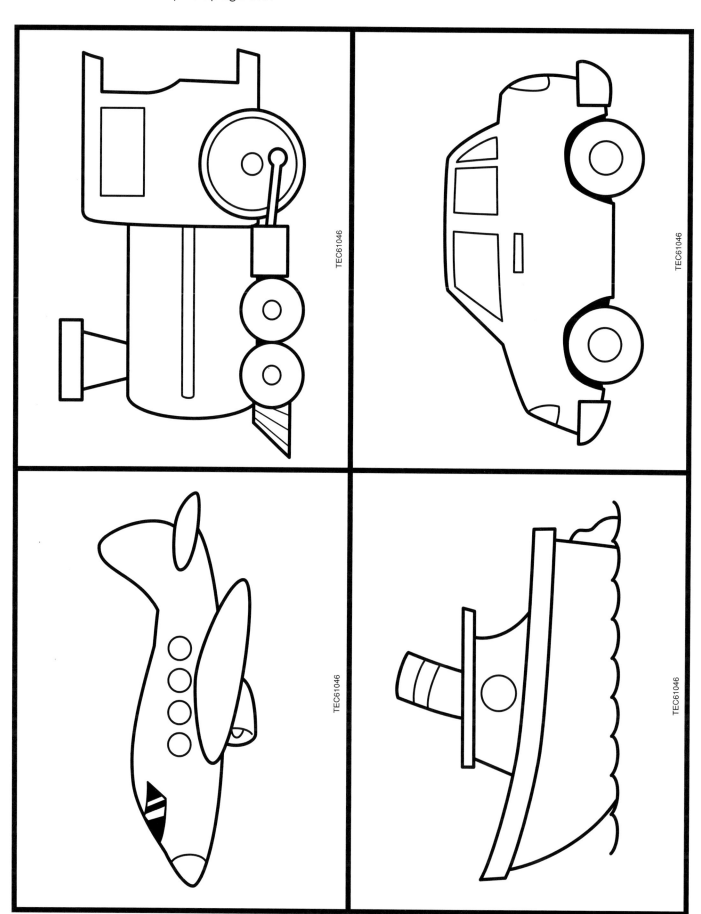

Ocean Centers

Math Center

Oceans of Fun

Youngsters will wade right into patterning! In advance, make several simple pattern strips by gluing colored fish-shaped crackers and pasta shells to tagboard strips. Place the strips at a center along with a beach bucket containing a supply of matching crackers and shells. A child selects a strip and copies the pattern. Then he continues in the same manner with additional patterns. **Patterns**

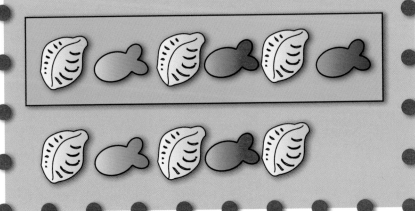

Sand Table

Beach Combing

A few plastic combs make this center "groovy"! Place a sand pail containing a sand shovel and various-size clean hair combs at your sand table. Dampen the sand. A child uses a comb to create a wave pattern in the sand. Then he tries a different comb and observes the different effects. When he is finished exploring, he uses the back of the shovel to smooth the sand for the next beachcomber. **Fine-motor skills**

Art Center

Simply Seahorses

These simple projects are sure to be admired! To prepare, use the pattern on page 205 to make a class supply of white construction paper seahorse cutouts. Also, cut a large supply of one-inch colorful tissue paper squares. Place the items at your art center along with a container of diluted white glue and an old paintbrush. A child paints a seahorse cutout with glue and then covers it completely with tissue squares, overlapping them for effect. When the glue is dry, trim the excess tissue paper from the edges and have the child use a marker to add an eye. Then display the finished projects on a window and watch them shine! **Using art media**

Literacy Center

Seaworthy Names

Reinforce concepts of print at this teacher-directed center. In advance, copy and cut out a supply of colorful construction paper shells from the patterns on page 206. Help a child count out one shell cutout for each letter in her name. Next, assist as needed as she prints one letter of her name on each shell. When she is finished, have her glue the shells in order on a sheet of blue paper. Then guide her to notice that each letter has its own space within her name. **Concepts of print**

Play Dough Center

Sizable Starfish

Place a set of small, medium, and large star-shaped cookie cutters at a center along with a batch of orange play dough and blue workmats (oceans). A child makes sets of starfish with the cookie cutters and places them in the "ocean." If desired, have older students make additional starfish without using the cutters. Fine-motor skills

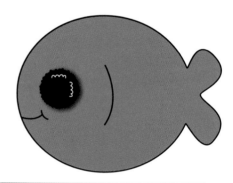

Gross-Motor Area

Fish Eye

To prepare this center, trim a large sheet of bulletin board paper into a fish shape. Add any desired details except for an eye. Place the fish on the floor in an open area of the classroom. Attach a length of tape to the floor a few feet from the fish. Then put a large pom-pom (eye) next to the tape line. When a student visits the center, he tosses the eye toward the fish. He retrieves the eye and tosses again. Once he has tossed several times from the tape line, he stands a distance behind the tape line and plays again. **Gross-motor skills**

TEC61046

Shell Patterns
Use with "Seaworthy Names" on page 204.

TEC61046

TEC61046

TEC61046

TEC61046

TEC61046

TEC61046

Pet Centers

Literacy Center

Schools of Fish

Youngsters are sure to enjoy helping these little fish find their friends! Cover a tabletop with blue paper to resemble water and cut out ten colorful copies of the fish pattern on page 209. Program each fish with the letters *B* or *F* (or other desired letters). Place the fish on the water. When a child visits the area, he sorts the fish into two schools, *B* and *F*. To make different schools, program fish to reinforce other skills such as uppercase and lowercase letters, shapes, or numbers! **Matching letters**

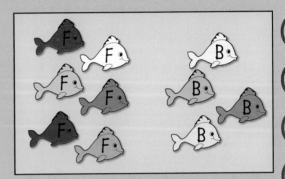

Play Dough Center

Pet Pals

Unique critters will be created at this play dough center! Stock the center with various colors of play dough and craft materials such as pipe cleaners, craft sticks, and feathers. Encourage youngsters to manipulate the play dough to make a pet. After the pet dries, send it home to live with its new family. Fine-motor skills

Math Center

Rolling for Bones

Cut out 12 copies of the bone pattern on page 209. Store the bones in a dog bowl and place the bowl at a center along with a large die. To play this partner game, each child in a pair rolls the die in turn and takes the corresponding number of bones from the bowl. After both partners have taken a turn, the twosome uses one-to-one correspondence to compare the sets of dog bones. To play another round, the duo returns the bones to the bowl and rolls again!
Making sets

Dramatic Play

The Doctors Will See You Now

Your little ones can be veterinarians in this role-playing center. To turn your dramatic-play area into a pet clinic, cover a table with a white sheet to create an examining table. Then set several pet carriers (or cardboard boxes cut to resemble cages) along one wall to make a kennel. Provide plenty of stuffed-toy patients and medical supplies such as bandage strips, gauze, wraps, masks, empty pill bottles, and toy medical tools. Clipboards and notepads are also handy for taking notes and writing prescriptions. Include an oversize white dress shirt or jacket for each doctor to wear. This setup is a sure cure for reluctant role-players. **Role-playing**

Writing Center

If I had ___a bird___ .
I would ___give him water every day.___

Sam

Textured Pets

Encourage youngsters to use their imaginations for a project that reviews pet needs. Program a sheet of paper with the words shown and make a construction paper copy for each student. Place the papers at a center along with a supply of craft items such as feathers, felt, and glitter. Arrange for an adult to assist youngsters at this center. When a child visits the center, the adult reads the sentence starter aloud and writes the youngster's dictated response on the lines. Then the child writes his name and illustrates his sentence. To complete the page, he uses the craft items to add texture to the scene. If desired, bind the completed pages into a book titled "Pet Care" for a kid-pleasing, textured story. Prewriting

Art Center

Seeing Spots!

Little ones use paint to match these spots! Cut out a copy of the dog pattern on page 210 for each child plus one extra. Paint colorful spots on one dog and post it in your painting area along with matching paint colors for student use. Then invite each center visitor to use the supplies to make a matching dog. For a new look, paint a different-patterned pooch for little ones to copy! **Visual discrimination**

TEC61046

Bone Patterns
Use with "Rolling for Bones" on page 207.

TEC61046

TEC61046

TEC61046

Dog Pattern
Use with "Seeing Spots!" on page 208.

TEC61046

BUG Centers

211

LITERACY CENTER

Just Buggy!

Expect a buzz of letter aware-ness around this center! To prepare, color and cut apart a construction paper copy of the bug cards on page 213. Place the cards and a container of magnetic letters at a center. A child selects a card, identifies the bug, and then matches the letters to copy the word. She repeats the activity with each card. **Letter matching**

ART CENTER

Bug Bracelet

In advance, make a class supply of cuffs by splitting cardboard tubes in half lengthwise and then cutting them into one-inch sections as shown. Also, cut a class supply of 1" x 6" green paper strips. Place the strips and cuffs at a center along with a red stamp pad, a black fine-tip marker, and glue. A child makes sets of three fingerprints on a paper strip to resemble bug bodies. Then he draws six legs on each bug body and adds eyes and antennae. To complete his bracelet, he glues the prepared strip to a cuff. When the glue is dry, invite him to don his bug bracelet. **Fine-motor skills**

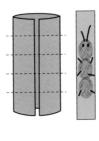

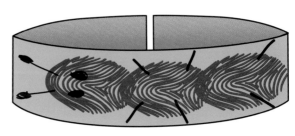

SAND TABLE

Hide an Ant

Make several moist sand mounds in your sand table to prepare for this center. Then poke several holes in each mound to resemble ant tunnels. Tuck a few small black pom-poms in the tunnels to represent ants. Also, place a container of black pom-poms nearby. Have a child try to remove the ants without collapsing the tunnels. Then invite him to build a mound, poke tunnels, and hide ants for the next center visitor. **Fine-motor skills**

Insect Exploration

Your little ones act as scientists at this hands-on center. Partially fill your sensory table with green and brown paper shreds and cardboard-tube logs. Next, hide large artificial bugs in the shreds and logs. Place a hand lens near the table. When a child finds a bug, he gently picks it up and examines it with the lens. Then he finds more bugs and compares them. After examining several bugs, he hides the bugs in the shreds and logs for the next center visitor. **Investigating insects**

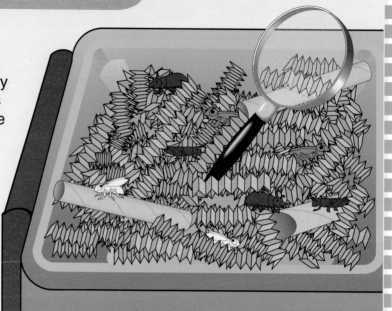

Fly, Buzz, or Crawl

For this partner center, cut apart two tagboard copies of the bug cards on page 213. Color each pair of bugs identically and then place the cards at a center. When a pair of youngsters visits the center, children spread the cards facedown and then take turns turning over two cards at a time. When a child finds a matching pair, he identifies the type of bug and then he and his partner both perform that bug's movement. If a matching pair is not found, the child turns both cards back over and ends his turn. **Visual discrimination**

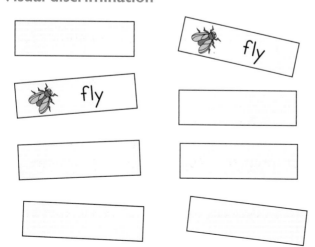

Comparing Caterpillars

Little learners make comparisons with caterpillars. To prepare, color and cut apart a tagboard copy of the caterpillar cards on page 214. Place the cards at a center. A child puts the caterpillars in order from shortest to longest. Then she scrambles the cards and arranges them in order from longest to shortest. **Seriating**

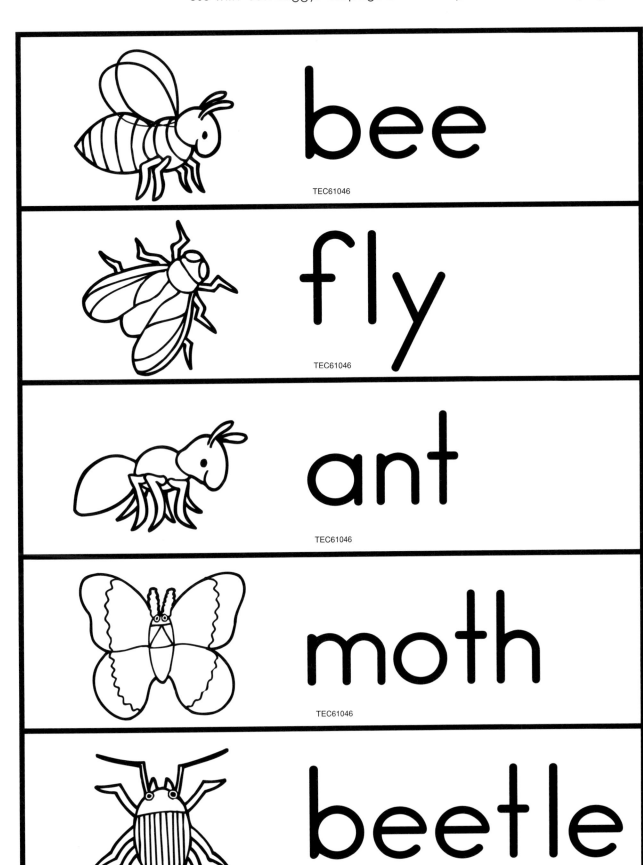

bee

TEC61046

fly

TEC61046

ant

TEC61046

moth

TEC61046

beetle

TEC61046

Caterpillar Cards
Use with "Comparing Caterpillars" on page 212.

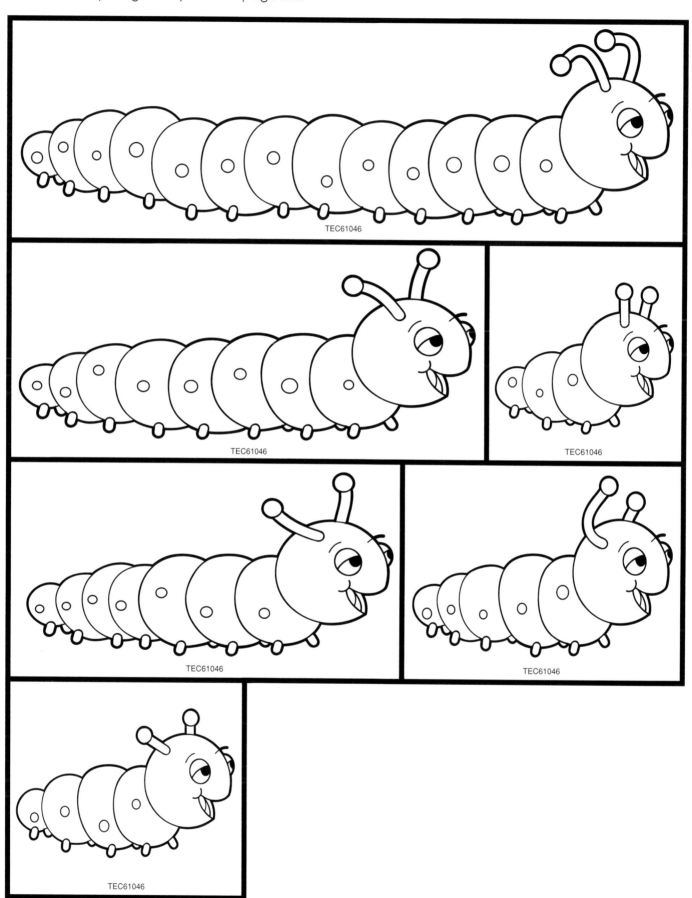

N ready reference image

Ready Reference

Making the Most of Every Center

Adding new and different items to your various centers can make them more enjoyable and stimulating for your students. Check out these suggestions; then scout around your house for the various items, ask parents for donations, or shop local yard sales. You may come across some great finds of your own!

Art Center

Besides the usual:
paper
crayons
markers
safety scissors
glue or paste
paint
paintbrushes
play dough

Try adding:
foam paintbrushes
mini paint rollers
sponges
glitter or textured paint
cookie cutters
small rolling pins
plastic knives
tissue paper
crepe paper
sheets of craft foam
gift wrap
index cards
wallpaper scraps
doilies
colored masking tape
stencils

glue sticks or rollers
shaped paper punches
colored chalk
decorative-edge safety scissors
hole punchers
rubber stamps
ink pads
crinkled gift wrap stuffing
pipe cleaners
craft feathers
fabric scraps
paper plates
paper lunch bags
colored sand
yarn
Magna Doodle toy

Sand and Water Table

Besides the usual:
sand
water
rice
plastic containers
scoops

Try filling the table with:
foam packing pieces
bubble solution
grits
shaving cream
crinkled gift wrap stuffing

Try adding to water:

ice cubes
vinyl sea animals
measuring cups and spoons
waterwheel
water pump

toy boats
eyedroppers
funnels
mild dish detergent
wire whisks or eggbeaters

Try adding to sand:

measuring cups
measuring spoons
funnels

plastic sand molds
toy construction vehicles
plastic baskets

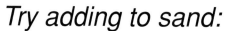

Reading and Listening Center

Besides the usual:
books
tape or CD player
cassette tapes

Try adding:
big books
class books
small rocking chair
small beanbag chair
floor pillows
stuffed animals
flannelboard
flannelboard stories

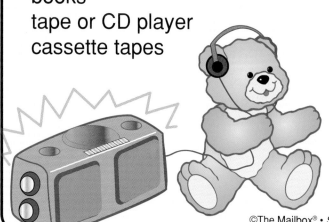

Block Center

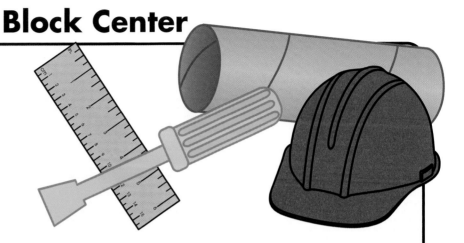

Besides the usual:
wooden blocks
DUPLO building sets
cardboard brick blocks
foam blocks
toy vehicles

Try adding:
toy traffic signs
wooden or vinyl people figures
wooden or vinyl animal figures
dollhouse
wooden or plastic train set
vinyl or carpet road map
paper and crayons

toy construction helmets
toy tools
pieces of PVC pipe
cardboard tubes
carpet squares
rulers or tape measures

Dramatic-Play Center

Besides the usual:
dress-up clothes
dishes and utensils
plastic foods
dolls
broom, mop, and dustpan

Try adding:
more clothing items, such as
   purses and wallets
   bandanas, ties, and scarves
   elbow-length gloves
toy telephone and directory
empty food containers

toy cash register and paper money
toy tools
placemats
silk flowers in a vase
kitchen towels
toy shopping cart or basket
baskets and trays
stuffed animals
puppets

(Also see pages 242–247 for ideas on transforming your dramatic-play center.)

CIRCLE Time

Turn-Taking Magic

Go head-to-head with the circle-time turn-taking challenge with this charming idea. In advance, create a magic wand by covering a ruler, dowel, or sturdy plastic tube with sparkly stickers or glitter fabric paint. To one end of the wand, attach a small item or construction paper cutout that represents your unit of study or an appropriate special occasion. For example, you might attach a silk leaf to the wand during your fall unit. Or use a plastic frog at the end of the wand during a study of pond life. Introduce the concept of taking turns by explaining that when a student's head is tapped lightly with the wand, it is her turn to talk. Ask the other students to listen quietly and attentively during each child's turn.

Places, Please!

Welcome little ones to circle time with this idea that reinforces visual discrimination skills. In advance, cut two identical shapes for each child. Adhere one shape in each pair to the floor in your circle area. Then, just before circle time, give each child a shape and have him find and sit on the matching shape in the circle. Collect the shapes for redistribution at your next circle time.

IMAGINATION BOX

Stir up youngsters' imaginations with this idea. Bring a decorative jewelry box to circle time. As you display the box, recite the chant shown. Invite the child named in the chant to remove the lid from the box and act out the imaginary item that she "finds" inside. Replace the lid, repeat the chant, and have the next child repeat the process, acting out his imaginary find.

Something is in our imagination box!
I wonder what that something could be.
[Child's name] thinks it's a [child names item].
Let's open the box and see.

Meow!

Do You See the Colors?

Color your circle time with this tune about colors. Each time you sing the song, replace the underlined word with the name of a different color. Appoint a child to sing the response and find something of that color in the room. If desired, expand the use of this song to include shapes and letters too.

(sung to the tune of "The Muffin Man")

Do you see the color [red], the color [red], the color [red]?
Do you see the color [red] somewhere in this room?

Yes, I see the color [red], the color [red], the color [red]?
Yes, I see the color [red] somewhere in this room?

THE NAME GAME

Dance youngsters into some name recognition with this simple idea. Print each child's name on a separate paper plate. Scatter the plates on the floor during circle time; then invite youngsters to dance to some lively music. When you stop the music, encourage each student to stand on the plate labeled with his name. Then collect the plates, randomly place them on the floor again, and start the music to play another round of this name game.

Sitting Pretty

Try this clever game to position youngsters for some attentive circle-time sitting. When youngsters have gathered for circle-time activities, toss a beanbag to a child. Ask that child to sit in any position she chooses; then challenge the rest of the class to imitate her position. Repeat the procedure, tossing the bag to a different child each time. Conclude the game by tossing the beanbag to yourself and modeling the preferred position—such as cross-legged—for youngsters to imitate. Now that youngsters are sitting pretty, circle time can begin!

Personal Treasures

Here's a neat twist to show-and-tell. Prepare a treasure box by spray-painting a large lidded box with gold paint. After the paint dries, use glitter pens and sparkling stickers to decorate the box. Give each child an opportunity to take the box home overnight (with a note of explanation attached) and place a special item inside. When the child returns the box to school, invite her to show and tell about her treasure during circle time. If desired, she might give clues to prompt her classmates to guess what her special item is before she reveals it.

If desired, extend the use of your treasure box to incorporate basic concepts and your unit of study. Attach a note requesting that parents help their child find an item related to a specific concept or topic. For instance you might request that a child bring in an item of a certain shape or color. Or you might suggest that she find an outdoor item related to fall or spring to put in the treasure box.

COOKING UP SOME FUN

This special two-sided board will surely attract attention to your circle-time activities. To create a double-duty magnet/felt board, purchase a large inexpensive metal cookie sheet. Hot-glue a sheet of felt to the back of the cookie sheet. Then use the felt-covered side of the board for flannelboard stories, finger-plays, and figures. Turn the board over to use magnetic figures and items during circle time. (Almost any item or picture can be backed with a piece of magnetic tape.) Invite youngsters to use the two-sided board to retell circle-time stories, and to practice the concepts and lessons reviewed during circle time.

THUMBS-UP, THUMBS-DOWN

Thumbs-up for good listening! Invite youngsters to demonstrate their general knowledge in this listen-and-think game. Explain that each time your make a true statement about something, students will put their thumbs up. If your statement is not true, children will give the thumbs-down signal. For starters use these examples; then make up your own statements relating to general knowledge, class rules, common courtesy, familiar stories, or even well-known facts about your community.

- Dogs have wings.   (Thumbs-down.)
- Bananas are yellow.   (Thumbs-up.)
- A refrigerator keeps food hot.   (Thumbs-down.)
- Chicks hatch from eggs.   (Thumbs-up.)

Knee to Knee

Preschoolers listen for directions while building body awareness. Seat youngsters and then ask each child to listen as you give a direction that includes two body parts, such as "Put your hand on your head" or "Put your elbow on your leg." Scan for accuracy as each child performs the action. Continue in this manner for several rounds. To increase the challenge, announce directions that include less familiar body parts such as ankle, wrist, or heel.

Lost My Opposite

Do-si-do and around you go with opposite partners. Cut apart a copy of the opposite cards on pages 225 and 226. Separate the opposites so that you have two groups of cards. Stick a piece of double-sided tape or rolled masking tape to the back of each opposite card in a set. Then separate students into two equal groups. Have each student in the first group choose a card from one group of opposites; then have each student in the second group choose a card from the other group of opposites. Instruct each student to stick his card to the front of his shirt. Line the groups up facing one another. Call out a word represented by one of the picture cards. Direct the student wearing that picture to skip along the opposite line, looking for his opposite, as the rest of the class sings "Lost My Opposite" to the tune of "Skip to My Lou."

Lost my opposite, what'll I do? *(Repeat three times.)*
Skip to my Lou, my darling.

When the student finds the child wearing the opposite picture card, have the two students join hands, swing around in the middle, and then go back to their original places as everyone sings:

Opposite, opposite, I found you. *(Repeat three times.)*
Skip to my Lou, my darling.

Flashlight Fun

Spotlight counting skills with this bright activity! Darken your classroom and then aim the beam of a flashlight on the floor in the center of your circle area. Explain that you're going to flash the light five times and ask students to help you count the flashes. Slowly turn the light on and off as students count the flashes in unison. Repeat with a different number. Then encourage students to count the flashes in order to figure out your number. Continue in this manner until students have successfully counted several sets of flashes.

Animal Antics

Following oral directions is lots of fun when preschoolers imitate animal actions and sounds. Have youngsters stand in a circle. Give a direction such as "tiptoe like a mouse," and invite students to move around the circle in that fashion. (See the list shown for suggestions.) Then direct youngsters to pause and listen while you name a different animal movement.

Animal Movement Suggestions:

Stomp like a dinosaur.

Scurry like a squirrel.

Flap like a chicken.

Waddle like a duck.

Gallop like a horse.

Slither like a snake.

Prowl like a lion.

Hop like a kangaroo.

Hide-and-Seek Letters

While students are out of the room, line up a set of magnetic letters in alphabetical order in your circle-time area. Remove several letters and then hide them in your class-room. During circle time, have youngsters help you recite the alphabet while you point to each letter in turn. When you reach a missing letter, act very surprised and tell students that some letters must be playing hide-and-seek. Continue reciting the alphabet to determine how many letters are missing. Next, ask youngsters to hunt for the missing letters. When all the letters have been found, help students identify each found letter and place it in the line. To conclude, enlist student help to recite the complete alphabet.

How Now, Brown Cow?

Reinforce letter identification skills with this "moo-ving" game! Use the pattern on page 227 to make one brown cow card and 26 white cow cards. Program each of the white cards with a different letter. Mix up the cards and then place them in a large circle on the floor. As you play lively music, have youngsters march in a circle behind the cutouts. After a few moments, stop the music to signal each child to stop behind the closest card. Then call out a letter. The child standing behind the named letter moos loudly. If a child is standing behind the brown cow, the class next recites the alphabet in unison. Then restart the music to begin the next round of play.

Special Delivery

Preschoolers are invited to a name-recognition party! To prepare, write a different child's name on each of a class supply of party invitations (or index cards). Give each child an invitation, help him read the name of the recipient, and then encourage him to deliver it to that child. When each child has his party invitation, have him confirm his name. Then play some fun music and invite youngsters to celebrate their growing name-recognition skills!

You're Invited!
Kaelan
Date: September 14
Time: 10:00

Moo!

A Little or a Lot?

Circle time becomes comparison time with this simple activity! In advance, place one or two same-size pom-poms in each of several resealable plastic bags. Next, fill the same quantity of bags with up to ten pom-poms. During circle time, invite two students to each choose a bag and decide if it contains many or few pom-poms. Then encourage the class to compare the bags and decide which contains more and which has fewer pom-poms. Help students count and compare the pom-poms to check their estimates. Repeat the activity with two different students. Continue in this manner as desired.

Hoop-de-do

To prepare for this set-matching activity, place a hoop (or yarn circle) in the center of your circle area. Display a number card and ask students to identify it. Then invite a youngster to count aloud as he places a matching set of blocks in the hoop. Confirm that the number and set match, and then have him count again as he removes the blocks from the hoop. Continue in this manner until a desired number of students has created sets.

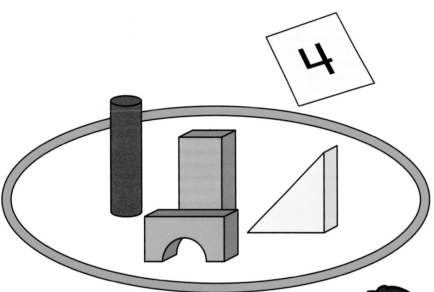

Surprise Boxes

Use the element of surprise to introduce new topics during circle time. Keep a variety of boxes on hand such as a jewelry box, a decorative gift box, a hatbox, and a gift wrapped copier-paper box. When you begin a new unit of study, place an item related to the topic in an appropriate size box. During circle time show the class the box; then invite students to guess what might be inside. Give clues to help them guess the box's contents. After youngsters have exhausted their guesses, open the box to reveal the surprise. Then use the item to draw students' attention to the new topic of study. Surprise!

PASS THE POTATO, PLEASE

Use this passing game to prompt thinking in categorical terms. During circle time explain that you will announce a category such as animals, food, toys, vehicles, or things that fly. Students will pass a beanbag around the circle until you give the signal to stop. The child holding the beanbag at that time will name an item belonging to the designated category. Then, on the go signal, students will resume passing the beanbag. Continue the game, periodically changing the category, for as long as student interest dictates.

happy

TEC61046

sad

TEC61046

day

TEC61046

night

TEC61046

on

TEC61046

off

TEC61046

up

TEC61046

down

TEC61046

above

TEC61046

below

TEC61046

asleep

TEC61046

awake

TEC61046

Note to the teacher: Use with "How Now, Brown Cow?" on page 223.

227

FINE MOTOR

Funny Families

Plenty of giggles are in store when youngsters use their fine-motor skills to create this funny family of faces. To make a family of faces, insert a piece of felt into each of three embroidery hoops: one large, one medium, and one small. Trim away the excess felt from each hoop. Attach the loop side of a self-adhesive Velcro fastener where each facial feature should be. Cut out eyes, noses, and mouths from magazines; then laminate them. Attach the hook side of a Velcro fastener to the back of each one. Store the hoops and cutouts in a tub; then place the tub in a center. To create a family of faces, a youngster presses the desired features onto each hoop to create facial expressions.

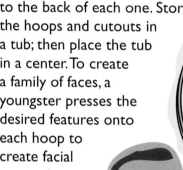

Feed the Alien

Your youngsters will practice hand-eye coordination and strengthen their finger muscles when they have a close encounter with this space creature. Remove the lid and label from an empty two-liter soda bottle. Use paint pens and other craft supplies to decorate the bottle to resemble an alien. Place the bottle, a supply of pom-pom moon rocks, and a pair of ice tongs on a tray; then place the tray in a center. Challenge a child to feed moon rocks to the alien by picking up pom-poms with the tongs and then dropping them into the bottle. For an added challenge, have the child count the moon rocks as he drops them into the bottle.

Transfer Station

Tap into strengthening small hand muscles with this activity, which is sure to cause a wave of excitement. Place two bowls and a sponge on a tray. Partially fill one bowl with water. Challenge a child to transfer the water from bowl to bowl by repeatedly dipping the sponge into the water, then squeezing it over the second bowl. Have him continue dipping and squeezing until the water has been moved. Drip, drop!

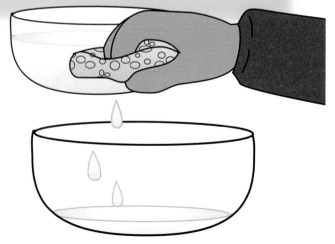

Confetti Collection

Put some punch into fine-motor practice with this creative center. Place colored construction paper strips; a few bowls; and several seasonal, thematic, or round-shaped hole punchers in a center. A student makes confetti by holding a construction paper strip over a bowl and then punching a series of holes into it. After each child has had several opportunities to make confetti, place the collected punches in your sensory table. Add bags of purchased confetti until the table is adequately stocked; then place some small scoops, spoons, cups, and containers in the table. Invite students to scoop and pour the confetti pieces.

I Can Serve

Use this small-group activity time and again to serve up some spooning and scooping practice. Seat a small group of youngsters around a table. Give each child a plastic plate. Fill a serving bowl with play-dough balls, nonmenthol shaving cream, or fingerpaint. Put a spoon in the bowl. Have the children pass the bowl from child to child so that each child can serve herself a ball of dough or a spoonful of the substance. When everyone has been served, invite each child to enjoy some sensory play with the material on her plate. Vary the activity on another day by putting a different substance in the bowl.

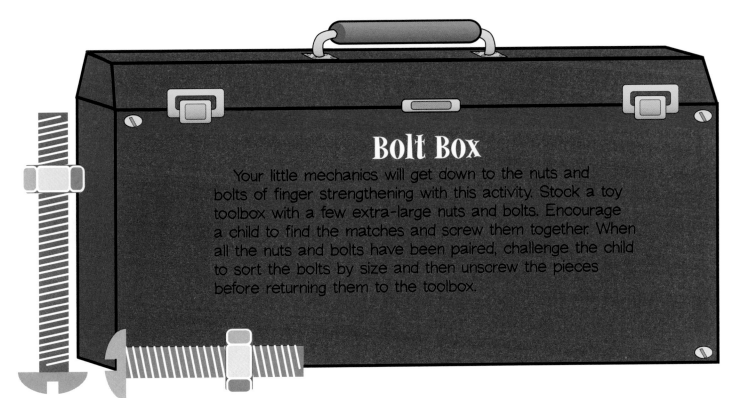

Bolt Box

Your little mechanics will get down to the nuts and bolts of finger strengthening with this activity. Stock a toy toolbox with a few extra-large nuts and bolts. Encourage a child to find the matches and screw them together. When all the nuts and bolts have been paired, challenge the child to sort the bolts by size and then unscrew the pieces before returning them to the toolbox.

Shoe Sort

Transform your dramatic-play center into a shoe store that has fine-motor exercise all buckled up. Collect a variety of shoes with different closures, such as buckles, snaps, ties, hooks, and Velcro fasteners. Place the shoes, shoehorns, a ruler, a mirror, and a small footstool in your dramatic-play center. Students are sure to enjoy measuring, fitting, and trying on the shoes, and the different types of closures will keep their fine-motor skills in step!

Birthday Blowout

You won't have to send out invitations to get your little ones to come to this fine-motor center. Make a birthday cake by gluing two or three Styrofoam circles together to create a cake shape. Decorate the cake with fabric, felt, ribbon, and trim pieces. Press several birthday-candle holders (available at craft or grocery stores) into the top of the cake. Remove the holders; then place a drop of glue in each hole. Replace the candle holders. When the glue is dry, place the cake and a supply of birthday candles in a center. To use the center, a child places a candle in each holder. For a variation, have a child pattern the candles or put a candle in the holder that is its color match.

Hanging Out the Wash

Your little ones will be proud to display their fine-motor fitness while hanging up laundry in this easy center. String a clothesline between two chairs. Place a quantity of spring-type clothespins and squares of colored felt near the clothesline. Invite your preschoolers to clip the felt pieces to the clothesline. For an added challenge, invite students to clip the felt pieces to the clothesline in a color pattern.

Twist and Serve

This center is the pick of the crop for strengthening hand muscles. Demonstrate for your youngsters how to use a citrus juicer by placing an orange half on top of it; then squeeze and twist the orange to extract the juice. Place the juicer, two orange halves for each child, and a class supply of disposable cups in a center. A child visiting this center uses the juicer to extract the juice from two orange halves. He then pours the juice into a cup and enjoys his delicious drink!

Colorful Canisters

Strengthen your youngsters' fine-motor skills while they practice matching colors! Place a roll of construction paper inside a film canister. Glue a matching color circle to its lid and close the canister. Repeat with other colors. Then place the canisters in a film case or a resealable bag. To play, a child removes the lids and scrambles them. Then he matches the colors and places each lid on its canister. The activity is ready for the next visitor, and you will quickly see who can match colors!

Select a Snack

Here's a snack idea that your little ones are sure to grab on to. In separate bowls, place a variety of small snack items, such as Cheerios, animal crackers, pretzel twists, and fish crackers. Add a pair of small tongs to each bowl. Place the bowls and a class supply of paper cups in your cooking center. To prepare a snack, a child uses the tongs to place her desired snack items in her cup. For an added challenge, tape a different numeral card from 1 to 5 on each bowl. A child then places the appropriate numbers of snacks in her cup. One, two, three. Snacktime is yummy!

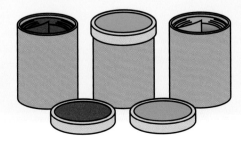

Drip-Drop Posies

Youngsters will squeeze in lots of pincer-finger practice while making these precious posies. Fill three plastic bowls with water; then add several drops of red, yellow, or blue food coloring to each bowl. Place an eyedropper in each bowl. Put the bowls and a supply of coffee filters on a work surface that has been protected with newspaper.

To make a flower, a child repeatedly drops different colors of food coloring onto a flattened coffee filter. When it is dry, gather the filter together in the center; then wrap one end of a green pipe cleaner around the gathered section as shown. Now that's a pretty posie.

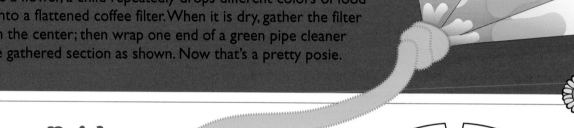

Lion Pride

On the back of a yellow paper plate, draw lines from the edge of the rim to the edge of the circle, as shown, for each student. Have each student cut along the lines on the rim and then fold forward some of the sections to create the lion's mane. On the front of the plate, have him use markers or other craft supplies to make the lion's face. Put the lions on display and your students are sure to take pride in their work!

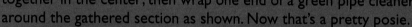

Basket to Basket

Here's an activity to help little ones improve their fine-motor skills. Place two baskets, a supply of cotton balls, tweezers, salad tongs, and spring-type clothes-pins in a center. Have youngsters visiting the center use the tools provided to transfer cotton balls from one basket to the other.

Check out the skill-building reproducibles on pages 233–236.

Buddy's Doghouse

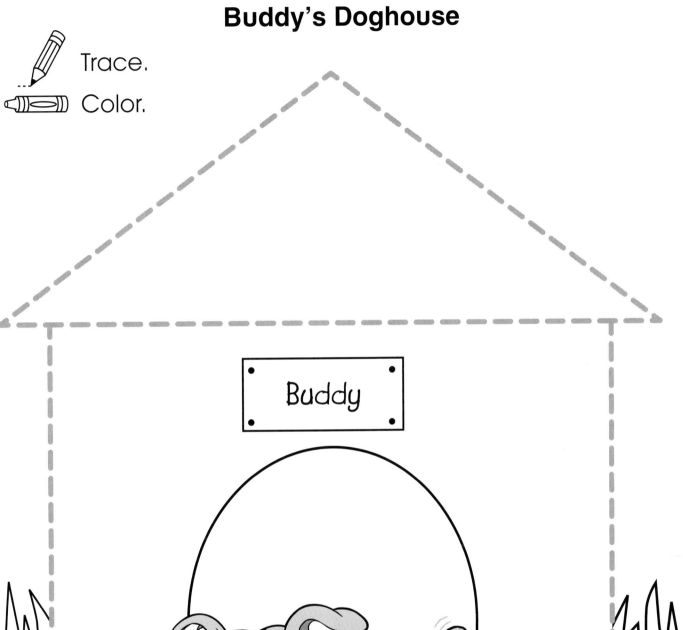

Trace.

Color.

Buddy

Name

Leaps to Lily Pads

Trace.

Up and Away

Color.

Cut.

Glue.

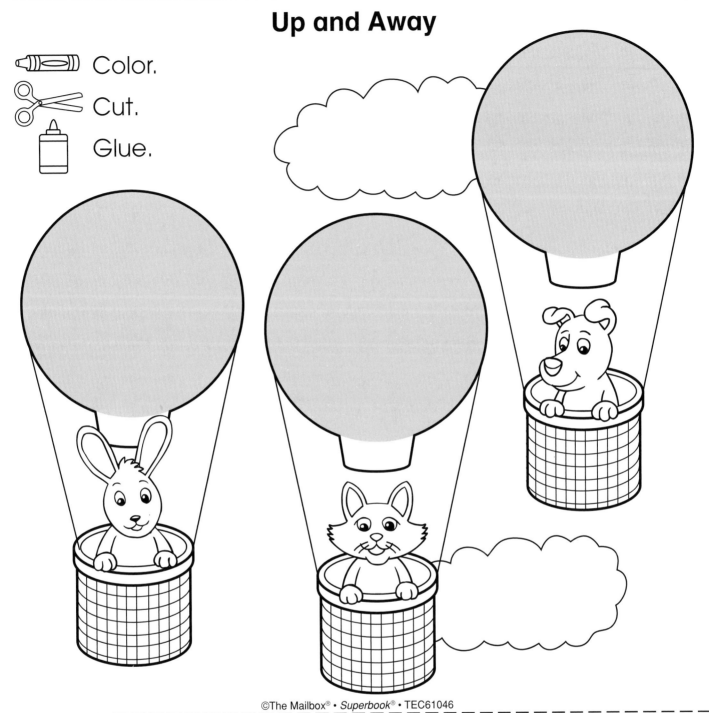

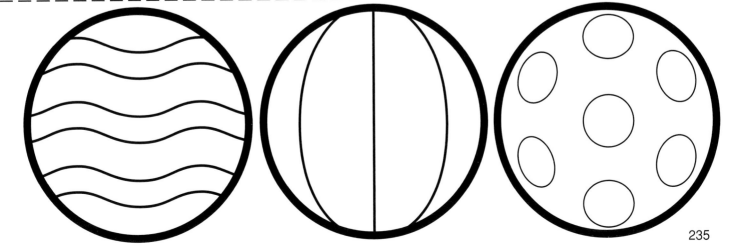

Saltwater Scene

 Color.

Cut.

Glue.

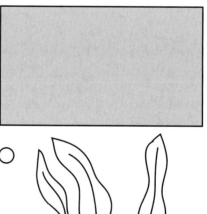

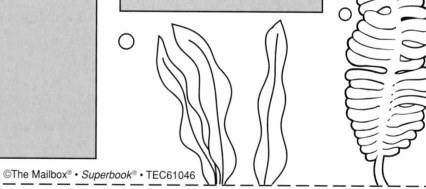

©The Mailbox® • Superbook® • TEC61046

Gross Motor

Dot-to-Dot

Youngsters move their bodies to connect the dots in this small-group activity. For each group member, use clear Con-Tact covering to secure a colorful construction paper circle to the floor. To begin, invite each child in the group to stand on a circle. Then announce a movement, such as hopping, and ask youngsters to perform that movement as they move to the next circle. Announce new movements for youngsters to perform according to their abilities.

Moving Right Along

Ask youngsters to share what they know about different outdoor things and how they move, such as leaves falling, sticks floating in water, snow-flakes blowing in the wind, or a spider crawling on a twig. Write their comments on chart paper; then invite youngsters to engage in some creative movements of their own. To begin, read a child's comment from the chart. Ask youngsters to perform that movement in their own ways. For example, a student might pretend to be a leaf falling straight down from a tree or he might float round and round before landing on the ground.

Animal Antics

Your little ones will move like animals during this activity. Prepare by cutting pictures of familiar animals from magazines. Glue each picture onto a sheet of tagboard.

To play, provide each student with an animal picture. In turn, encourage each youngster to dramatize movements that could be made by her pictured animal. As she is moving, invite the remainder of the group to guess the name of the pictured animal.

ROAR!

Bouncing Balls

Invite your little ones to be rubber balls when acting out the following poem.

I'm a little rubber ball,
(Squat on the floor.)

As round as round can be.
(Bend arms; rest hands on hips.)

Watch me bounce,
1...2...3!
(Jump up and return to a squatting position after each count.)

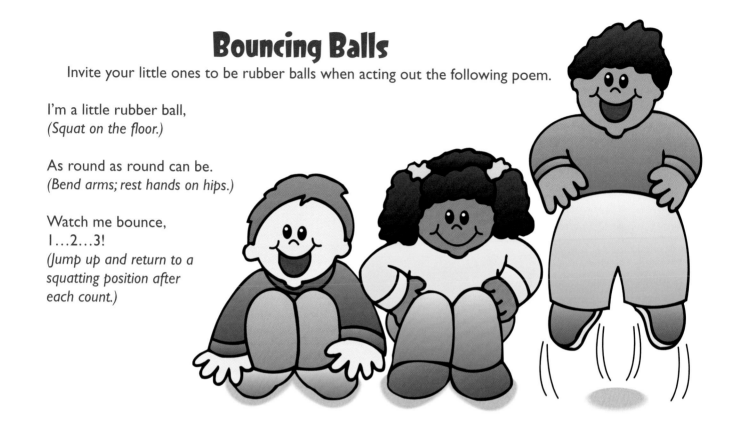

HERE TO THERE

Be prepared for lots of giggles and wiggles when you challenge students with this movement activity. Invite a small group of students to stand along a line in an open area of your classroom. Place a ball in front of each child. Then direct each student to move the ball across a designated finish line some distance away, using a suggested body part. For example, have students move the balls using only their elbows. When each child has moved the ball over the finish line, direct a different group of students to move the balls back to the starting line using a different body part. Repeat with a new group of students until each child has had a turn.

Toss It In

Use a wide variety of containers to give youngsters a fun way to practice aiming and tossing. Gather several large containers such as baskets, plastic flowerpots, sand buckets, and gift bags. Arrange the containers in an open area along with a supply of beanbags. Have a small group of students stand at a desired distance from the containers. Then invite them to take turns tossing the beanbags into the containers.

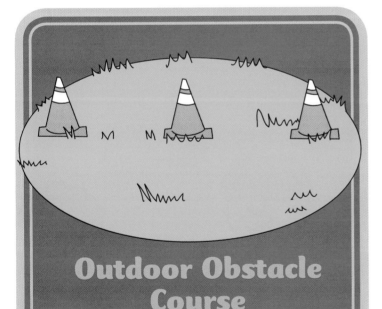

Outdoor Obstacle Course

Challenge your little ones' movement abilities by setting up an obstacle course! Make a row of markers using an item such as cones in an open area outdoors. Encourage each student, in turn, to run in a zigzag formation around the markers. Repeat the activity as desired, each time announcing a different way for youngsters to move around the markers, such as hopping, skipping, or galloping.

STUCK LIKE GLUE

Your little ones will be using their bodies and imaginations to get into these sticky situations. Invite each student to use an imaginary paintbrush to brush glue over his body. Stand away from the group; then give directions such as "Stick your elbow to your knee" or "Stick your hand to your head." Next, challenge each child to walk to you; then wash away the glue by pouring an imaginary pail of water over the top of him. Now that's some super glue!

Jump the Brook

This gross-motor game will leave your youngsters jumping for joy. In advance, prepare a supply of fish cutouts. Then place two parallel lengths of blue yarn on the floor, leaving just enough space to place one fish in the "brook" between them. Invite youngsters to line up behind a piece of yarn and jump over the brook one at a time. If a child cannot jump the brook without the fish "nibbling" at her toes, she is out of the game. After each youngster has tried to jump the brook with one fish, move the yarn lengths far enough apart to add a second fish and invite little ones to jump over the brook again. Continue adding one fish at a time and moving the pieces of yarn farther apart until only a small number of jumpers remains.

Watch Me!

Invite your youngsters to take charge of movement time. To begin, select one child to act as the teacher. Encourage him to lead the class in an exercise such as knee bends, toe touches, or arm circles. Help the class count to ten as it does the exercise. Then choose a different child to lead the class in the next exercise. Continue in this manner until each child has had a turn to play the role of the teacher.

Limbo Like Me!

Everyone will want to play this limbo game that's similar to Simon Says. Ask a volunteer to hold one end of a broomstick while you hold the other end. Play some music; then invite a child to be the limbo line leader. Challenge him to find a way to move under the broomstick without touching it, such as slithering, crawling, or rolling. Direct the remainder of the group to copy the leader's movement. When each child in the line has gone under, lower the stick. Have students continue to follow the leader under the stick. Play continues in this manner until a child touches the broomstick while going under. Then choose a different limbo line leader.

Where's the Dinosaur?

A pretend dinosaur hunt is a fun way to get your youngsters moving. Have each child stand and spread out in an open area. Explain that you are leading a dinosaur hunt. To begin, invite students to imitate you as you walk through the forest (walk slowly in place). After a few moments, announce that you've spotted one of the obstacles from the list shown and demonstrate the corresponding movement for students to perform. For example, announce that you have spotted a cave and lead children in crawling through it. Repeat with additional obstacles and their corresponding movements as desired. To conclude, pretend that you spot the dinosaur, but it moves too quickly and gets away! Better luck next time!

Obstacle	Movement
stepping stones	leaping
a cave	crawling
thick vines	climbing
a river	jumping
a mountain	climbing
a log	walking on tiptoes

Seasonal Shape-Up

Introduce your little ones to seasonal symbols by putting them on your classroom floor. Use masking tape to form a seasonal symbol (such as a Christmas tree in December or a heart in February) on open floor space. Then encourage your youngsters, in turn, to move along the lines in various ways. Ask them to walk, hop, tiptoe, or crawl along the lines to form the seasonal shape as they practice the movement.

Traveling Motions

Get students headed in the right direction by adding a transportation twist to the classic game Follow the Leader. Ask youngsters to form a line, one behind the other, and take your place at the front. Call out a form of transportation, such as a car. Demonstrate a corresponding movement, such as pretending to steer, and encourage children to copy your movement as you lead the line around the room. To continue the activity, announce other modes of transportation—such as an airplane, a bicycle, a train, roller skates, or a horse—and then invite children to imitate the corresponding movements.

Dramatic Play
and Role-Play

THIS IS THE WAY WE GO TO SCHOOL

Every child will have experiences to draw upon for this activity. During group time, discuss different means of transportation; then ask students, "How did you get to school today?" Write their responses on a sheet of chart paper. Guide children in selecting classroom items to use as appropriate props to help them act out the different means of transportation listed on the chart. For example, arrange chairs in rows to create a bus. Transform a large cardboard box into a car. Or place a length of bulletin board paper on the floor to resemble a sidewalk. Then encourage each child to act out how he got to school.

Set the Scene

Add new dimensions to your little ones' dramatic play with simple backdrops. Use a black marker to draw an outline of a scene, such as a row of houses, on a length of bulletin board paper. As you draw, encourage students to suggest details for you to add, such as flowers, mountains, and trees. When the outline is complete, invite your students to color in the scene using markers, crayons, or paints. Attach the backdrop to a wall in your dramatic-play center. When you are ready to change the focus of the center, roll the paper into a scroll; then secure it with a rubber band. Then draw a new scene to coordinate with your current theme.

Preschool Express

Grab a ticket and get on board for some dramatic-play fun that is sure to keep your little conductors on the track. Collect a variety of large cardboard boxes. Place the boxes on the floor in your group area. During a group time, show students photos of trains and locomotives, pointing out important features such as wheels and doors. Supply students with craft materials such as markers, construction paper, scissors, and glue. Invite students to decorate the boxes to resemble train cars. When the cars are complete, line up the boxes end to end to create a long train. Make a dining car by adding some play food to one of the boxes; then add some stuffed-animal passengers to the other cars. Invite youngsters to climb on board and chug away on an imaginary train ride.

Let's Play School!

Give preschoolers an opportunity to walk in your shoes as they role-play the teacher in the dramatic-play area. Setting up this scene is easy; just look around! Include chalk, an eraser, an easel, a big book, a pointer, a puppet, paper and crayons, and plenty of rewarding stickers for the teacher to use. Provide the teacher with a school-themed sweater or T-shirt to wear. Encourage students to take turns; then watch as they emulate their favorite educator in action—you!

CANINE CAPERS

Prepare a doggie headband for each child by cutting out two ear shapes from white construction paper. Staple the ears onto a construction paper headband. Invite each student to color her headband as desired. When she is finished, fit the headband to her head; then staple the ends together. Have students wear their headbands as they howl along to "How Much Is That Doggie in the Window?" or any favorite song about dogs. Then encourage your little ones to act out doggie behaviors from tail waggin' to hole diggin'.

All in the Family

Family fun will take center stage when you add a family prop box to your dramatic-play area. Cover a large cardboard box with bulletin board paper. Cut pictures of family members and family groups from magazines; then glue them onto the box. Collect an assortment of men's, women's, and children's dress-up clothes and shoes. Include a baby doll, baby clothes, a blanket, and a bottle in your collection. Place all the items in the box. Introduce the items in the family prop box to your students; then place the box in your dramatic-play center. Soon your little ones will be role-playing family situations. There may be no place like home—but this center comes close!

SONG DRAMA

Your little ones will be Broadway-bound after performing in this musical extravaganza! Write the words to some favorite songs on a length of bulletin board paper; then post the chart near your group area. Sing the songs with your students; then brainstorm ideas about how the words to each one might be dramatized and what props may be needed. Write youngsters' responses next to the appropriate phrases on the chart. Then collect the needed materials using classroom supplies, family donations, or thrift-store purchases. After the props have been collected, encourage one small group of children at a time to dress up in its choice of play clothes. Encourage the children to act out the lyrics of one song as the remainder of the group sings. Continue with the remaining groups and songs until your musical revue is finished.

Row, row, row your boat.

I am a <u>cat</u> .
I can <u>arch my back</u> .
I can <u>meow</u> .
I feel <u>soft</u> .
I smell <u>like fish</u> .
I am <u>happy</u> .
I am <u>orange</u> .
I am a <u>cat</u> .

POET'S CORNER

Introduce your youngsters to the magic of poetry by having them dramatize their own poems. Program a sheet of paper with the poem framework shown below; then duplicate a page for each student. During a group time, brainstorm a list of different things students can pretend to be such as an elephant, a princess, a tree, etc. Then, working with each individual student, write her responses as she completes each sentence. After completing her poem, encourage her to act it out, using props if she desires. When each child has had an opportunity to create a poem and dramatize it, place the poems in a box labeled "Poetry Play." During center time encourage students to select their own or other poems from the box to dramatize.

I am a [person, place, or thing].
I can [movement].
I can [sound].
I feel [texture].
I smell [scent].
I am [emotion].
I am [color].
I am a [repeat first line].

CHORE-TIME CHARADES

Involve youngsters in the movements of routine chores with this charades-style game. To play, model a movement to simulate the performance of a particular household chore such as vacuuming, washing windows, or scrubbing a bathtub. Ask youngsters to imitate your movements, but do not tell them which chore is being performed. After a designated time, signal for students to stop their activity; then ask them to name which chore they were doing. After all the guesses have been exhausted, tell youngsters which chore was being represented. Continue the game, modeling the actions of a different chore each time.

ANIMAL ANTICS

Your little ones will move like animals in this cooperative game. Prepare by cutting pictures of familiar animals from magazines. Glue each picture onto a separate sheet of tagboard; then laminate the sheets for durability. Cut each picture in half using a different cutting line such as zigzag, straight, or curved.

To play, provide each student with half of a picture. Encourage each youngster to find her partner by locating the child who has the matching picture half. When each child has found her partner, challenge the pair to work together to dramatize movements that could be made by their pictured animal. As the pair is moving, invite the remainder of the group to guess the name of the pictured animal.

COOL COMBOS

For a dramatic change of pace, combine other classroom centers with your dramatic-play center. For example, add a water table and invite youngsters to wash dishes or doll clothes. Or provide a collection of building blocks for making baby beds and furniture. Or place a basket of favorite books in your dramatic-play center and encourage little ones to "read" to doll babies or act out the stories. Invite youngsters to suggest creative ways to combine different centers with the dramatic play center. You'll be surprised at what their active imaginations will cook up!

TREASURE TROVE

Ahoy, matey! Your little pirates will love hunting for this treasure! Cover a lidded or hinged cardboard box with wood-grained Con-Tact paper to resemble a treasure chest. To make coins, glue gold or silver foil gift wrap to sheets of construction paper and then cut circles from the paper. Place the coins into the box along with a variety of beaded necklaces and glitter pop-pom "jewels." Place the treasure chest in your dramatic-play center. Your youngsters will soon unlock the wealth of creative opportunities this treasure box holds!

Smile!

This role-playing experience is sure to bring lots of toothy grins! Transform a center into a dentist's office with simple props such as wide mouthed puppets (patients), toothbrushes, an unbreakable hand mirror, and medical scrub tops. Also, set up a waiting area nearby with a toy phone, appointment book, chairs, and magazines. Youngsters take turns pretending to be hygienists, dentists, and parents of the puppet patients.

Mail Call

Mailing and receiving letters has never been more fun! Stock a center with a variety of postcards, envelopes, paper, pencils, and stickers to represent stamps. Be sure to include a bag that resembles a mailbag and a blue button-down shirt for the mail carrier's uniform. Encourage a student to pretend to be a customer writing and mailing letters. Invite another student to role-play a postal worker sorting and delivering mail.

Lemonade Stand

Here's a refreshing imaginary-play activity! Set a table with a plastic pitcher, several paper cups, and a play lemon or two. Enlist student help to make a sign for the lemonade stand. Then invite little ones to take turns pretending to make lemonade and serve lots of thirsty customers.

Super Scoopers

Youngsters create cool treats in this make-believe ice-cream parlor! Place clean, empty whipped-topping bowls, syrup containers, and ice-cream cartons at a center. Add red pom-pom cherries, play dough in a variety of colors, ice-cream scoops, plastic bowls and spoons, and some aprons. Include a small table and chairs for customers to order and enjoy their special sundaes.

Down by the Sea

Invite your beach bunnies to use these props to re-create a "sun-sational" day by the shore. Tape a length of white bulletin board paper to a low section of a wall in the dramatic-play area. Provide a variety of markers and colored chalk and invite children to draw a background scene complete with sun, sand, and surf. (For younger preschoolers, you may want to sketch the outlines of the sun, waves, and sand for them to color.) Move the sand table into the area or fill a plastic swimming pool with sand. Put in plastic shovels, buckets, castle molds, assorted containers for building, and craft foam seashell cutouts. Spread several beach towels on the floor; then shine a desk lamp into the area for basking in the "sunshine." Flip-flops, sunglasses, a picnic basket, swimming floats, sun hats, and some background beach music will complete this beach-lover's paradise.

Music & Movement

Butterfly Bop

This imaginative movement activity will have youngsters all a-flutter! For each child place a large colorful paper flower cutout on the floor. As you play soft music, have youngsters move like butter-flies around the room. After a few moments, stop the music to signal each child to stop on a flower. Then restart the music to begin the next round of play.

Rhythm Rods

These personalized rhythm sticks will prompt youngsters to rap and romp to their own beats. To make a set of rhythm rods, a child decorates two paper towel tubes with crayons, paint, or colored markers. Edge each end of each rod with a strip of colored vinyl tape to prevent the tubes from unraveling. Invite youngsters to create their own music by tapping the rods together like rhythm sticks or using them like drumsticks on a tabletop, a chair seat, or the floor. Encourage student pairs to experiment with the different beats and tempos of various music styles such as marches, rap, jazz, and rock-and-roll.

THE BEAT GOES ON

This listening activity will give students some valuable practice in detecting rhythms and in following directions. To begin, play a musical selection with a steady, rhythmic beat. Begin a simple pattern to the rhythm of the music. For instance, you might clap your hands, then snap your fingers. Invite youngsters to join you in repeating the pattern. After a short time, begin another simple pattern such as tapping your shoulders and then raising your arms. Continue in this manner throughout the selection, encouraging youngsters to watch and repeat each new pattern you introduce. Then, on the next round, you might increase the complexity of the pattern to three parts. If desired, have students take turns creating patterns for the class to copy.

Free to Fly

Freedom of expression is the way to fly in this activity. To prepare, tie two large scarves together. Explain that the scarves represent the wings of a bird, a butterfly, or any other flying creature that a child might want to imagine himself to be. Then play some peaceful, flowing music. Invite each child, in turn, to position the tied scarves across his back so that he can use them like wings. Encourage him to create his own flight pattern as he flies, flaps, flutters, and floats to express his interpretation of the music. Adjust the flight times of each student so that every child has a turn to fly.

Ribbon Rings

These colorful rings are the perfect dance companions and tools for movement exploration. To create a ribbon ring, tie several colorful ribbons in different widths and lengths to a shower-curtain ring or plastic bracelet. Then invite each youngster to rhythmically move her rings and her body to different styles of music. Or have youngsters mirror a leader as she moves with her ribbon ring to a simple rhythm, a musical selection, or no music at all. Students might also explore the movement of the wind using their special rings.

Elephant Size

Youngsters enjoy a huge workout when imitating elephant-movements! Invite students to spread out in an open area. Then give elephant-related directions, such as "Walk on all fours," "Clasp your hands together and raise your arms like a trunk," "Stand on one foot," "Pretend to pick up peanuts with your trunk," and "Use your trunk to spray water on your back." Continue in this manner for several rounds. Then end the activity by asking your little elephants to kneel down and take a bow.

Dancer's Choice

Preschoolers boogie on over for this movement activity! Encourage youngsters to don an accessory from your dress-up box, such as a hat or scarf. Then play some lively music and lead students in a parade around the room. Periodically stop and perform a dance action for each child to copy, such as clapping your hands to the beat, wiggling your hips, or bending your knees. Once youngsters have the hang of it, select a student leader to continue the dancing fun.

Balancing Act

Here's an activity that balances movement and fun! In advance, place a long length of wide colored tape on the floor in an open area. Then play music and direct each child to move appropriately along the tape line. For example, a slow classical selection might be accompanied by long, slow steps. An energetic tune might go with marching or jumping. A fast tune may be accompanied by quick tiptoeing. Challenge older preschoolers to stay on the line as they move to the music.

Symbolic Cymbals

These paper plate cymbals will give youngsters the feel and excitement of using the real things—without the earsplitting noise level! Give each child two sturdy paper plates to decorate with markers or crayons. Using a real pair of cymbals, show younsters how to clap the paper cymbals together to create a rhythm. Play some music with a steady beat; then have youngsters imitate your cymbal dance as you play the instrument in different positions such as over your head, behind your back, to the right and left sides, and in front of your knees. Give each child an opportunity to play the real cymbals and lead the cymbal dance as you take the role of follower with the rest of the class.

Dancing Shoes

These special shoes can transform any child into a dreamy waltzer or a disco dynamo. To create a pair of dancing shoes, simply have a child personalize a pair of paper plates with markers or crayons. Then have him slip his feet into the imaginary shoes (stand on the plates). Play a musical selection and encourage each child to slide along the floor in his special shoes, keeping rhythm to the music. Challenge students to partner-dance and try interesting slide-steps and backward and sideways moves. Be sure to play a variety of music as youngsters break in their imaginary dancing shoes.

The Circle Dance

What time is it? It's time to do the circle dance! Give each child an opportunity to show off some movement while she's in the spotlight. To create the special stage, simply place a large plastic or yarn ring on the floor; then have your students form a larger loose circle around the ring. Invite a child to stand inside the ring while you lead the class in singing this song naming the featured child where indicated. While you sing, encourage the child in the ring to dance, move, or even act as silly as she wishes. Then call a different child to switch places with the first child, and repeat the song. Continue until each child has had a turn to do the circle dance.

(sung to the tune of "If You're Happy and You Know It")

Oh, it's time to see the special circle dance!
Oh, it's time to see the special circle dance!
Dancing's fun for you and me.
Now it's [Paige] we will see.
Oh, it's time to see the special circle dance!

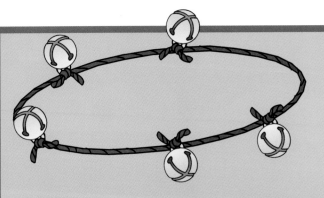

JINGLE-BELL BRACELETS

These simple pieces of jewelry will have children jingling right along with any catchy tune. To make a bracelet, sew or tie several small jingle bells onto a ponytail holder. Have each child slip the jingle-bell band onto her wrist or ankle; then play some rhythmic selections of music. Invite youngsters to shake their wrists or ankles or to dance while jingling to the beat of the music. At the end of the activity, be sure to collect the bells for safekeeping.

BODY MUSIC

Youngsters will be amazed to discover the musical instruments that are attached to their own bodies! Challenge students to explore the many different musical sounds they can make with different parts of their bodies. First, ask youngsters to create rhythmic sounds by breathing in different ways, then by clicking their tongues, smacking their lips, humming, and whistling. Then have them experiment with the many sounds their hands can make—clapping their hands together, snapping their fingers, and patting their hands against other body parts. Next, encourage students to create different musical sounds with their feet. Finally, invite youngsters to make music with their different body instruments while following the rhythms of some lively recordings.

BODY TALK

Students will be rocking and wiggling as they move various body parts in this group activity. Play some lively music. As you name a body part, have each student move that part of his body to the beat of the music. For added fun, have students wiggle their noses, raise their eyebrows, or blink their eyes in time with the music. As children become more confident, encourage volunteers to be the leaders in this game of following directions.

Art Explorations

Kitchen Collage

Little ones cook up some creative printing with kitchen gadgets! Place interesting utensils such as mashers, spatulas, spoons, colanders, and whisks in your art area. Add shallow trays of colorful paint and a container of rinse water. To make a collage, have a child select a utensil, dip it in paint, and print it on a large sheet of paper. Invite her to repeat the process with other utensils and colors of paint, making sure to rinse utensils before changing colors.

Color Combing

Pick this idea for an unusual painting technique that's sure to engage your preschoolers! To prepare for one child, dab alternating colors of fingerpaint along the edges of a sheet of fingerpaint paper. Have the child use a large plastic pick comb to swirl and spread the paint around the paper, blending the colors and creating pretty designs!

"Sew" Pretty

In advance, cut a square of rug canvas for each child. Also cut a supply of various colors of curling ribbon lengths. Give each child a canvas square and several ribbons. Have him lace and weave a length of ribbon through the holes in his canvas square. Then show him how to turn the canvas and repeat the process with a different ribbon. Have him continue in this manner until the canvas is full of colors and designs.

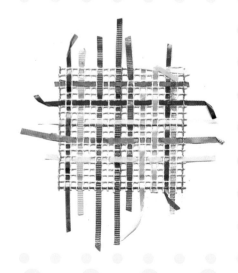

Makin' Tracks

Preschoolers track down some fun with this exploration. Cover a tabletop with paper. Place a variety of toy vehicles nearby, along with shallow trays of colorful paint. Invite a child to choose a vehicle, dip its wheels in paint, and "drive" it on the paper. Have him continue in this manner to make several interesting tracks. When the paint is dry, encourage each child to match each set of tracks with the appropriate vehicle.

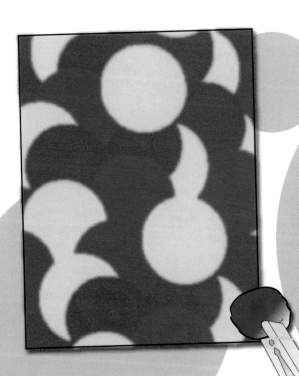

Dips and Dabs

Simple cotton ball printers lead to lots of artistic exploration! Help each child clip a cotton ball to a clothespin. Then have her dip it into the paint color of her choice and dab it onto her paper to create a design. Next, invite her to repeat the process with a fresh cotton ball and different color of paint. Encourage each child to overlap the colors to softly blend them. If desired, invite each youngster to work in a third color for further color-blending investigation.

Circles and More Circles

Stock your art area with a variety of small round plastic jars, cups, and containers. Place paper plates and shallow trays of paint nearby. To make a circle collage, invite a child to dip a container into paint and print the circle onto a paper plate. Encourage her to overlap various circles and colors to create an interesting collage.

Roll Out the Colors

Youngsters roll their way to beautifully blended artwork! In advance, fill each of several squeeze bottles with a different color of paint. Help a child squeeze two to three colors of paint squiggles on a sheet of construction paper. Then have him cover the paper with a same-size sheet of waxed paper. Next, direct him to roll a rolling pin over the paper, sandwiching the paint in between to blend the colors. Help him carefully peel off the waxed paper and discard it.

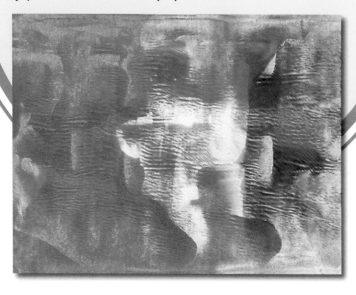

Chunky Drawing

In advance, collect old and broken crayon pieces. Have youngsters peel off all the paper wrappings and sort the pieces by color. Melt the pieces and then pour the hot wax into separate compartments of an ice cube tray. Let the wax harden. Pop out the resulting crayon cubes and place them in a center with large sheets of paper. Invite students to draw and color with these super size crayons.

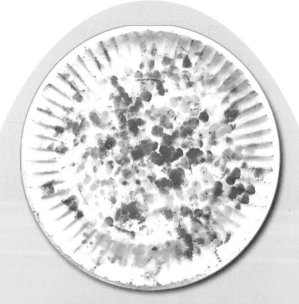

Tickle Painting

This fun technique is sure to result in plenty of giggles! To make a tickle painting, a child folds a plain facial tissue several times. Then he dips the corners and edges into various colors of diluted washable paint. Next, he places the tissue on a plain paper plate and unfolds it as desired. Using only his fingertips, he tickles the tissue by moving it around on the plate until the plate is covered with colorful dots.

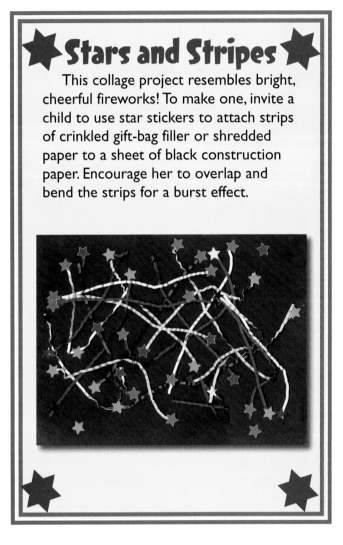

★ Stars and Stripes ★

This collage project resembles bright, cheerful fireworks! To make one, invite a child to use star stickers to attach strips of crinkled gift-bag filler or shredded paper to a sheet of black construction paper. Encourage her to overlap and bend the strips for a burst effect.

Celery Roses

Looking for a simple yet beautiful print technique? Just reach for celery! To prepare, slice the stalks from a bunch of celery, leaving the base intact. To make roses, have a child dip the celery base into colorful paint and print it on a sheet of paper. Repeat with other colors as desired.

Clip Art

Clothespins make interesting and accessible painting tools! In advance, place a spring-type clothespin beside each of several shallow trays of paint. Have a child dip the tips of a clothespin in the selected color of paint and then squeeze the clothespin open and shut on a sheet of paper. Invite her to repeat the process with different colors until a desired effect is achieved.

Changeable Chalk

Preschoolers discover the properties of chalk with this technique! Ask a youngster to rub various colors of sidewalk chalk on a sheet of construction paper, overlapping the colors to fill the sheet completely. Then help him use a spray bottle to lightly mist the sheet with water. Encourage him to watch as the colors change and intensify. As the paper dries, lead him to notice that the colors soften again. If desired, invite him to gently rub more chalk on the damp paper to explore the effects.

Fluff Paint

This fluffy paint is meant to be spread and swirled! In advance, prepare fluff paint by mixing equal parts of nonmenthol shaving cream and white glue. If desired, divide the mixture among several small bowls and use tempera paint to tint each batch a different color. Place craft sticks nearby. Invite a student to use a craft stick to scoop some paint onto a sheet of construction paper. Have him spread the paint around the paper to make a pleasing design. Let the painting dry flat overnight.

Crayons-on-a-String

If your art center routine is "crayons at the table, paints at the easel," then think again! Attach one end of a long length of yarn to the top of your easel, and tie the opposite end around a crayon. (You might add a dab of hot glue for security.) Youngsters will love drawing with this crayon-on-a-string. Tie two or three crayons together for a multicolored effect.

A "Hole" Lot of Creativity

Encourage children to think creatively about shapes and spaces with this idea. Before hanging a sheet of art paper on an easel, cut a hole in it. The hole can be any shape—try circles, squares, stars, or diamonds for starters. If desired, hang a solid piece of paper behind the one with the hole. Then observe how your youngsters react: Do they paint inside the cutout shape or around it?

Sticky Stuff

Want youngsters to stick with their artistic endeavors? Stock your art center with some of these peel-and-stick materials. Youngsters will be creating with new media and building fine-motor skills as they peel and place these materials.

stickers
adhesive bandages
colored masking tape
magnetic tape
scraps of Con-Tact paper
adhesive Velcro

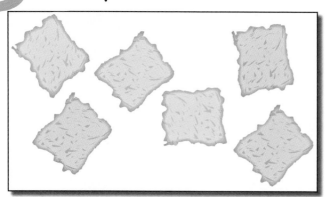

Carpet-Square Prints

Looking for a new art idea? Look down—on the floor! Carpet squares will provide interesting textures for paint prints. Visit your local carpet or home improvement store and ask for some carpet samples. Try to gather a few different textures such as berber, sculptured, and plush carpeting. Use a utility knife to cut the samples into smaller, more manageable squares or rectangles. Set out large sheets of construction paper or pieces of bulletin board paper and shallow trays of tempera paint. Encourage youngsters to press the carpet samples into paint, then onto paper. Invite them to compare the prints created by different textures of carpeting.

Egg Roll

This alternative to traditional marble painting is perfect for some artistic exploration. Place a sheet of drawing paper in a box lid. Drizzle a little tempera paint on the paper; then invite a child to lay a plastic egg in the box lid. Have him gently tilt and rock the box lid to make the egg roll through the paint. Continue by adding other paint colors until the child is satisfied with the design.

Wrap It Up

Here's an art supply that makes both a great painting surface and a great painting tool: bubble wrap!

 Use a length of bubble wrap in place of fingerpainting paper.

 Clip a piece of bubble wrap to your easel.

 Make a print from a painted bubble-wrap design by pressing a sheet of drawing paper over it.

 Create a bubble-wrap mitt. Just wrap a length of bubble wrap around a child's hand and tape it to fit snugly. Then invite the child to use the bubble-wrap mitt to daub paint onto paper to create a design.

Smash Painting

This idea will be a smash with your preschoolers! Set out tempera paints, paper, margarine-tub lids, and a few hammers or mallets. Invite a child to drip a bit of paint onto his paper, place a margarine-tub lid over the paint, and tap the lid. Have him lift the lid and observe how the paint has moved. Invite him to use other paint colors and repeat the process as many times as he desires.

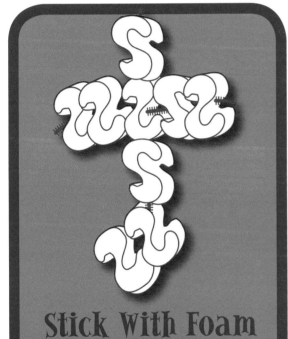

Stick With Foam

Gather up packing peanuts and put them to good use! Set out a supply of foam or biodegradable packing pieces, along with a variety of items that can be used safely to stick the packing pieces together. You could include pipe cleaners, twist-ties, tiny twigs, craft sticks, coffee stirrers, or toothpicks. (Use materials appropriate for your students' age level, and be sure to provide adequate supervision.) Encourage your students to create sculptures of their own designs with the materials.

Starched-Yarn Designs

Don't get hung up about process art—hang it up instead. To make a starched-yarn design, dip yarn of various lengths, colors, and thicknesses into liquid starch. Then arrange these pieces inside a plastic lid lined with waxed paper. Let the design dry at least overnight. (It may take a few days to dry, depending on the thickness of the yarn and how saturated it becomes. If necessary, turn the design over partway through the drying time.) When the design is stiff and dry, remove it from the waxed paper. Use fishing line to suspend the projects in your classroom.

RECIPES
for Arts & Crafts

BAKING DOUGH

2 cups flour
1 cup salt
water

Mix the dry ingredients; then add enough water to create a workable dough. Invite children to sculpt figures or roll and cut the dough with cookie cutters. Bake the dough at 300°F for 1 to 1 ½ hours (depending on the thickness of each figure). Finished products can be painted.

MILK PAINT

evaporated milk
food coloring

Divide one or more cans of evaporated milk evenly among several containers. Add a few drops of a different color of food coloring to each container and mix until the desired shades are achieved. Have youngsters paint with this mixture on construction paper to create a creamy, pastel look.

MAGIC CRYSTALS

2 cups water
2 cups Epsom salts
food coloring (optional)

In a saucepan, combine the water and Epsom salts, and bring to a boil. Stir the mixture and allow it to cool. If desired, add a few drops of food coloring. Have students paint with this mixture on construction paper. The paint will dry to create clear or colored crystals.

DECORATIVE DYE

1 tablespoon rubbing alcohol
food coloring
large dry pasta shapes

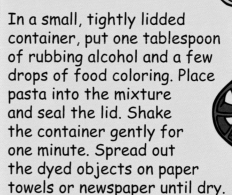

In a small, tightly lidded container, put one tablespoon of rubbing alcohol and a few drops of food coloring. Place pasta into the mixture and seal the lid. Shake the container gently for one minute. Spread out the dyed objects on paper towels or newspaper until dry.

TEACHER-MADE PLAY DOUGH

1 cup flour
½ cup salt
2 teaspoons cream of tartar
1 cup water
1 teaspoon vegetable oil
food coloring

Mix the dry ingredients together. Then add the remaining ingredients and stir. In a heavy skillet, cook the mixture for two to three minutes, stirring frequently. Turn the dough onto a lightly floured surface and knead it until it becomes soft and smooth. Mix up a separate batch of dough for each color desired. Store the dough in an airtight container.

COLORED GLUE

food coloring
white glue

Add a few drops of a different color of food coloring to each of several empty squeeze bottles. Gradually add glue, using a drinking straw to stir the glue until it's evenly tinted.

EXTRA-BRIGHT TEMPERA PAINT

2 cups dry tempera paint
1 cup liquid soap (clear or white works best)
1 cup liquid starch

Mix the paint and soap; then add starch and stir. If the mixture becomes too thick, add more liquid soap. Store the paint in a plastic lidded container.

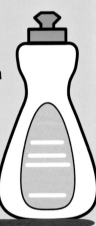

CORN SYRUP PAINT

light corn syrup
food coloring

Divide one or more bottles of corn syrup evenly among several containers. Add a few drops of a different color of food coloring to each container and mix until the desired shades are achieved. This paint requires a few days of drying time.

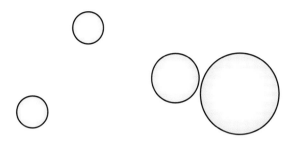

BUBBLE MIXTURE

¼ cup dishwashing liquid
½ cup water
1 teaspoon sugar
food coloring

Mix the dishwashing liquid, water, and sugar together in a container. If color is desired, mix in a few drops of food coloring.

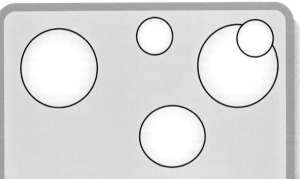

KOOL-AID DOUGH

2 ½—3 cups flour
½ cup salt
1 package unsweetened Kool-Aid mix
1 tablespoon alum
2 cups boiling water
3 tablespoons corn oil
1 cup additional flour

Mix the first six ingredients into a dough. Using some or all of the additional flour, knead the dough until it reaches the desired consistency. Store the dough in an airtight container.

EASY PAPIER-MÂCHÉ

liquid starch
cold water
newspaper torn into strips

Mix equal parts of liquid starch and cold water. Dip the newspaper strips into the mixture before applying to a form of chicken wire or rolled newspaper.

SALT PAINT

2 teaspoons salt
1 teaspoon liquid starch
a few drops of tempera paint

Mix the ingredients together. The salt gives a frosted appearance to the paint.

COLORED GRITS

liquid tempera paint
grits

In a large bowl, mix the ingredients, being careful not to let the grits get too wet. Spread the mixture onto cookie sheets to dry for a day or two, stirring occasionally. Use as you would colored sand.

SHINY PAINT

1 part white liquid glue
1 part liquid tempera paint

Mix the ingredients. This paint will retain a wet look after it has dried.

GLUE

Cover a bulletin board with a green plastic tablecloth and a fall-leaves border. Cut a basket shape from cardboard. Draw lines on the shape to make it resemble a bushel basket; then staple it to the board. Have each child sponge-paint a construction paper apple shape. When the paint is dry, attach the apples around the basket.

Cut a tree shape from brown bulletin board paper and staple it to one side of a bulletin board. Using the patterns on page 275, cut out a supply of construction paper leaves; then label each leaf with a different title from your classroom book collection. Attach the leaves to the tree. During storytime have a student pick a leaf from the tree. Read the corresponding book; then attach the leaf to the right side of the board to form a pile.

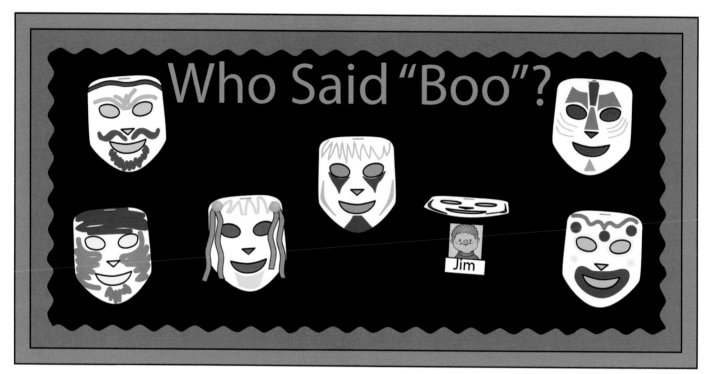

Give each child a construction paper mask shape. Have her decorate her mask with markers, pom-poms, ribbon, sequins, colored glue, or other craft materials. Staple the tops of the masks to a black background. Tape each child's photo to the background under her mask. Encourage children to guess who's under each mask, then flip it up to find out. Boo!

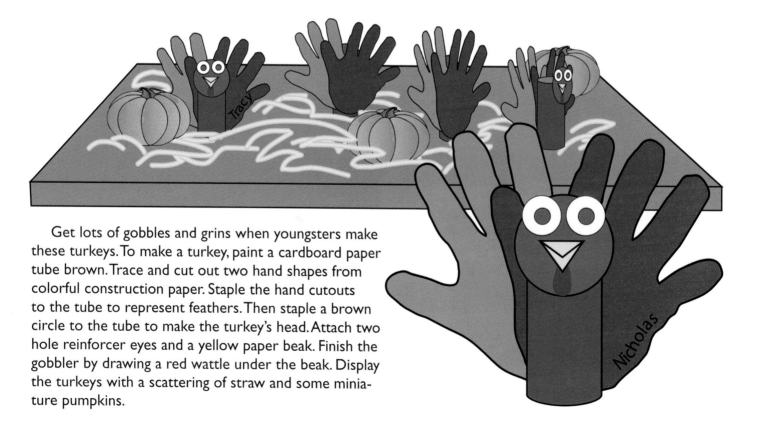

Get lots of gobbles and grins when youngsters make these turkeys. To make a turkey, paint a cardboard paper tube brown. Trace and cut out two hand shapes from colorful construction paper. Staple the hand cutouts to the tube to represent feathers. Then staple a brown circle to the tube to make the turkey's head. Attach two hole reinforcer eyes and a yellow paper beak. Finish the gobbler by drawing a red wattle under the beak. Display the turkeys with a scattering of straw and some miniature pumpkins.

Create a snow scene using blue and white bulletin board paper as shown. Have youngsters add paper snowflakes and cotton snow on paper building rooftops. Next, have each child put on his snow gear and lie on the floor as if he were making a snow angel. Take a snapshot of him. (Do not use instant film.) Cut the photos closely around each child's body as shown. Have each child use an angel template (cut a bit larger than the photo cutouts) to sponge-paint a blue angel on the snow. When the paint is dry, staple each photo atop a different angel.

Enlarge the chilly penguin character on page 276 to fit the corner of your bulletin board. Duplicate the ice-pop pattern, also on page 276, onto each of the nine basic colors of construction paper. Cut out the ice pops; then label each one with the correct color word. Use clear-drying glue and iridescent glitter to give each pop an icy look. Tape two tongue depressors to the back of each ice pop.

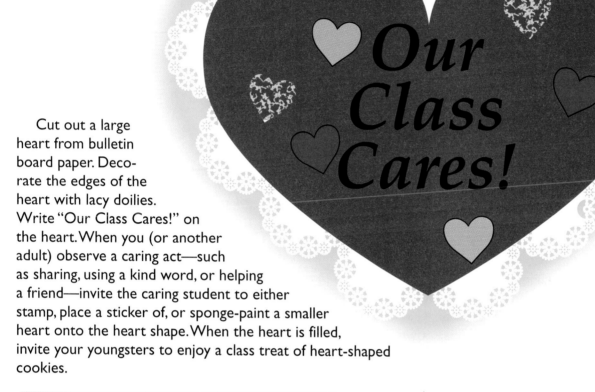

Cut out a large heart from bulletin board paper. Decorate the edges of the heart with lacy doilies. Write "Our Class Cares!" on the heart. When you (or another adult) observe a caring act—such as sharing, using a kind word, or helping a friend—invite the caring student to either stamp, place a sticker of, or sponge-paint a smaller heart onto the heart shape. When the heart is filled, invite your youngsters to enjoy a class treat of heart-shaped cookies.

Encourage each child to decorate a personalized shamrock cutout with an assortment of green craft materials, such as tiny sequins, glitter glue, and ribbon. Staple the tops of the shamrocks to a bulletin board so that they can be flipped up. Each morning, before students arrive, hide a small leprechaun cutout under one of the shamrocks. Invite children to guess where the leprechaun is hiding. Designate that shamrock's lucky owner as your helper for the day.

Cut a length of pastel bulletin board paper to fit a classroom board. Have each child create a chick by using the bottom of a plastic cup to print a yellow circle onto the paper. Direct him to add two hole reinforcer eyes and glue an orange craft-foam beak onto the circle. Have him add legs with an orange marker. Then glue a yellow craft feather onto each chick. Have each child create an eggshell by using the open end of a plastic cup to print bright colors of paint onto a construction paper egg cutout. When the paint is dry, puzzle-cut the eggs to resemble broken eggshells. Glue the eggshells to the pastel paper and mount it with a title to the board.

Have each child bring in a photo of his mother or female caregiver. Cut a large vase from bulletin board paper. Use a marker to write the title on the vase. Cut out a class supply of colorful construction paper flowers. Cut a hole in the center of each flower. Tape each photo to the back of a flower so that the picture is showing through the hole. Use crepe paper to represent stems, and add a few construction paper leaves.

Cut a large circle from white poster board. From yellow paper, cut a sun ray for each student in your class. Invite a few children to finger-paint the center of the circle with red paint. Then add some yellow paint and have another group of children fingerpaint. Continue adding yellow paint until the whole circle is painted. After the paint dries, staple the circle to a blue background. Write each child's name and favorite summer word on one of the rays; then attach them all around the circle. Add the title to complete the display.

Have each child bring in a photo of his dad or male caregiver. Cover a board with aluminum foil. Make two sticks of dynamite by taping two short pieces of rope to the ends of two red tagboard rectangles. Staple these to the board as shown; then add a yellow gift bow to the end of each piece of rope. Title the board; then attach the photos. If desired, staple yellow or gold starburst cutouts between the photos.

Cut a length of light brown bulletin board paper to fit one of your classroom boards. Before covering the board with it, print each child's footprints on the paper with brown paint. After the paint dries, have children use large paintbrushes to spread diluted glue around the footprints. Sprinkle sand onto the glue; then staple the paper to the board and add the title. To complete the display, hot-glue some real seashells to it.

Put color and texture within children's reach with this display. Cut a flowerpot from bulletin board paper. Print the title on the pot; then mount the pot near the bottom of a wall. Cut a large tagboard flower from each of the nine basic colors. To each flower, add a white center labeled with the color word. Cover the petals of each flower with a different-textured material, such as felt, cotton, foil gift wrap, satin, corduroy, or denim. Attach the flowers, along with crepe-paper stems, to the wall above the flowerpot.

Draw and cut out a supply of brown hexagons; then glue them to a length of white bulletin board paper to resemble a honeycomb. Then mount the paper on a wall. Duplicate the bee patterns on page 277 so that there are 55 bees total. Laminate the bees if desired. Label the honeycomb with numerals 1 through 10; then attach the correct number of bees around each numeral. Buzz, buzz!

Mmm...mouthwatering math! Cut ten pizza slices from yellow felt. Color the edge of each slice and label each one with a different numeral from 1 to 10. Cut 55 circles from red felt, and back each one with the hook side of a piece of self-adhesive Velcro. Mount the slices on a low bulletin board along with the title. Store the felt circles (pepperoni) in a pizza box nearby. Invite youngsters to stick the corresponding number of pepperoni pieces to each pizza slice.

We're on Track With Shapes

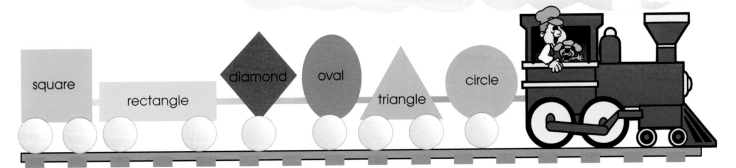

Let shapes chug around your classroom with this display. Enlarge and color the train engine pattern on page 278; then cut each of the basic geometric shapes from a different color of construction paper. Label each shape with its name; then attach it to a wall. Connect the train pieces by adding aluminum-foil rails and wheels.

| 3 Sean Johnson |
| 7 Anna Parker |
| 19 Danny Craigman |
| 23 Kristin Smith |

| 4 Mandy Dixon |
| 10 Scott Lyons |
| 16 Liza Jones |
| 30 Allen Brady |

| 2 Debbie Walker |
| 5 Donna Teal |
| 5 Hannah Lloyd |
| 21 Billy Apple |

| 6 Jackson Crane |
| 12 Jesse Horton |
| 15 Susan Hill |
| 26 Cathy Bruce |

How about a "beary" special birthday display? Make 12 enlarged copies of the bear pattern on page 279 on brown construction paper. For each bear, cut a party hat from different-colored construction paper and a gift box from birthday wrap. Label and assemble a bear for each month as shown; then laminate the bears. Add personalized strips with children's birthdates to the gift boxes. Mount the display on a classroom wall and add gift-bow hat toppers; then add an uninflated Mylar balloon above the current month's bear.

Make several enlarged fishbowls from the pattern on page 280. Label each bowl with a classroom chore; then have children use diluted blue paint to fingerpaint water inside the fishbowls. Using different colors of construction paper, duplicate a fish from the pattern on page 277 for each child. Personalize each fish; then laminate the fish and the fishbowls. Attach the fishbowls and the title to a door or wall. Assign helpers by attaching fish to each bowl.

Stir up some good help with this tasty display. Use a checkered tablecloth as a bulletin board background. Enlarge and color the chef on page 280. Tear off several lengths of aluminum foil to resemble baking sheets. Use a permanent marker to label each one with a class job. For each child, duplicate the cookie pattern on page 277 onto manila paper. Personalize the cookies; then laminate them. Assemble the board as shown, changing the helpers often. Yummy!

TEC61046

TEC61046

TEC61046

Penguin and Ice-Pop Pattern

Use with "Cool Colors" on page 267.

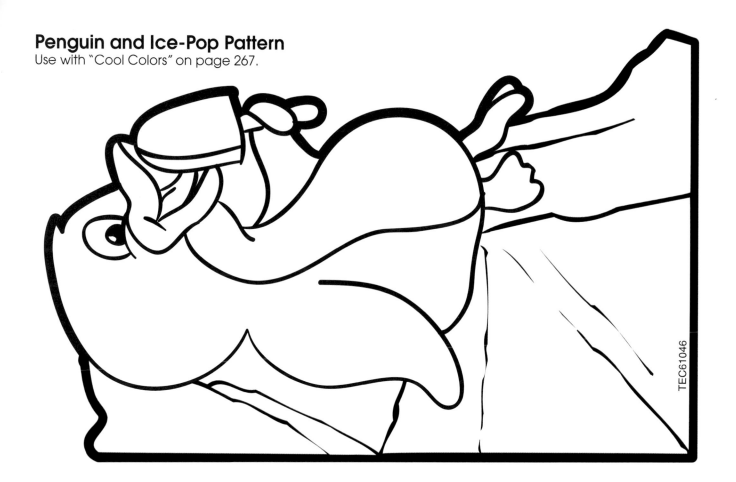

TEC61046

TEC61046

Bee Patterns

Use with "One, Two, Three,...Count These Bees!" on page 272.

Fish Pattern

Use with "Need a Helper? Go Fish!" on page 274 and "Swimming Right Along" on page 311.

Cookie Pattern

Use with "A Batch of Good Help" on page 274.

TEC61046

TEC61046

Fishbowl Pattern
Use with "Need a Helper? Go Fish!" on page 274.

TEC61046

Chef Pattern
Use with "A Batch of Good Help" on page 274.

TEC61046

Assessment Tips

It's in the Notebook!

Need a way to easily record and retrieve student assessment notes? Try this! Label a divider page for each child; then place the dividers alphabetically in a three-ring binder. Behind each divider, label a sheet of paper for each standard or skill you plan to assess. As you assess student progress, write key information on a personalized sticky note or mailing label. Then simply transfer the notes onto the corresponding pages. The resulting pages are a neatly organized resource for monitoring progress, tailoring instruction, and planning for parent conferences.

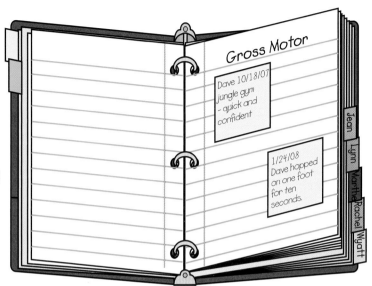

Smooth Assessments

Minimize interruptions during individual or small-group assessments with this idea! Show youngsters a special scarf, a silly hat, or another unique clothing item. Explain that when you wear the item, it is a signal to hold all questions and comments until it is removed. Short blocks of uninterrupted time are sure to be gained while student independence is fostered.

Fill and File

Keep track of observational assessments with this record-keeping folder. To make a folder, write each student's name on the bottom of an index card. Then tape the cards to the inside of a folder as shown. When you want to record an observation, simply write it on the corresponding card. When a card is full, remove it from the folder and file it in an index card box. If desired, make different folders in this manner for specific skills, such as letter knowledge, social skills, or fine-motor skills.

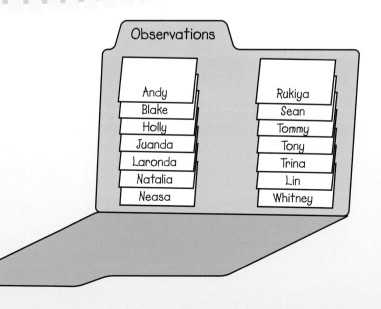

Colorful Fish

Students demonstrate color knowledge with these spectacular swimmers! Jot down desired directions for students to follow, such as "Use the colors green and yellow to color the fish." Then give each child a copy of the fish pattern on page 209. Read the directions aloud and encourage each youngster to use his crayons to color the fish as described. When a youngster finishes, ask him to point to or name specific colors to verify color knowledge. Finally, attach a copy of the directions to each completed page for an easy assessment of colors.

Tree of Knowledge

This color-coded system enables you to instantly interpret your students' progress. Program the leaves on a copy of page 284 with desired skills. Copy the programmed page to make a class supply. Then personalize a paper for each student. At the end of an assessment period, color each leaf by the code to chart student progress. Each completed assessment is not only a helpful way to individualize instruction, but it is also a perfect tool to explain a progression of skills during parent conferences.

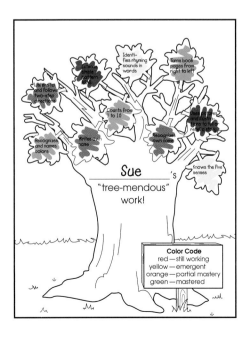

Busy-Bee Assessment

Use this honey of an idea to keep track of student progress! Program a copy of the beehive pattern on page 283 with desired skills. Then personalize a yellow construction paper copy for each student. If desired, cut out the beehives. When a youngster masters a skill, invite him to place a bee sticker on the appropriate section of his hive. Little ones are sure to buzz about their accomplishments!

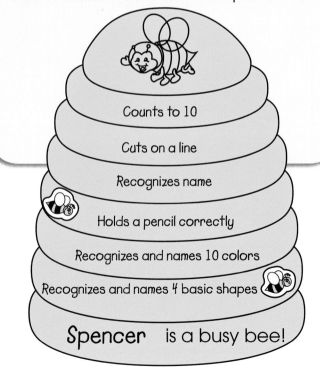

is a busy bee!

TEC61046

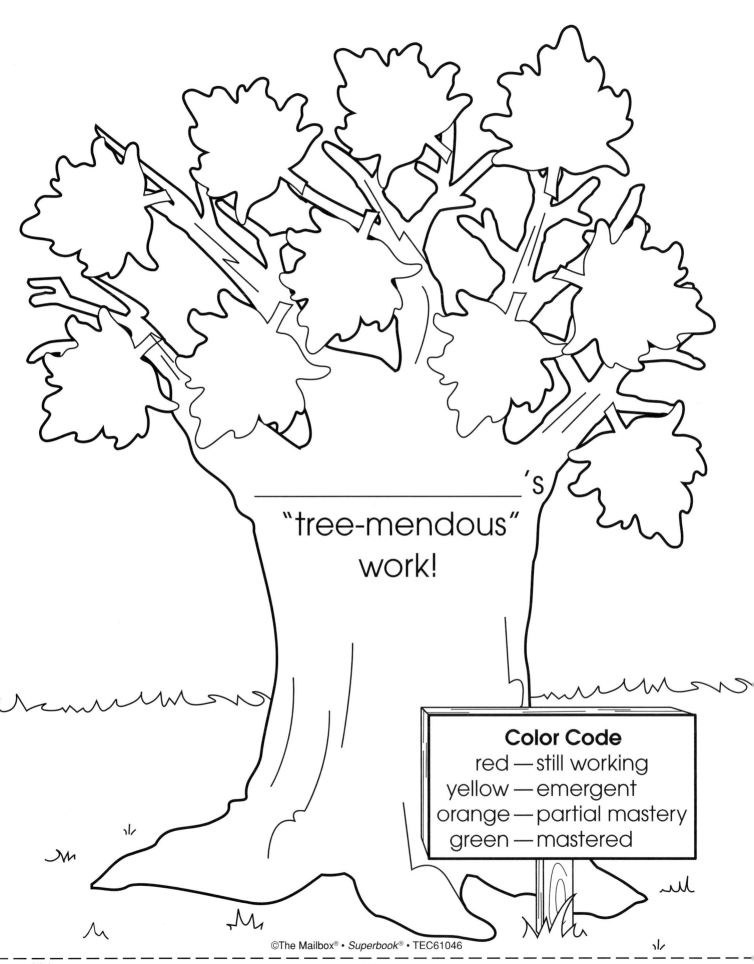

_____'s

"tree-mendous"
work!

Color Code
red — still working
yellow — emergent
orange — partial mastery
green — mastered

Note to the teacher: Use with "Tree of Knowledge" on page 282.

English Language Learners

Picture-Perfect Day

Instead of just telling students what activity is next, show them! To prepare this schedule idea, take photos of students during routine activities. Each morning, post the day's schedule as desired. Then display selected photos beside the corresponding times. Since students will know what to expect, they're sure to feel comfortable in your classroom!

8:15 Centers

8:45 Morning Snack

9:00 Outdoor Play

Vocabulary Builders

Here's a perfect way to increase students' English vocabularies! Cut out a copy of the picture cards on page 288 and store them in a resealable plastic bag. Label three blank cards as shown. Display one prepared card in a pocket chart and read it to youngsters. Invite a child to remove a card from the bag and name the pictured item. If the item belongs to the displayed category, she places it in the pocket chart. If it is not in the category, she sets it aside. Continue in the same manner for each remaining card. After reviewing the pictured items, repeat the process for the other categories.

Things we wear

Things with wheels

Things we eat

See It, Say It, Draw It!

Introduce common vocabulary words with this repetitive idea! For each word you would like youngsters to become familiar with, obtain a picture or a photo. Show students the picture and lead them in saying the name of the item several times. Then give each child a sheet of paper and have her draw the item while she names it. Label the completed student papers and display them in a prominent location. Periodically refer to the posted pictures to further reinforce the vocabulary word.

Valuable Storytimes

When it comes to developing vocabulary and language skills, read-alouds are some of the best teaching tools. Use these storytime suggestions and the recommended titles to reinforce a variety of skills.

- **Alphabet Books:** Use grade-appropriate selections to introduce chosen words. Then guide youngsters to use the words in sentences.

- **Predictable Books:** Promote oral expression by inviting youngsters to join in the reading. Then encourage students to revisit the books on their own.

- **Wordless Books:** Introduce key words as you discuss the pictures with students. Then write student-generated phrases or sentences that tell about the pictures.

Alphabet Books

Eating the Alphabet: Fruits and Vegetables From A to Z
   by Lois Ehlert
Alphabet Under Construction by Denise Fleming
26 Letters and 99 Cents by Tana Hoban
Action Alphabet by Shelly Rotner

Predictable Books

I Was Walking Down the Road by Sarah E. Barchas
The Very Hungry Caterpillar by Eric Carle
Have You Seen My Cat? by Eric Carle
The Chick and the Duckling by Mirra Ginsburg
The Doorbell Rang by Pat Hutchins
Jump, Frog, Jump by Robert Kalan
Brown Bear, Brown Bear, What Do You See?
   by Bill Martin Jr.
It Looked Like Spilt Milk by Charles G. Shaw

Wordless Books

The Snowman by Raymond Biggs
Pancakes for Breakfast by Tomie dePaola
Rosie's Walk by Pat Hutchins

Songs and Chants

What better way to promote oral language than with repetitive songs and chants? After all, they provide plenty of opportunities for modeling, and every student can successfully participate. Incorporate actions or props to enhance students' understanding.

Find the Shape

Cut out different shapes from colorful construction paper. Then gather youngsters in a circle and place a shape in the center. Lead students in singing the song shown, substituting the name of the shape where indicated. Continue in the same way for each remaining shape.

(sung to the tune of "There's a Hole in the Bucket")

There's a shape on the carpet,
The carpet, the carpet.
There's a shape on the carpet.
What shape do you see?

Oh, the shape is a [circle],
[A circle, a circle].
Oh, the shape is a [circle].
Please hand it to me.

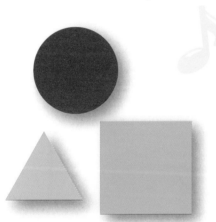

On the Move!

Spotlight names of different body parts with this action chant!

Pat your shoulders.
Touch your lips.
Nod your head.
Wiggle your hips.
Clap your hands.
Tickle your feet.
Twirl around.
Then take your seat!

Where Is Teddy?

With this catchy song, students gain experience with the position words *in* and *on*. Obtain a stuffed toy bear and introduce it as Teddy. Ask students to cover their eyes as you place Teddy in a box. Then have students open their eyes, and lead them in singing the song shown. Repeat the song, placing the bear in different locations (see suggestions).

(sung to the tune of "Are You Sleeping?")

Where is Teddy?
Where is Teddy?
[In the box, in the box].
How did Teddy get there?
[Child's name], please go get him.
Silly bear, silly bear.

Suggested locations: on the box, on the floor, on the table, on the chair, in the bag, in the sink

Picture Cards

Use with "Vocabulary Builders" on page 285.

TEC61046   TEC61046   TEC61046

TEC61046   TEC61046   TEC61046

TEC61046   TEC61046   TEC61046

TEC61046   TEC61046   TEC61046

PARENTS AS PARTNERS

what's Going On?

Keep families informed about the skills and concepts you are covering at school. On a monthly or quarterly basis—whichever works best for you—send home a list or simple chart showing the new skills and concepts you'll be working on with your class. Encourage parents to work on these skills and concepts at home too.

As a variation, send home a note each time you begin a new theme. List some of the activities you have planned and explain how they fit into various curriculum areas. Give a few suggestions for activities parents can do at home to support your thematic unit.

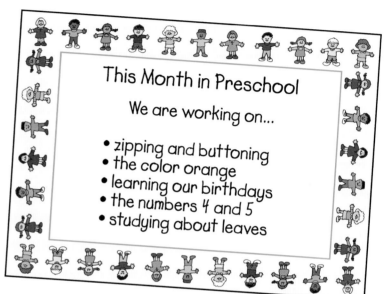

This Month in Preschool

We are working on...

• zipping and buttoning
• the color orange
• learning our birthdays
• the numbers 4 and 5
• studying about leaves

Keeping Track

If you like the idea of regularly communicating with parents about their children's personal progress but are wary of keeping track of whom you've contacted, try this simple idea. Purchase a set of index cards. On each card, print the names of three children in your class. Then stack the cards and leave them in a handy location. The names on the top card are the students whose parents you'll contact that day. Send home a quick note with those three children, noting at least one positive aspect about each child's learning or behavior. (If you're really pressed for time, consider using preprinted notes available at your teacher supply store.) Then move the top index card to the bottom of the stack and you're ready to make the contacts for the next day!

Anita
Thai
Nicholas

"what Did You Do at School Today?"

Help little ones answer this often-asked question by providing them with a visual reminder. If you've spent the day reading a story about Johnny Appleseed, doing apple artwork, and preparing an apple snack, provide each child with a sheet of paper from an apple-shaped notepad to take home. Or stamp an apple shape on each child's hand as she walks out the door. Make sure you explain the reminders to parents ahead of time so they can be on the lookout for these visual clues and ask appropriate questions. Once children are accustomed to taking home these clues, they may no longer need a visual reminder. Try telling youngsters a key word, such as "bubbles" or "eggs," that they can remember to help spark discussions about the school day's events.

A Loaning Library

Preschoolers are usually bursting with pride over special class projects and books they help to create. Share the joy by allowing families to borrow some of these class treasures for an overnight look-see. Simply package each book or tape (or a video showing large projects) in a large zippered plastic bag. Label the bag with a permanent marker and provide a sign-out sheet with a matching label. Then invite families to check out their little ones' accomplishments from this very special class library!

Help with Show-and-Tell

Often preschoolers need guidance in selecting items to bring to school for show-and-tell. Make this an easier task—and one in which caregivers can be involved—by centering sharing time around your current theme. Send home a duplicated note with a simple message such as "Tomorrow, please bring something [red] for show-and-tell." Parent and child can work together to find an appropriate item.

Tomorrow, please bring something red for show-and-tell.

Monthly Treasure Hunts

This activity will do double duty by encouraging parents and children to spend time together and by helping you out with classroom supplies. Each month send home a note asking families to work together to gather specific items for use at school. For example, in September you might ask that families go on a nature walk and collect pinecones. In December you might ask for scraps of ribbon and wrapping paper. And in May, ask families to collect all kinds of flowers. You'll receive lots of treasures, and parents and children will have some treasured time together.

Home Cookin'

If you've ever seen the look on a youngster's face when she walks into your classroom with a plateful of her mom's homemade cookies, then you know the pride that accompanies providing a snack for the class. Ask each of your students' families to take a turn providing a snack or special treat. Encourage each family to involve its child in preparing an easy recipe, perhaps a family favorite or one that reflects the family's heritage. If desired, ask parents to write up their recipes; then compile them into a recipe book and make copies for each child to take home once everyone has participated.

It's December

Please work with your child to collect extra wrapping paper, ribbons, or bows. We'll do lots of fun things at school with your donations!

Thank you!

Learning at Home

Preschoolers' parents are often anxious to find out how to help their children extend their learning experiences at home. Consider sending home a newsletter with suggestions for activities and reading material that will tie into your topics of study. You might want to give suggestions every week, every other week, or only once a month, depending on your schedule and curriculum. Simply duplicate the form on page 296; then fill in each box with appropriate ideas and information. Make a copy for each family and send home these nifty notes with your youngsters.

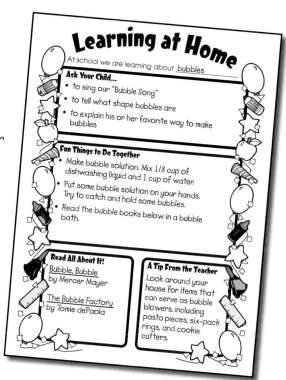

Learning at Home

At school we are learning about _bubbles_

Ask Your Child...
• to sing our "Bubble Song"
• to tell what shape bubbles are
• to explain his or her favorite way to make bubbles

Fun Things to Do Together
• Make bubble solution. Mix 1/8 cup of dishwashing liquid and 1 cup of water.
• Put some bubble solution on your hands. Try to catch and hold some bubbles.
• Read the bubble books below in a bubble bath.

Read All About It!
Bubble, Bubble by Mercer Mayer

The Bubble Factory by Tomie dePaola

A Tip From the Teacher
Look around your house for items that can serve as bubble blowers, including pasta pieces, six-pack rings, and cookie cutters.

Read and Find Out

Here's a fun and easy way to encourage parents and children to read together. Each month choose a good children's book and write one or two questions about the story on a piece of paper. For example, if you select *The Very Hungry Caterpillar* by Eric Carle, one question might be "How many things did the hungry caterpillar eat through?" Package the book and questions together in a large zippered plastic bag. Invite each child, in turn, to take the bag home. Ask parents to first read the questions, then the book, to their children. Have them jot down their children's answers to the questions on a sheet of paper and return the bag to school the next day. Then the story can continue on its way until every child has had a turn to read and find out!

Theme Riddles

What's a great way for parents and children to practice critical-thinking skills together? A theme riddle! Each time you begin a new theme, make up a very simple riddle related to it. For example, if you are studying animals, your riddle might say, "I have four legs. I am black and white. I look like a horse. What am I?" Include the riddle as part of your regular newsletter, or write it on a separate sheet of paper and duplicate it for each child to take home. Encourage parents to present the riddle to their children as part of their dinnertime conversations. Now that's good thinking!

Hey, Diddle, Diddle—
Can you guess this riddle?

I have four legs.
I am black and white.
I look like a horse.
What am I?

Word of the Week

Parents can try this weekly activity to help build their youngsters' vocabularies. Each week select a word related to your current theme and draw or cut out clip art that represents it. (Nouns will be easiest, of course.) Duplicate the picture for each child to take home. Ask each child's parents to post the picture on their refrigerator. They may want to provide the magnetic letters that spell the word or simply write the word on a slip of paper and post it next to the picture. Before you know it, your little ones will be word wizards!

Family of the week

What better way to get families involved in your classroom than to get them talking about themselves? Each week send home a copy of the invitation on page 297 with a different child. Set aside time each week for the children to learn about the family of the week. This project will help emphasize the differences and similarities in family structures, as well as help classmates get to know one another better.

You Are Invited to Be Our
Family of the Week

Our preschool class would love to get to know your family better! Please consider one of the following options to share some information about your family with our class:

- Come to school one day next week to tell about your family. Bring along photos and special mementos that will help us learn more about you.
- Make a poster about your family. You could include pictures, magazine cutouts, and drawings that tell us about you.
- Send a family photo album to school. Jot some notes to tell us about some of the special pictures.

Please call me or send a note to let me know which day next week would be convenient for you.
Thank you!

Family Blocks

If you don't have time in your schedule for the "Family of the Week" idea (above), try this simpler way for families to share information about themselves. Create a set of family blocks for the children to share, discuss, and play with. For each child, collect a cube-shaped tissue box, or tape together two clean, dry juice boxes. Cut a sheet of white or light-colored construction paper so that it matches the height of the block and wraps completely around it, slightly overlapping on one edge. Send the cut-to-fit paper home with each child, along with a copy of the note on page 297. After each family returns its decorated paper, wrap the paper around a block and tape it in place. Then invite each little one to describe the pictures on his block and tell about his family. Leave the family blocks in a center where children can use them during their free-choice play.

Classy Accomplishments

"Hip, hip, hooray! We reached a goal today!" That's what little ones will be cheering when you send home class accomplishment notes. Whenever your class reaches a milestone, such as every child being able to write her name, program a copy of the note below. Then send a copy home with each child. Parents will enjoy being a part of their children's success!

HIP, HIP, HOORAY! WE REACHED A GOAL TODAY!

We can all write our first names!

Note
Use with "Classy Accomplishments" above.

HIP, HIP, HOORAY! WE REACHED A GOAL TODAY!

©The Mailbox® • Superbook® • TEC61046

Learning at Home

At school we are learning about _____.

Ask Your Child...

Fun Things to Do Together

Read All About It!

A Tip From the Teacher

Note to the teacher: Use with "Learning at Home" on page 292.

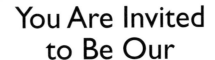

You Are Invited to Be Our
Family of the Week

Our preschool class would love to get to know your family better! Please consider one of the following options to share some information about your family with our class:

- Come to school one day next week to tell about your family. Bring along photos and special mementos that will help us learn more about you.
- Make a poster about your family. You could include pictures, magazine cutouts, and drawings that tell us about you.
- Send a family photo album to school. Jot some notes to tell us about some of the special pictures.

Please call me or send a note to let me know which day next week would be convenient for you.
Thank you!

©The Mailbox® • *Superbook®* • TEC61046

Parent Note
Use with "Family Blocks" on page 294.

Dear Family,

Our preschool class would love to get to know your family better! So we are constructing a set of family blocks for the children to share. Please decorate one side of the attached paper with photos, drawings, magazine pictures, and words that tell about your family members. Please return the decorated paper to school by _____. Then stop in to see our finished family blocks!
(date)

Thank you for your cooperation!

©The Mailbox® • *Superbook®* • TEC61046

PARENT CONFERENCES

Dear Kent Family,
Welcome to a new school year! I would love to meet with you on _____ to discuss the _____ upcoming year. Please answer the following questions so that we can talk about them during this conference time.

— List three topics your child would like to learn about this year.
— List three skills you would like your child to acquire this year.
— What does your child look forward to most about school?
— What does your child look forward to least about school?

I'm looking forward to meeting you.

Sincerely,
Mrs. Goren

BRIGHT BEGINNINGS

Get the new school year off to a bright beginning by scheduling a conference with each family prior to the start of school! Before the first day of class, mail a letter to each family scheduling a specific conference time and requesting that parents write down responses to these suggested prompts and questions:
— List three topics your child would like to learn about this year.
— List three skills you would like your child to acquire this year.
— What does your child look forward to most about school?
— What does your child look forward to least about school?

During each conference, discuss the responses. Encourage the child to participate in the conversation by asking him to tell you what he would like to learn about. Then end the conference by showing the family around your classroom, pointing out important areas such as the child's cubby, bathrooms, and play areas. Later, use the information gathered from students to help plan thematic units based on their interests.

Draw-a-Man Journal

Parents will clearly see the developmental progress of their children when you share these journals during conference times. Prepare a journal for each child by stapling several sheets of paper—equal to the number of months in your school year—between construction paper covers. Personalize each journal with a child's name.

During the first week of school, provide each child with crayons and his journal; then have him complete the first page. Instruct him to draw a picture of a man or "Daddy." Do as little prompting as possible, allowing the child as much time as needed to complete his picture. When he has completed his drawing, write the date on the page. Have each child complete one drawing a month. Then, during parent conferences, share each child's journal with his parents, pointing out the progress made throughout the year. At the end of the school year, send home each student's journal as a meaningful keepsake for parents.

9-27-07

Storyboards

Let pictures tell the story of your classroom activities for parents who are waiting for their scheduled conferences. Use tape to hinge together two sheets of poster board (or cardboard). Attach to the poster board photographs of students participating in classroom activities such as circle time, center time, and recess. Write a caption under each photo that explains what is taking place. Decorate the poster board with cutouts and stickers that correspond to the pictures. Then display the completed storyboard on a tabletop near the entrance to your classroom. Parents will be delighted to get a picture-perfect view of their children at school.

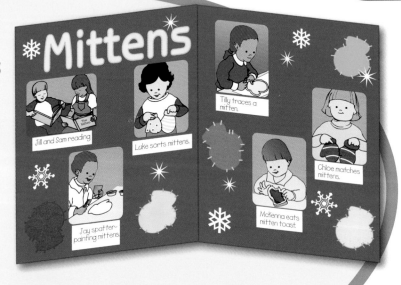

Tea for Two—or Three

Create a warm and inviting atmosphere for parents during conference time with this cozy idea. The day before scheduled conferences begin, invite your students to prepare a batch of cookies using your favorite recipe. On the day of conferences, make a pot of tea or coffee; then arrange some of the cookies on a decorative plate.

Before each conference, spend a few moments getting to know parents over a cup of tea and cookies. Parents will welcome an opportunity to chat with you before you share conference information.

Very Important Preschooler

Parents will know they have a V.I.P. in their family when you use this nifty way to share information during parent conferences. Make a class supply of the V.I.P. report on page 300. Use information gathered from classroom observations and evaluations to fill in the skill boxes on each child's report. Then list the goals you have for that child in the appropriate box. Invite each student to tell you his goals (what he would like to learn during the year) and write those in the corresponding box. Finally, make a copy of each child's V.I.P. report to give to parents.

During parent conferences, share the information on the sheet with each family. Encourage parents to share their goals for their child; then write those goals on your copy of the report. File your copy for reference throughout the school year.

Check out the helpful reproducible on page 301.

Very Important Preschooler

Name _____

Date _____

Student Goals

Social

Motor

Language

Math

Teacher Goals

Parent Goals

Note to the teacher: Use with "Very Important Preschooler" on page 299.

Dear Parent,

    I would like to meet with you on _____ at _____
to discuss _____. Please complete the bottom portion of
this form and return it to me as soon as possible.
    I look forward to talking with you!

Sincerely,

_____
teacher signature

- ☐ I plan to attend my child's conference at the scheduled time.
- ☐ I will need to reschedule our conference. A more convenient time for me would be

_____.

_____
parent signature

_____
child's name

Dear Parent,
    Becoming involved in your child's education helps strengthen the home/school
connection and provides your child with a sense of continuity. You can help enhance our
preschool program by sharing your time, talents, and expertise with the children. Please
look over the following list of ways you can help in our classroom and check those that
interest you. Please return this survey as soon as possible.

Thanks for making a difference!

Name of Parent(s) _____

Telephone Numbers: Work _____ Home _____

____ Read a story to a group of children.
____ Assist with or plan a special project or holiday event.
____ Share a hobby or your occupation and show tools used in your hobby/career.
____ Prepare classroom learning materials at home (tracing, cutting, coloring, etc.).
____ Provide materials for special projects.

CLASSROOM MANAGEMENT

Trays for Storage

Five-drawer office organizers are a great way to save space and store small manipulatives. Label the outside of each drawer with the name of a different manipulative. If desired, hot-glue a corresponding manipulative piece next to each name. Each drawer holds a large supply of manipulatives and the traylike design makes it easy for little hands to handle.

Clean as a Whistle

Make short work out of cleaning and sanitizing small plastic manipulatives by letting your washing machine do all the work. Place some manipulatives inside a mesh lingerie bag. Toss the bag into your washer along with some laundry soap and a small amount of bleach. Set your machine on the gentle cycle; then sit back and relax. Your manipulatives will come out sparkling clean and sanitized.

Divide and Conquer

Use this creative idea to conquer the battle over limited storage space and define classroom center areas. Collect several lidded boxes similar to those that hold copier paper. Cover each box and its lid separately with Con-Tact covering. Place storage materials in each box; then label its lid with the contents. Line the boxes up; then stack them one atop the other to create a portable storage wall that helps define and separate classroom centers.

Hang It Up

If you're hung up over a way to store all of your charts, posters, and large bulletin board pieces, try this easy management tip. Simply use clothespins to clip the desired item onto a clothes hanger. Hang the hangers from a rod suspended in a storage closet or on a rolling garment rack placed in an unused corner of your classroom. Now all of your large materials are stored neatly and are available right at your fingertips.

Easy Stringing

Whenever you have an activity that calls for students to use yarn to lace or string objects, use a length of curling ribbon instead. The colorful ribbon is inexpensive and the ends don't fray, making it easy for little fingers to handle. Plus, the gently curling ends add interest to any project!

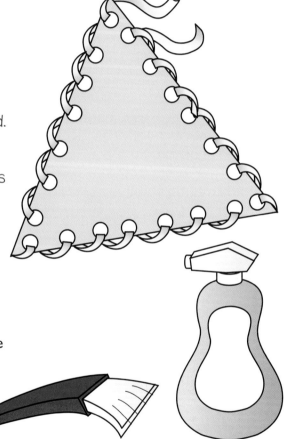

Spritz and Scrape

Here's a quick tip to help keep your tables nice and clean. Simply spray the surface with all-purpose cleaner and then use an ice scraper to scrape off dried glue and other residue. Wipe away the mess with a paper towel and you're all set!

Simple Seating

For an extra-easy seating arrangement, try colorful duct tape. Mark each seating spot in your circle-time area with a square of tape. Then invite each child to sit on a square. Seating is a snap!

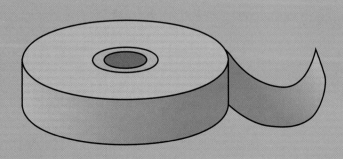

Sign In, Please

Use this daily attendance recording system to promote—and even assess— youngsters' name-writing skills. To prepare a sign-in board, laminate a sheet of poster board to display on your classroom door or on a wall near the door. Attach one end of a length of yarn to an erasable marker; then attach the other end of the yarn to the poster. To use, have each child sign her name (or her mark) on the poster each day as she arrives at school. Then use the sign-in board to note which children are present for the day. Before erasing the names at the end of the day, record anecdotal notes about each child's name-writing skills. A sign-in sheet that pulls double-duty—cool!

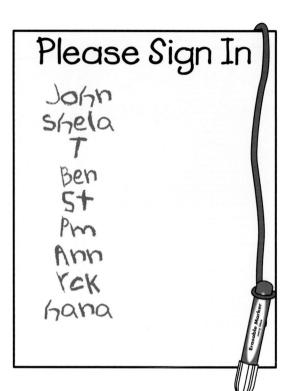

Come-and-Play Trays

As your little ones arrive, capture their attention while reducing their separation anxiety with these instant tray activities. To prepare, obtain a tray or box lid for each child. Arrange on each tray materials for a different activity, such as cookie cutters and play dough for sensory play, laces and short lengths of straw for stringing, or crayons and paper for drawing. As each child arrives, invite her to use a tray of materials. You can almost hear the tray say, "Come and play! Come and play!"

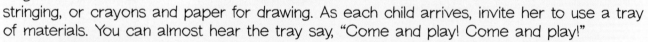

Chores Chat

Youngsters will swell with pride and a sense of responsibility when they tell about how they keep their belongings organized and in place! After students arrive each day, call them together for a brief group time. During this time remind them of their routine arrival chores—such as putting away bookbags, hanging up coats, or putting lunchboxes in an assigned place—and ask each child to tell the group which chores he remembered to do. Give those children who may have left out a chore the opportunity to do it at this time; then invite the class to sing the song below to the tune of "Row, Row, Row Your Boat." After singing, praise the students for helping to keep the class running smoothly. This daily chores chat will go a long way toward creating proud, responsible citizens.

We've done all our chores.
We've done all our chores.
Listen, and we'll tell you now,
We've done all our chores!

Birthday Bags

Save time by preparing birthday gift bags for the whole year all at once! Decorate a class supply of small paper bags. For each child, fill a bag with inexpensive items, such as crayons, coloring sheets, decorative pencils, paperback books, stickers, small toys, and candy. Store the bags in a closet or cabinet. Before a birthday child arrives at school on his special day, personalize a bag and place it at his seat or in his cubby. What a way to start the day!

Summer Birthdays

Honor students who have summer birthdays with a day-long celebration at the end of the school year. Plan a day filled with birthday-related activities and treats. Be sure to include the usual birthday activities that are done throughout the year, too. Now each student with a summer birthday will be able to share his special occasion with his classmates!

Spread a Center

Make more room for centers in a flash with this quick and easy idea. Purchase a vinyl tablecloth and spread it in an unused corner, a hallway, or an open area of your classroom. Place a center activity, such as small manipulatives, on the tablecloth. The cloth visually defines the center area and cleanup is a breeze. Just gather the manipulatives into the center of the cloth; then pour them back into their proper container.

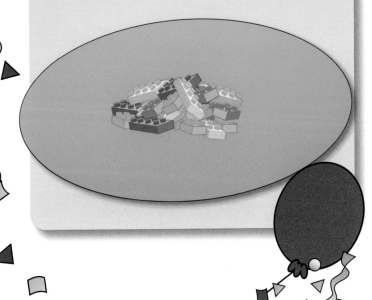

Birthday Certificate

No matter how you choose to celebrate students' birthdays, be sure to present each child with a copy of one of the birthday certificates on page 313.

A Place for Me

These easy-to-clean placemats are just right for designating individual work areas or center activities. Use a permanent marker to personalize a plain vinyl placemat for each child. If desired, tape each child's photo next to his name. Arrange the mats as desired; then invite each child to sit by his mat.

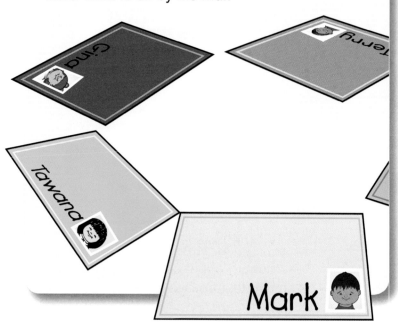

"Place-maps"

Setting tables for snacks or mealtimes is a snap wiith this tip! On each plain vinyl placemat in a class supply, use a permanent marker to outline a plate, a cup, a napkin, and eating utensils. Then, when it's time for meals, have each child match the corresponding table items to the appropriate places on her mat. Lunch is served!

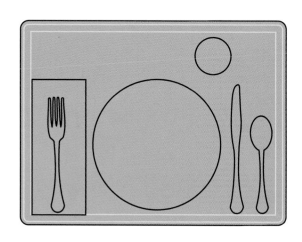

Snacktime Song

Prepare your students for snacktime with this tasty tune.

(sung to the tune of "Row, Row, Row Your Boat")

Snack, snack, snacktime is here.
Won't you have a seat?
Fold your hands right in your lap.
Let's get set to eat!

I See You

Use this song to help little ones get settled and ready to listen before a group activity.

(sung to the tune of "Frère Jacques")

I see brown eyes.
I see green eyes,
Blue eyes too!
I see you!
Quiet all the talk now.
Show me that you know how.
Take a bow! Take a bow!

Dream Sweet Dreams

Lead youngsters in a quiet rendition of this tune as they prepare their cots or mats for rest time.

(sung to the tune of "Frère Jacques")

Time for resting.
Time for resting,
Preschool friends,
Preschool friends.

Close your tired eyes now.
Close your tired eyes now.
Dream sweet dreams.
Dream sweet dreams.

It's Time to Wiggle

Try this tune when your students have an overabundance of energy.

(sung to the tune of "Ten Little Indians")

Wiggle, wiggle, shake, and jiggle!
Shake your arms and giggle, giggle.
Shake your legs; it's time to wiggle.
Now let's all sit down!

Picture Me

Making transitions from one activity to another will be a snap with this idea. To prepare, mount a photo or self-portrait of each child on a separate tagboard card. At the end of a group activity or at line-up time, place each child's picture—one at a time—in a pocket chart. Have each child move to his assigned area or stand in line when his picture is placed in the chart.

Give the Signal

Here's an efficient way to direct outbound traffic from your classroom. To make a simple traffic signal, label an eight-inch red construction paper circle with "Stop" and a same-size green construction paper circle with "Go." Glue the cutouts together back-to-back; then string a length of yarn through a hole punched near the rim of the circle. Tie the yarn ends together. Hang the traffic signal—with "Stop" facing out—beside your classroom door. After lining youngsters up to go to a different school location, explain that you will switch the signal to "Go" when the class is quiet and ready to leave. Quiet. Ready. Let's go!

Cell Phone

A very special phone call may provide the perfect incentive for youngsters to make a transition from one activity to another. To receive such a call, keep a toy phone handy on a high shelf in the classroom. Just before a transition time—such as cleanup or snacktime—ring the phone; then answer it, pretending to talk to a storybook character, the president, or even your school's director/principal. During your phone conversation, be sure to mention that it's time for a specific transition; then conveniently repeat your caller's reminders about expected behaviors for that transition. For example, you might say, "Yes, Gingerbread Man, I'll remind the children to pick up *all* the toys and put them away. Thanks for your call. And watch out for that fox! Bye-bye." Then return the phone to the shelf to await your next special caller.

I'm Ready

Prepare youngsters for the next activity with this quick chant. Invite students to repeat each line and gesture after you perform it. Then conclude with a "thank-you" to students for showing their readiness by making eye contact with you.

Big ears to hear.	Cup hands behind ears.
Big eyes to see.	Loop fingers like pretend glasses in front of eyes.
Now I'm ready.	Point to self.
One, two, three.	Clap hands three times; then put hands in lap.

It's No Small "Feet"!

If standing in line is difficult for your little ones, try this tip. Draw a pair of feet on several colors of construction paper. Cut out the feet; then arrange the pairs in an area of your classroom that requires children to stand in line, such as by the door or sink. Cover each pair of feet with a piece of clear Con-Tact covering. When it is time to line up, simply have each child stand on a pair of feet. Your little ones are sure to enjoy stepping from one pair of feet to another as they wait for their turns.

Softly Singing

Keeping youngsters quiet while walking in the hallway is easy with this musical tip! Simply lead students in whisper-singing a familiar song, such as the "Alphabet Song," as you move through the hallways together. Little ones stay engaged all the way to your destination!

Songs for Lining Up

Make this daily routine fun for your preschoolers by singing either of these catchy songs.

(sung to the tune of "Good Night, Ladies")

Line up, children.
Line up, children.
Line up, children.
It's time to line up now.

(sung to the tune of "Jingle Bells")

Let's line up.
Let's line up
Quick as one, two, three.
Come and form a nice straight line
Right here in front of me.

Special Delivery

Make sure important notes and student work make it home with these special delivery tubes. To make a tube, cover a clean potato chip canister with construction paper or Con-Tact covering. Use a permanent marker to label the canister with "Special Delivery." To use, roll up papers to be sent home with a child and slip them into the canister; then place the lid on the canister. Explain to the child that he will be taking home a special delivery to his parents. Encourage him to return the empty canister the following day so that it can be used for his next special delivery.

Quiet as a Mouse

Shhhh! This little mouse helps youngsters remember to use their inside voices. Place a small toy mouse in a visible area and tell students that the mouse wants to be part of their class. Explain that noise scares the mouse, so youngsters must remember to talk in soft voices in order to keep the mouse in his spot. When they get too noisy, the mouse will hide. At the end of the day, if the mouse is still visible, reward students with a mouse sticker or other small award or special privilege.

Give 'em a Roll!

When acknowledging positive moments in your classroom, teach students to give a silent roll instead of clapping. To do this, a child makes a fist and rolls it in front of his body. If something is really terrific, give 'em a double roll by using both fists!

Collection of Compliments

Reinforce positive student behavior with this idea. Gather a clean, empty container and a supply of pom-poms. When the class receives a compliment from you, another staff member, or a parent, drop a pom-pom into the container. When the container is full, offer a class incentive, such as a special snack or extra recess time. Then empty the container and begin again.

Seasonal Incentives

Motivate youngsters to behave appropriately year-round with this idea. At the beginning of each season, create a display that corresponds with that season. For each child, add to the display a seasonal cutout labeled with her name. For example, you might display cutouts of leaves for fall, snowmen for winter, flowers for spring, and suns for summer. Throughout the year, as you randomly catch a student behaving appropriately, invite her to attach a sticky dot to her cutout. When a child's cutout is filled with dots, have her exchange it for a special treat. Then give her a new cutout so she can work toward another prize.

Swimming Right Along

Youngsters will be swimming right along in the pool of good behavior with this self-checking system. To prepare, create an ocean scene display by layering several different shades of blue and green paper strips to represent the ocean water. Place a pushpin in the bottom water layer for each child; then randomly place pins along the other layers. For each child, cut out and label a construction paper fish (pattern on page 277). Punch a hole in each fish cutout; then hang each on a pin in the bottom layer of water. To use, help a child move his fish up a layer each time he is caught in appropriate behavior. When his fish reaches the top, reward him with a treat; then have him return his fish to the bottom to swim his way to the surface once again.

The Sweet Smell of Success

What does a great day in preschool smell like? How about vanilla, cherry, or perhaps pineapple? At the end of the day, use a cotton swab to dab a tiny bit of extract (found in the baking aisle) on the back of each child's hand. Vary the scent so that students stay motivated to use their best behavior in order to find out what the day's scent will be.

SUBSTITUTE Teacher Tips

Substitute Savvy

Transform a three-ring notebook into an informative binder for your substitute teacher. Inside the binder, place a class set of nametags and tabbed sections containing the essential information your substitute will need for a successful day, such as

- a labeled class photo
- a list of emergency and contact information
- a list of classroom procedures, such as those for dismissal, fire drills, and inclement weather.
- a classroom map with materials and student seating assignments
- a school map
- a schedule that includes daily routines and special weekly activities
- lesson plans
- blank paper for notes to and from your substitute

Classroom map:

Manipulatives — pattern blocks
Storage — first aid kit, treats
Teacher's Desk
Library Center
Door — fire extinguisher
Meeting Area Rug
Supplies — extra clothes
Game Center — dominoes
Art Supplies — bag of tricks
Computer Center
Listening Center — tape player
Blocks

Time	Monday	Tuesday	Wednesday	Thursday	Friday
8:30-9:30	Explorations/ Free Choice Centers				
9:30-10:00	Circle Time	Music	Circle Time	Music	Circle Time
10:00-11:00	Work Centers	Circle Time / Whole-group activity	Work Centers	Circle Time / Whole-group activity	Work Centers
11:00-11:45	← Lunch →				
11:45-12:15	← Recess →				
12:15-1:30	← Rest/Quiet Time →				

OUR SCHEDULE

Check out the reproducibles on pages 314–316.

Bag of Tricks

What does the substitute do when she's at the end of the lesson plans with time to spare? Reach into this bag of tricks, of course! Collect the materials needed to play several quick games and insert them into a large gift bag. Write simple directions for each game on separate index cards. Punch a hole in the corner of each card, bind them together with a loose-leaf ring, and then put them in the bag too. Be sure to explain the bag of tricks in your plans.

HAPPY BIRTHDAY!

_____

©The Mailbox® • Superbook® • TEC61046

IT'S YOUR BIRTHDAY,

GO WILD!

©The Mailbox® • Superbook® • TEC61046

Note to the teacher: Duplicate cards on construction paper. Cut out and personalize each card. Distribute a card to each child on his birthday.

313

OUR SCHEDULE

Time	Monday	Tuesday	Wednesday	Thursday	Friday

Note to the teacher: Duplicate and use this form for planning.

Preschool Plans

We're Learning About

Date

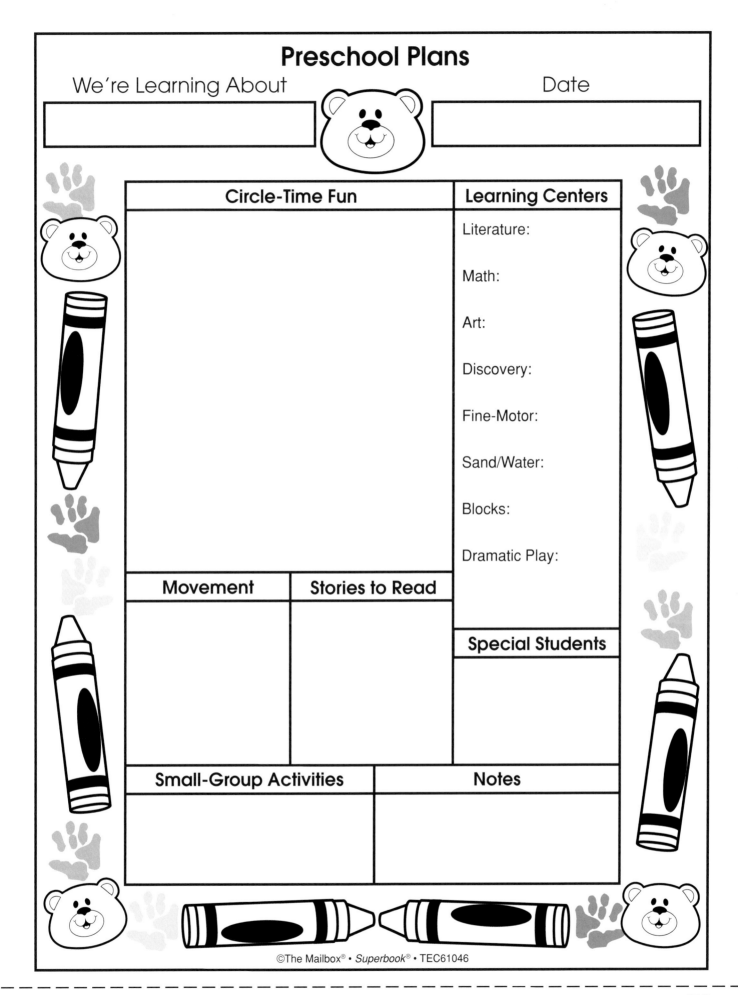

Circle-Time Fun	Learning Centers
	Literature:
	Math:
	Art:
	Discovery:
	Fine-Motor:
	Sand/Water:
	Blocks:
	Dramatic Play:

Movement	Stories to Read	
		Special Students

Small-Group Activities	Notes

Sunday	Monday	Tuesday	Wednesday	Thursday	Friday	Saturday

Note to the teacher: Duplicate and use this calendar for monthly planning.

Index

addresses, 117

all about me, 113–120

animals, 91–98, 130, 222, 237, 243, 245, 250

art explorations, 254–261

arts and crafts

    fall, 128, 130, 131, 132

    recipes, 262–264

    spring, 152, 153, 154, 155

    summer, 165, 166, 167, 203, 204

    winter, 140, 141, 142, 143

assessment tips, 281–284

back-to-school, 9–15, 273, 274, 298

beginning sounds, 23, 24, 31

birthdays, 117, 176, 230, 273, 305, 313

blocks, 24, 82, 200, 217

body parts, 113, 114, 221, 253, 287

book awareness, 35

book knowledge, 35, 36

books

    Brown Bear, Brown Bear, What Do You See? 51

    Caps for Sale, 56

    Green Eggs and Ham, 53

    Jamberry, 55

    The Very Hungry Caterpillar, 54

    Where the Wild Things Are, 52

    Brown Bear, Brown Bear, What Do You See? 51

bugs, 211–214

bulletin boards, 265–280, 311

Caps for Sale, 56

centers, 189–198

    art, 195, 203, 208, 211, 215

    block, 82, 200, 217

    bug, 211–214

    dramatic play, 82, 100, 200, 208, 217

    fine motor, 194, 229, 231

    games, 212

    gross motor, 196, 197, 204

    literacy, 20, 33, 42, 43, 166, 194, 195, 199, 204, 207, 208, 211, 216

    management, 189–193, 215–217, 305

    math, 77, 80, 81, 82, 83, 194, 195, 196, 197, 199, 203, 207, 212

    pet, 207–210

    play dough, 194, 204, 207

    puzzle, 199

sand table, 83, 197, 203, 211, 216

    seasonal

        fall, 133

        spring, 157

        summer, 168

        winter, 145

    sensory, 196, 212

    water table, 200, 216

Christmas, 142, 143, 150

circle time, 218–227

classroom displays, 265–280, 311

classroom management (see management)

colors, 63–67, 124, 196, 219, 231

comparing, 223

concepts of print, 33, 34, 204

counting, 80, 81, 82, 83, 93, 94, 140, 155, 174, 197, 221, 272

dinosaurs, 241

dramatic play, 82, 100, 143, 167, 200, 208, 217, 230, 242–247

Easter, 154, 155, 156, 178, 260, 269

English language learners, 285–288

environmental print, 36

fall, 128–139, 180, 265

family, 115, 180, 243, 294

Father's Day, 156, 164, 270

fine motor, 68, 73, 74, 75, 90, 129, 138, 141, 150, 162, 173, 194, 203, 204, 207, 211, 228–236

following directions, 16, 17, 199

Fourth of July, 165, 257

friendship & kindness, 10, 121–127

Green Eggs and Ham, 53

gross motor, 69, 94, 167, 196, 197, 204, 237–241

Halloween, 131, 132, 175, 180, 266

holidays and seasonal, 128–188 (see specific holiday or season)

home-school connection, 10, 70, 83, 117, 179–188, 220, 289–301, 309

insects, 211, 212

Jamberry, 55

letter formation, 43, 44, 50

letter identification, 44, 195, 223

letter matching, 40, 41, 49, 151, 166, 194, 207, 211

letter recognition, 39

letters, 33, 39–50, 222

listening, 16, 17, 220

listening & speaking, 16–19

literature, 51–62, 286

making sets, 81, 82, 83, 207, 224

management, 302–316

    assessment, 281–284

    attendance, 9, 304

    centers, 189–193, 215–217, 305

    classroom helpers, 274, 304

    discipline & motivation, 295, 309, 310, 311

    organization, 190, 302, 303, 306

    snacktime, 306

    substitute teacher, 312

    transitions, 23, 113, 151, 304, 307, 308, 309

matching, 197, 199

matching letters, 151, 207

matching numerals and sets, 197

months, 52

Mother's Day, 156, 269

motivation, 295, 310–311

movement (see gross motor and music and movement)

music and movement, 248–253

name recognition, 9, 32, 219, 223

New Year's, 143

number awareness, 81

numbers, 80–90, 195, 197, 223, 224

ocean, 167, 203–206, 236, 247

one-to-one correspondence, 80, 89, 207

opposites, 221

parent conferences, 298–301

parent resource, 10

parts of the body, 113, 114

patterns, 77, 132, 196, 203

pets, 207–210

phonological awareness, 20–31

plants, 99–104

positional words, 155, 287

prewriting, 208

print awareness, 36

print awareness & book knowledge, 32–38

profile of a preschooler, 4–8

ready reference pages, 215–217

recipes, 65, 262–264

reproducibles

    fine motor, 73, 74, 75, 90, 138, 150, 162, 173, 233, 234, 235, 236

    literacy, 30, 31, 49, 50, 67, 151, 163

    management, 13–15, 175–178, 179–188, 193, 314, 315, 316

    math, 67, 73, 74, 75, 89, 90, 174

science, 112

visual discrimination, 139

rhyming, 20, 21, 30, 163

role-playing, 208, 243, 246

self-esteem, 10, 114, 115

sequencing, 101

seriating, 212

shapes, 68–75, 76, 131, 143, 194, 199, 218, 241, 273, 287

sharing, 123, 124

sink and float, 200

songs and fingerplays, 11, 16, 23, 32, 35, 36, 52, 69, 76, 77, 93, 101, 105, 107, 116, 121, 124, 131, 140, 142, 144, 152, 153, 156, 166, 219, 252, 287, 304, 306, 307, 309

sorting, 64, 69, 76, 99, 129

sorting and patterns, 76–79

speaking, 17

spring, 152–163, 186, 187, 271

St. Patrick's Day, 152, 177, 185, 268

substitute teachers, 312

summer, 164–174, 188, 247, 270, 271

syllables, 22

Thanksgiving, 132, 175, 181, 266

transitions, 23, 113, 304, 307, 308, 309

transportation, 199–202, 241, 242, 255

uppercase and lowercase letters, 42, 166

Valentine's Day, 143, 144, 177, 184, 268

Very Hungry Caterpillar, The, 54

visual discrimination, 17, 139, 142, 156, 194, 208, 212, 218

vocabulary, 285, 286

weather, 105–112

welcome to school (see back-to-school)

Where the Wild Things Are, 52

winter, 108, 140–151, 176, 182, 183, 267

word awareness, 22